THE POWER TO MANAGE

By the same author

TRADE UNIONS
WHAT'S WRONG WITH THE UNIONS?

THE POWER TO MANAGE

A History of the
Engineering Employers' Federation

ERIC WIGHAM

'The employers have the right to manage their
establishments and the trade unions have the
right to exercise their functions.'

MACMILLAN

First published 1973 by
THE MACMILLAN PRESS LTD
London and Basingstoke
Associated companies in New York Toronto
Dublin Melbourne Johannesburg and Madras

SBN 333 12812 5

Printed in Great Britain by
WESTERN PRINTING SERVICES LIMITED
Bristol

Contents

APPENDIXES

Foreword

The Engineering Employers' Federation commissioned this history because they believed that the part played by the Federation in the development of industrial relations in Britain justified the compilation of a permanent record. Such a work, we felt, would be of most value if prepared by a completely independent person with a knowledge of industrial relations. It was decided that all the Federation's records should be placed at the author's disposal and that he should be given a free hand. We believe that the result is worthy of publication but there are inevitably many points in the analysis and interpretation of facts which are the author's own.

THOMAS CARLILE
President

April 1972

Author's Note

My thanks are due to the Engineering Employers' Federation and to Mr Martin Jukes, QC, the Director-General, for commissioning me to write this history, for allowing me complete freedom to explore their records, and for their toleration of the result. The full responsibility for everything in the book is mine. I am grateful too, to past and present office-bearers and officials of the Federation and of many local Associations who gave me unstinted co-operation. I should particularly mention Mr John Paterson, the publications editor, who smoothed away practical problems and who read the proofs. A few of the many others are referred to in Appendix N on sources.

Mr Robin Moss and Mr Howard Gospel gave me invaluable help with the research work and by reading some of the chapters. Mr Oliver Clarke gave me at the beginning the benefit of his unrivalled knowledge of the history of the Federation and read my manuscript at the end. He pointed out some of my worst mistakes and is in no way to blame for those that remain.

The Federation began life in 1896 as the Employers' Federation of Engineering Associations. In 1899 it became the Engineering Employers' Federation, in 1919 the Engineering and National Employers' Federations, in 1924 the Engineering and Allied Employers' National Federation and in 1960 the Engineering Employers' Federation. I have referred to it throughout as the Federation with a capital F. The Federation executive board from 1899 to 1924 and the management board from 1924 onwards are the Board. The provisions for avoiding disputes are the Procedure. The National Confederation of Employers' Organisations from 1919 to 1939 and the British Employers' Confederation from 1939 to 1965 are the Employers' Confederation. The '*status quo*' argument is frequently mentioned. This is the dispute which has gone on throughout the Federation's history as to the extent to which managements are entitled to introduce contested changes in their factories without first going through the Procedure for avoiding disputes.

I have tried to be sparing with initials but the following will often be found:

Iron Trades Employers' Association (1872–1900)	ITEA
The Federation's Emergency Committee (1897–1916)	EC
Amalgamated Society of Engineers (1851–1920)	ASE
Amalgamated Engineering Union (1920–1968)	AEU
Trades Union Congress (1868 onwards)	TUC
Federation of British Industries (1916–1965)	FBI
Confederation of British Industry (1965 onwards)	CBI
Confederation of Shipbuilding and Engineering Unions	CSEU

Other organisations may be referred to by initials where their full title has just been used.

The quotation on the title-page is the first sentence of the 'managerial functions' agreement of 1922. It remained unchanged until the Procedure was terminated in 1971.

CHAPTER I

Introduction

Origins of Employers' Organisations – The 1852
Lock-out – Struggles for Workshop Power – Collective
Bargaining and Conciliation – New Functions in a
Changing World

The Engineering Employers' Federation is much the largest and
most important organisation of its kind in Britain. At the end of
1971 it was made of up 22 local associations with nearly 5000
member firms in Britain and Northern Ireland employing more
than two million workers in an industry which produces 40 per
cent of the nation's manufactured products and 40 per cent of
the nation's exports. The annual wage and salary bills of its
members amount to £2500 m.

Unlike some other employers' federations, for instance that of
the builders, the Federation is not concerned with trade matters
but confines itself to labour relations. It has always been careful
not to go outside that field and no less insistent that no other
organisation obtrudes into it. This is one reason why it long had
the reputation of being the toughest employers' organisation.
Trade associations tend to be preoccupied with maintaining
production and may want to do so even at the cost of concessions
to employees which are hard to justify in the long run. Employers'
organisations must seek to keep labour costs within reasonable
bounds (even though they incur losses through stoppages of work
in the process), and to maintain the controls they regard as
essential for efficient management. They are always on the other
side of the negotiating table from the trade unions, not necessarily
in conflict but inevitably taking a different view.

Employers' organisations grew up as defensive alliances. They
were not uncommon in the early part of the last century, in
engineering as in other industries, but they were usually local and

temporary. They were formed in reply to the organisation of workers into trade unions, to resist particular demands which they regarded as excessive and in general to prevent the unions from enforcing rules which interfered with their freedom to run their factories as they wished. Three times in the past 120 years the employers and unions in the engineering industry have engaged in an all-out power struggle. The first was in 1852, the year after the formation of the Amalgamated Society of Engineers, the second in 1897, the year after the formation of the Employers' Federation, the third in 1922, two years after the formation of the Amalgamated Engineering Union. Consciousness of new power contributed to all of them. All three were general lock-outs by employers' organisations in reply to limited trade union action which they considered was interfering with their prerogatives. All three were won by the employers. After all three the employers imposed settlements which re-established their authority in their own undertakings. And each time the unions, after they had recovered from the set-back, extended their functions until once more they intruded painfully into management. And gradually the employers have come to accept an extension of union rights. They demanded much less in the settlement of 1898 than in 1852 and less still in 1922. They were ready to concede much more in negotiations for a new procedural agreement for manual workers in 1970 and 1971, but it was still over the right to manage that the negotiations broke down.

It has never been easy for employers, in daily competition with each other, to make a firm alliance, and in the early days their associations were usually short-lived bodies formed to deal with an immediate threat and drifting apart again when it was over.

The employers [said the Royal Commission on the Organisation and Rules of Trade Unions and other Associations in 1869] cannot fail to see the advantage which the trade unions, in the conduct of strikes, have in attacking the employers in detail. The strike is with this view directed against a single employer or against the employers in a single district, the workmen on strike being supported by those still in the employment of other masters; the intention being, on the success of the first strike, to take others in succession. To defeat this policy, the employers resort to such expedients as they deem best for their own protection. The ordinary course is to form an association of their own, in which they agree, in the event of a strike against any member of the association, to close the workshops of all, and in some cases, by a subscription among themselves, to give pecuniary assistance to the employer against whom the strike is directed. These associations are described as being frequently of a temporary character, and dissolved as soon as the contest with the workmen, which has given rise to the association, comes to an end.

The dispute of 1852 was conducted by an association which for the first time in engineering was more than local, the Central Association of Employers of Operative Engineers. This was set up at a joint meeting of employers from Lancashire and London and later brought in others from Yorkshire and its object was to defeat a demand by the ASE for the abolition of overtime and piece-work. Its aim was quite simply to smash the union. The members got together in a London coffee house on 24 January and agreed on recommendations which they considered

indispensably necessary for the protection of the operative and labouring classes from the annoyances, intimidation, personal violence and exclusion from employment, to which they have been habitually subjected by the influence, organisation and ascendancy in the various shops of members of unions, and for the relief of employers from the interference and dictation thereby inflicted on them.

No member of the association, it was agreed, would engage or knowingly employ a member of a union. No deputation of work-men or unions would be received, any workman taking part in such a deputation would be dismissed forthwith. (But employers were recommended to be at all times open to personal representa-tions by individuals.) Employers would as much as possible avoid delegating the engagement of workmen to make sure the rules were observed. No member would engage or continue in employ-ment any workman until the latter had read, in the presence of at least one witness, the rules of the establishment, and signed a dec-laration that he was not and would not become a union member. Furthermore, no member would engage any workman with-out ascertaining from what establishment he was discharged and whether he had infringed the declaration. If one member was involved in a strike, for reasons approved by the association, he would be supported by all the others.

The lock-out had begun on 1 January, when the men refused to work overtime or piece-work. In February the employers opened their workshops and workers began to trickle back and sign the declaration. The following month the union asked the masters to receive a deputation but were refused on the grounds that the masters were 'strongly opposed to all combinations'. By the end of April most of the men were back at work but many, although they signed the declaration, did not leave the union on the grounds that they had signed under duress. Some preferred to emigrate and laid the foundation of union branches in Australia and Canada. The union was not broken, as many had been by such defeats in earlier decades, and within a few years had more than restored its membership and funds. But the employers' organisation faded out.

The attitude adopted by the employers in 1852 was not remarkable at the time. In a *laissez-faire society*, many people regarded the activities of trade unions as an artificial interference with the natural economic relationship between masters and men. When a report on the lock-out was given to a meeting of the Social Science Association in 1860 by Thomas Hughes, a lawyer later to become famous as the author of *Tom Brown's Schooldays*, there was a lively debate on the subject. Another paper by Edmund Potter FRS, of Manchester, expounded the view that 'labour must be considered as a mere purchasable article, like all other commodities, and ought to be bought and sold, and weighed and measured accordingly'. His explanation of the formation of unions was simple: 'Two-thirds of the working class might save; not one third does save; hence their want of power and their anxiousness for combinations.' Hughes and others contested this.

A committee on trade societies and strikes, set up by the society, thought it would be 'most mischievous' to return to the old policy of prohibiting combinations, but had their qualifications. They said many employers believed that 'without combination workmen in their trades could not secure the fair market rate of wages' but 'when a trade society constantly interferes with processes of manufacture, the annoyance and element of uncertainty thus introduced renders a large average rate of profit necessary to tempt capital into the trade, and therefore a less margin is left'.

Whatever the economic justification for unions, the survival and progress of the ASE after the lock-out demonstrated that they had come to stay. The ASE was the first of the 'new model' unions, providing extensive friendly society benefits for members and achieving a financial stability based on an efficient administrative system. Unions in other industries were quick to adopt its methods. Their steady if unspectacular advance led to the creation of the TUC in 1868 and was followed by a change in public attitudes which resulted in the Trade Union Act of 1871 which gave unions protection under the law such as they had never previously enjoyed. In this new situation, employers began to realise that the old evanescent alliances were not enough, and in one industry after another permanent organisation began to appear. In the middle sixties in Scotland and in Belfast and the early seventies in England lasting local associations of engineering employers were established. The industry's first stable national organisation, the Iron Trades Employers' Association, came into existence in 1872 with headquarters in Manchester, to be succeeded by the Federation in 1896.

The object of the 1897 lock-out was very different from that of 1852. The employers did not hope or even want to smash the unions, but to stop them from interfering in matters which the employers regarded as the prerogative of management such as who should man the new machines, how much overtime should be worked, how many apprentices should be employed, whether men should be paid on piece or time rates. They accepted collective bargaining with the unions in limited fields – national negotiations on wages did not arrive until the First World War – and they established a jointly operated disputes machinery. The lock-out of 1922 was to re-establish the prerogatives which had been eroded during the war.

The three basic functions of the Federation remained unchanged from 1897 for about seventy years. The first was by collective action to prevent individual firms or local associations from being picked out by the unions one by one. For this purpose the general lock-out or threat of lock-out in support of members continued to be used until the late twenties but was increasingly replaced by national collective bargaining, while threats of workshop conflict could usually be handled by the disputes machinery. The possible use of the collective lock-out was talked of again several times after the Second World War, when the draughtsmen's union adopted a policy of attacking individual firms and to a lesser extent as a reply to unofficial local action, but each time the Federation decided against it. National conflict was near more than once, but arising out of the breakdown of national negotiations, not the need to defend a member or group of members.

The second basic function, which could be regarded as an aspect of the first, was the preservation of the power to manage. This resulted not only in the lock-outs of 1897 and 1922, but also in the attitude adopted by the Federation to any proposal to increase the participation by unions in the control of the industry at national or local level. It partly accounted for the Federation's rejection of the idea of a national joint council when such councils were advocated by the Whitley Committee during the First World War and by successive courts of inquiry into engineering disputes after the Second World War; it accounted for the leading part played by the Federation in opposing the Mond-Turner plan after the 1926 General Strike, for their anxiety to avoid a statutory basis for joint production committees during and after the Second World War and again in 1964, for their reluctance to negotiate a national redundancy agreement lest they might be obliged to give the unions some say in the way redundancies were handled. Some concessions were made in successive revisions of the disputes machinery, restricting more closely the circumstances in which managements might make contested changes without going through the Procedure first, but the cause of a breakdown of negotiations for a new procedure in 1971 was their insistence that managements must be responsible for the day-to-day running of their factories.

It is not difficult to find reasons for the preoccupation of engineering with their management rights. Their industry above all others has been characterised by continual growth and change. From the making of textile machinery and railway engines it went on to marine engineering and then to electrical appliances and motor cars and aircraft and electronics. Within each section changes in methods of production have never ceased, and if an employer is hindered from bringing in rapidly new machines and techniques, or from using them effectively, he is at once placed at a disadvantage with his competitors at home and abroad. The problem has not, of course, been confined to engineering. Other industries have from time to time had similar struggles. But because of its size and importance, engineering naturally had to bear the brunt of the battle and over the years has set a pattern which others have followed.

A factor in the background at every testing time, though its importance is hard to assess, is the fear that union intervention in the workshops is a stage on the way to socialism and the sweeping away of private employers altogether. In 1852, the Christian socialists and co-operative workshops were much talked of. The ASE was impressed by the idea, which was thought of by some as a means of making profitable use of the society's funds and by some as a road towards a new society. A factor in the 1897 lock-out was the revival of socialism which began in the eighties and in which many leading members of the ASE, including the general secretary, played a part. Similarly, the 1922 lock-out was in part a reaction to the shop stewards' movement of the First World War, with its advocacy of workers' control.

Anxieties have naturally been greatest during the two wars and when Labour governments have been in power. When the negotiations for a new procedure agreement were begun in 1970, Labour Ministers had been talking sympathetically of workers having a share in control. Worker directors had been appointed in the steel industry and further experiments in the same direction were proposed for the ports. Employers noted with suspicion that Hugh Scanlon, President of the engineers' union, and Jack Jones, General Secretary of the Transport and General Workers' Union, were prominent in an organisation called the Institute for Workers' Control.

The third basic function of the Federation, arising from and complementary to the other two, was to keep the peace. The creation of defensive machinery to meet the attacks of the unions inevitably resulted in frequent conflicts which imposed heavy losses both on the the employers and on their workers. It was natural that both sides should look for ways other than trials of strength to settle their differences. During the latter part of the nineteenth century many industries experimented with methods of doing this, such as the creation of conciliation and arbitration boards, and automatic ways of dealing with wage movements, such as sliding scales based on prices.

The method chosen by the Federation in 1898, its outstanding contribution to the development of labour relations in this country, was the creation of the provisions for the avoidance of disputes. This provided for conciliation to be kept within the industry, where alone the causes of disputes would be fully understood, while at the same time unresolved differences could be shifted away from the point of conflict to local and if need be national conferences, where they could be considered dispassionately before any stoppage of work took place. It did not take long for the value of the arrangement to be accepted by union leaders as well as employers, and the Procedure was used more and more, even in the sixties and seventies of this century when there were also many strikes in breach of it. For many employers, belief in the Procedure was almost an article of faith and it was largely because of this that the Federation so often resisted the introduction of different principles, such as that of outside arbitration or the establishment of some form of joint industrial council. Even when in 1970 the Federation proposed big changes in the Procedure, they did not accept that the old way had failed. It was part of the industry's way of life.

During the past decade the Federation has begun to develop a fourth basic function, obvious to the observer but somewhat hard to define. It can perhaps be described as labour relations leadership. One of the main activities of local associations, and to a lesser extent of the Federation itself, has always been to give advice to members on their labour problems. But this new development goes further than that. It is an attempt to influence members to create a new kind of relationship at factory level. The conditions in which the Federation has had to operate since the Second World War have made such a development essential. A continuous high level of employment, the ever closer integration of industry so that a stoppage by a few men could lay thousands idle, financial payments to strikers, governments walking on an economic tightrope, gave a new power to the workers at plant level so that collective bargaining was to a large extent taken over by shop stewards and went back to factories. National collective bargaining became confined largely to the establishment of minimum rates and some standard conditions.

But the Federation no longer defends its member firms by strong-arm methods as it did in the old days. Absentee owners of conglomerate firms are reluctant to face the cost of a stoppage to pull someone else's coals out of the fire as the engineer-owners did more than half a century ago. Governments have been unwilling to face a national stoppage of manual workers in so vital an industry. A crisis in 1957, when the Federation was induced by the Government to back down after throwing down the gauntlet to the manual workers' unions, reduced its prestige and cohesion to the lowest level in its history.

The shock made the Federation realise that it would have to change itself and its approach to its job. For more than sixty years it had been a powerful bargaining and conciliating body but little more. It had become an inward-looking body, shunning publicity. Planning for the future was not thought of. Training and safety were for members. But lately it has been gradually reforming itself to take its place in a changed world. In 1953 it appointed a publicity officer, in 1959 a training officer, in 1966 a safety officer, in 1969 a publications editor. It has stimulated mergers of associations to enable them to provide more comprehensive services. It has been encouraging and helping associations to establish training schools. It has called in consultants to improve its organisation and bought a computer to extend the scope of its information. It has been improving communications with its members and building up a system of consultation which has widened their participation in decision making. In 1967 it set up a research department and in 1969 a productivity advisory service, through which it is encouraging members to move towards a new kind of management, not so much by prerogative as by consent. No one at Broadway House would claim that the new objectives are fully accepted or even understood by all the members, but there is movement.

CHAPTER 2

Towards Federation 1872–1896

The 54-hour Strike – Formation of the Iron Trades
Employers' Association – Union Aggression Grows –
Trouble with the Shipbuilders – Federation at Last

On 1 June 1871, the engineering workers on the Tyne struck
for a reduction in hours from 59 to 54 a week, Sunderland
workers having secured the reduction the previous month after a
brief battle. There followed a classic nineteenth century industrial
struggle which lasted five months and resulted in a victory for the
men. Previous attempts to secure the reduction on the Tyne and
on the Tees had failed, but now the workers were in a stronger
position than they had been for many years. Foreign competition
had almost disappeared because the United States was not yet a
serious rival and Continental firms were busy repairing the
damage caused by the Franco-Prussian War. Business was boom-
ing and the trade union movement was entering upon one of its
periods of most rapid expansion. The report of the Royal Commission and the Trade Union Act of 1871 established the moral
and legal right of unions to exercise their functions. The Reform
Act of 1867 had given votes to many of their members.

There were as yet not many trade unionists in the engineering
trade in Newcastle, but the strikers set up an *ad hoc* organisation,
the Nine Hour League, under the skilful leadership of John
Burnett, later to become general secretary of the ASE and afterwards the Board of Trade's first labour correspondent. The
employers also established an *ad hoc* association led by Sir
William (later Lord) Armstrong, tough, resourceful and determined, one of the outstanding engineers and industrialists of his
time. It was ten years since the first iron warship had been built
and the expanding shipbuilding and marine engineering firms of
the North-east and the Clyde were feeling their strength. Black-

legs were brought in not only from other parts of Britain but from
a number of Continental countries, but many were met on the
docks and persuaded to return. The First Socialist International
(in spite of opposition by Karl Marx because the ASE was not
affiliated) deputed a Belgian union leader to counter the
employers' recruiting efforts on the Continent. Many strikers got
jobs elsewhere, particularly in the south. The employers found
themselves increasingly on the defensive.

The strike was 'a struggle on the part of the men for mastery',
according to the *Newcastle Journal*. The *Newcastle Chronicle*,
sympathetic to the men, said some employers were reasoning:

> The men have been 'petted and spoiled' of late years. They
> have got far too much their own way and have become too
> independent. They have got political and now they want social
> and trade power. In a short time they will, if not checked,
> become both masters and workmen. If they were turned adrift
> for a few months and made to feel their position, they would
> be more submissive when they resumed work.

The Newcastle masters, like the strikers, sent deputations round
the country seeking financial support and found employers elsewhere feeling the need of collective organisation if they were to
regain managerial control. A meeting was arranged in Newcastle
on 8 August 1871, under Armstrong's chairmanship, which was
attended by employers from Glasgow, Stockton, Middlesbrough,
Hartlepool, Hull, Leeds and Liverpool. On a motion from Glasgow a committee was set up 'for the purpose of considering and
reporting upon the best mode of establishing an association of
employers in the engineering and shipbuilding trades throughout
the United Kingdom'.

Percy Westmacott, managing director of Armstrong's Elswick
works, and John Ure, of John Elder and Company, Clyde shipbuilders, were asked to sound out employers in districts not represented and two months later reported that

> with two or three individual exceptions, it was universally
> admitted that the combination and perfect organisation of
> trades unions, aided by powerful agitation to enforce unwar-
> rantable demands upon employers chiefly by intimidation, is
> damaging to the interests of the several trades, being contrary

to the natural law of supply and demand, and opposed to the freedom of labour and freedom of contract, and that it now behoves employers in self-defence to secure unity of action and mutually to aid, counsel and support each other by forming and organising a General or National Association of Masters.

After further meetings, the Iron Trades Employers' Association was inaugurated on 4 April 1872, in the Westminster Palace Hotel, London. But somewhere along the road the firms of the Tyne and the Clyde, who began it all, had pulled out – and with them those of Stockton, Middlesbrough, Hartlepool and Hull. The leaders of the association were drawn from Manchester, Liverpool, London and Leeds.

What had gone wrong? It looks as if the message had been spread so successfully that the great firms of the Tyne and the Clyde found themselves outnumbered and outvoted by the very different ones of the inland towns. According to William Boyd, who became managing director of the Wallsend Slipway and Engineering Company about this time, the main reason was that 'the class of work turned out in the Tyne district was very different from that done in Lancashire and Yorkshire'. Renewed efforts to bring in the Tyne were made in 1873 and 1874, when the employers there replied that 'though they were feeling the disastrous result of their isolated position, they were from local causes still disunited as a district and had no prospect of being able to join the national association'.

One gets the impression that some bad feeling developed during the preliminary meetings. When the ITEA was formed, Armstrong's offered £2000 to the funds of a new Tyne association if it was set up within twelve months. This was achieved with a few weeks to spare when an association of Tyne Shipbuilding and Engineering Employers was formed on 22 March 1873. The chairman, a shipbuilder named C. Mitchell, said that in view of differences that had arisen over former attempts to consolidate an association, because of stringent conditions, there would now be the simplest possible basis of association. Remembering how strikers got jobs elsewhere in 1871, there was insistence on only one rule: 'That each member shall pledge himself not to employ any workman who may be on strike against any other member.'

The subscription was fixed at £10 a year for firms employing more than 500 workers and £5 for firms employing fewer. Secretarial expenses were to be paid for by the interest on Armstrong's gift and on a sum of £96 7s. 11d. left over from the strike fund. But within a few months the shipbuilding employers were meeting separately and after the first year, though there is no evidence of a formal break, the engineering employers dropped out completely. The association became one of shipbuilders only – the first of a number of instances of shipbuilders acting as cuckoos in the nest. The Tyne engineering employers did not get together again for ten years.

Permanent associations were already in existence in Scotland and Belfast at this time. The first in Britain was set up in Edinburgh as the result of a demand by engineering craftsmen for a reduction in hours from 60 to 57 a week 'in order to allow the workmen more time for the cultivation and elevation of their minds'. The intention was to negotiate with firms separately but within a week of the workers' announcement of their claim, the employers got together and on 2 November 1865, established the East of Scotland Employers' Association of Engineers and Ironfounders. The 57-hour week was granted shortly afterwards.

The following year there was a series of strikes on the Clyde followed by a general demand for a reduction in hours of labour from 60 to 55. The employers got together informally, as was usual, and after a three-day conference with the men's leaders conceded 57 hours. They then discovered that the men expected 60 hours' pay for the shorter week. Their rejection of this was followed by a number of strikes and at this stage, on 30 April 1866, the employers set up the Clyde Shipbuilders' and Engineers' Association.

The first action of the new association was to declare an immediate lock-out of more than 17,000 men in reply to the strikes. The men eventually resumed work on the employers' terms, though some stuck out for eighteen weeks. There were thirty-five member firms, mostly in shipbuilding, who paid no subscriptions. Promissory notes were given by members at the rate of £4 for every man or boy they employed. These notes guaranteed a sum of between £90,000 and £100,000, available at a day's notice.

The same system of promissory notes was adopted in Belfast when the Belfast Engineers', Shipbuilders', Founders' and Machine Makers' Association was formed in the summer of 1866 with eighteen members employing 4250 workers, including 1126 at James Combe and Co., and 1013 at Harland and Wolff.

In 1873, therefore, there were in existence the Iron Trades Employers' Association, with members in most of the main centres in England except the North-east, and independent associations in Glasgow, Edinburgh and Belfast. The ITEA established their headquarters in Manchester and appointed as general secretary Ephraim Hutchings, who held the office for eighteen years. Hutchings, son of a Buckinghamshire osier-grower, had been secretary of mechanics institutions in Sheffield and Manchester and afterwards built railways in Brazil and the Argentine, returning to England about the time when Manchester and Leeds employers were looking for someone to organise the association. A picture of Hutchings in the Iron Trades *Record* – a year-by-year account of ITEA activities published when the Association dissolved itself in 1900 – shows a fierce-looking character with bushy hair, eyebrows and whiskers.

Probably greater influence in the association was exercised by a solicitor named Sidney Smith – the 'notorious' Sidney Smith as James B. Jefferys describes him in his history of the engineers' union – who became financial secretary. He had been secretary of the employers' association during the 1852 engineers' lock-out, was concerned in a Lancashire cotton strike in 1853, was joint employers' secretary during a big builders' strike in 1858–9, and organised a meeting of London engineering employers to try to enlist support during the 1871 Newcastle strike.

In the ITEA's first year, fifteen engineering districts established branches including 190 firms employing 66,406 men and boys. The association's income in the eleven months to the first annual meeting was £8259 and they were left with a balance of £6530.

A year after its formation, the ITEA took the initiative in setting up, with employers in other industries, the National Federation of Associated Employers of Labour to counter the political activities of the TUC Parliamentary Committee. A manifesto sent out with the federation's rules said it had been formed 'in consequence of the extraordinary development – oppressive action – far-reaching, but openly-avowed designs – and elaborate organisation of the trade unions' and went on to paint a remarkable picture of union power and efficiency. Their leaders resembled 'the staff of a well-organised, well-provisioned army for which everything that foresight and pre-occupation in a given purpose could provide is at command'. They showed 'skilful and ceaseless energy'. The result of this organisation and of the pecuniary and other sacrifices which workers made in its support 'must be to give it to a large extent control of the elections, and consequently of Parliament; the power to dictate terms everywhere between employers and employed, and the mastery over the independence of the workmen, as well as over the operations of the employers'.

There was much more in this vein, which the gratified unions hastened to reprint. The manifesto went on to contrast the weakness of employers' organisations 'with a few associations mostly confined to one town and rarely displaying any sign of vitality except under the influence of urgent local necessity'. So the Federation offered a 'centre of action for associated employers'.

John Robinson, of the Atlas Works, Manchester, the first president of the ITEA, was also the first chairman of the federation. The federation campaigned unsuccessfully against the amendment of the Criminal Law Amendment Act, 1871, which the unions considered excessively restrictive on picketing, but in a few years faded out.

The ITEA was more solidly based. It was not a negotiating body like a modern employers' organisation. In fact it had no direct contacts with trade unions. Its main activity was to help employers in disputes by financial assistance and providing non-unionists to take the place of strikers. It constantly urged upon its members the use of the 'Inquiry Note'. This was a form which every management was expected, before signing on a new worker, to send to his previous employer to get information on his record and reason for leaving. It was intended to prevent strikers getting work elsewhere, as they did during the Newcastle strike, and could also be used to avoid the employment of 'trouble-makers'. One of the early disputes in which the association was involved was an unsuccessful demand in Nottingham that the use of the note should be discontinued. In London the form had been in use ever since the 1852 lock-out.

From the beginning, the association claimed a long list of successes. 'From every district reports were received that the masters felt themselves stronger than they ever were before, and that they were now able to resist unreasonable demands from trades unionists, which in similar cases would have had to be agreed to.' The ITEA *Record* contrasted this with 'the case of the Tyne masters, who in the absence of such a combination were forced, without a day's resistance, or even consideration, to yield an advance of 15 per cent to all classes of labour'.

During 1873–4 the association started a registration office for unemployed workers, a forerunner of the more elaborate organisations started in the nineties to provide strike-breakers. The account in the *Record* of many disputes ends with words like: 'In time the places of the strikers were filled by non-unionists, and the strike was broken down' or 'Labourers, after the strike, were working machines which previously were in the hands of highly-paid mechanics'. They were not always successful. In Bolton, it is recorded, 'the association obtained 600 non-unionists to fill the places of men on strike, but owing to the determined action of the pickets very few of these men ever reached the works'.

The employers concerted their action at district level, but not nationally. On a number of occasions a strike against one firm was met by all the local firms dismissing 10 per cent of their workers every fortnight. The union demands, however, were often made to employers in a whole district. The *Record* says that in Sheffield in 1873–4 the men first tried to establish minimum district wage rates. Some 1,500 went on strike but were 'entirely defeated'. Disputes were most commonly over the introduction of piece-work, overtime rates, the manning of machines and wage movements.

From the middle of 1874 trade began to deteriorate and steadily worsened until the country found itself in the midst of a great depression which reached its climax in 1879, a year which came to be looked back upon with the same sort of emotion as did the year 1931 in later times. 'The year opens with Labour completely at the mercy of Capital and with Capital gloating over its power to inflict the most cruel pangs upon Labour, and exercising that power with a venom that will work an inevitable terrible retribution', said the journal of the Boilermakers' Society. But so far from gloating, many of the engineering firms were fighting for existence.

More and more employers reduced wages. 'Thirty per cent of the skilled labour were unemployed,' says the *Record*. 'The profitless character of nearly every engineering undertaking led employers to simultaneously revise their pay-sheets.' In London and Liverpool and Birkenhead the men went on strike against the proposed reduction. 'The supply of men was so abundant that the association was able to obtain the number of non-union men required, and in spite of picketing and intimidation the reductions were carried out in these as in all other branches of the association,' said the *Record*.

The ITEA also worked hard for an increase in hours. They tried to get 'some important industrial and commercial organisations' to combine with them in a joint movement but their efforts were not successful. So they arranged a more limited conference between the leading engineering and shipbuilding employers in England and Scotland, in the belief that any action to be successful must be concerted. They afterwards sent a questionnaire to the employers to test their opinion, which did not justify any further steps.

What happened, according to union sources, was that a copy of Sidney Smith's invitation to the conference, declaring that the time had come 'when the idle hours which have been unprofitably thrown away must be reclaimed', fell into the hands of John Burnett, now the ASE secretary. Burnett immediately sent copies, with a reply, to the press as well as to employers and union branches, and hostile public reaction prevented the ITEA from proceeding further. The union resisted the attempts to increase hours by individual firms with the utmost obstinacy, because any change was likely to last longer than a change in wages. Both sides accepted the dictum of Sir William Armstrong during the Newcastle strike: 'Wages fluctuate with demand, but shortened hours of work do not alter.' The Huddersfield employers succeeded in getting hours increased to $57\frac{1}{2}$ and the Bradford employers to $56\frac{1}{2}$, in both cases after strikes, but no other ITEA branch made the attempt. Employers in Scotland, where hours had been reduced to 51, succeeded in restoring the 54-hour week.

The ITEA was paying increased attention in this period to the position of foremen.

It was noted by the committee [says the *Record*] that nothing satisfactory could be done while foremen were retained who were members of trade unions, and the committee were so convinced as to the desirability of foremen not belonging to any union, that they offered to give every assistance possible to any member of the association who desired to make the change without any cost to the member. A number of applications were received by the association in response to this offer and applicants were supplied with the foremen they required.

The longest strike in the engineering industry, lasting more than two years, began in Sunderland in June 1883. It arose over a demand from the ASE local executive for a restriction in the number of apprentices. The boilermakers and shipwrights were at this time maintaining a strict policy of limitation, an easier matter in the more compact shipbuilding industry, with the result that large numbers of lads were finding their way into engineering shops. The union was also demanding the end of the inquiry note. At first work in the factories was carried on by apprentices, but the strike committee managed to get a large number of them to come out. The employers then took out hundreds of summonses to force them to resume work. After three months, the employers began to import workers from other districts and appealed for help from employers on the Tyne and elsewhere and from the ITEA.

Although the Sunderland employers were not members, the ITEA were able to give them a good deal of advice and assistance, and as a result both the Wear and Tyne employers formed branches of the association. In the following years there began to appear on the executive the names of some of the legendary figures who were to lead the great lock-out of 1897. Benjamin Dobson, from Bolton, was already on the executive. Colonel Dyer, from Newcastle, came on in place of Percy Westmacott a few years later and a year after that Benjamin Browne, who had joined the Tyne firm of Hawthorn, Leslie only a few months before the 1871 strike.

Industrial relations during the late eighties became more embittered. It was a decade of social ferment. There had been a socialist revival, accompanied by demands for the eight-hour day, exposures of conditions of life among the poor in the great cities and the movement which led to the creation of the general unions. In 1886–7 there was a strike in Bolton about overtime and a $7\frac{1}{2}$ per cent wage claim which, according to the *Record*, was carried on 'with riotous destruction of property'. 'Some of the trade unions assumed a very hostile attitude towards employers,' the *Record* says two years later, 'and under repeated threats of expulsion from their unions and the forfeiture of their monetary rights in their funds, the men were ordered to take steps in regard to individual employers, the injustice and immorality of which were of the most glaring type.'

Claims for the eight-hour day were not making much progress but the Tyne and Wear men got a reduction from 54 to 53 hours in 1890 after a strike known locally as the 'football dispute'. The men wanted to stop work on Saturdays at noon instead of 1 p.m., as was already done in shipbuilding, building and a number of other industries. Working the extra hour, they complained, prevented them from attending the local football matches unless they went direct from their work. After an eight-day strike, the employers conceded the point and the 53-hour spread to some other districts.

There was a series of damaging disputes in the North-east in the early nineties. One was on overtime, when the men succeeded in getting some restriction on the amount to be worked, another a demarcation dispute between fitters and plumbers – perhaps the worst of a growing number of demarcation disputes – which led to a lock-out by the engineering and shipbuilding employers, and yet another over a pay claim affecting iron founders and patternmakers on Tees-side in 1894. The settlement with the iron founders provided for the establishment of a board of conciliation.

In addition to helping their branches to fight disputes, the ITEA did a limited amount of research work and supplied information to members and the public. For instance it got an actuary to prepare documents questioning the security offered by the ASE to its members in respect of its sick and superannuation funds. It conducted a survey of the effect of piece-work in increasing earnings as well as output. It circulated tables showing the rates of wages paid in different districts, and the rules and customs in force on holidays, overtime, nightshift and allowances.

It was also active in making representations to Royal Commissions and to the Government on proposed legislation. Five representatives of the ITEA from different districts gave evidence to the Royal Commission on Labour in the early nineties. One of them was Sir Andrew Noble, chairman of the Tyne and Wear association and future Federation president, who favoured the formation of boards of conciliation and ballots of strikers on employers' proposals for settlement under the supervision of an officer or arbitrator appointed by the State. He said that the ITEA hardly included *most* employers but it did include a very large number.

Among the parliamentary measures on which the association was active were those dealing with employers' liability and workmen's compensation. When the Employers' Liability Act was passed in 1880, the ITEA started a mutual insurance scheme which, it claimed, 'by the low rate charged was the means of forcing the insurance companies to reduce their rates from the excessively high figures they were quoting and thus saved not only members of the association but every employer of labour in the trade a very large sum of money.' With the passing of the Workmen's Compensation Act in 1897, they put this on a more formal basis by creating the Iron Trades Employers' Insurance Association – the ITEA's permanent legacy to the industry. The insurance association still flourishes and over the years has extended its activities.

Meanwhile the Clyde masters had initiated a new attempt to start a national federation covering Scotland, England and Northern Ireland. In June 1889, they circularised employers' organisations in other centres and followed this up with deputations to the Tyne and Wear, the Mersey and Barrow. A widely representative meeting agreed that federation was desirable and that it should be a first principle to form a board of conciliation with ultimate powers to refer all forms of trade dispute to arbitration. The rules were approved at a general meeting at Carlisle on 11 November, when it was agreed that the ITEA should appoint six members as a consultative committee to sit with the executive without voting powers.

Once again, however, the attempt to form an all-inclusive federation failed. Of the 67 firms which had originally shown interest, only 32 joined. There were only 5 from England, all from the north, whereas there were 17 from Glasgow and the Clyde, 5 from other parts of Scotland and 5 from Belfast. There were 13 firms which were shipbuilders only, 13 mixed shipbuilders and engineers and 6 engineers only. And even before the first annual meeting the shipbuilders were proposing that the engineering firms should leave the federation.

The engineering firms in the Clyde Shipbuilders' and Engineers' Association decided in principle to secede and form a separate association in 1890. They did not do so immediately but two years later the association received appeals for help from the Tyne employers, reinforced by the ITEA, who had locked out 5000 engineers as a result of the plumbers' and fitters' demarcation dispute already mentioned. As the dispute concerned only engineers, the Clyde shipbuilding firms did not feel inclined to give much support and it was generally agreed that the time had come to make the break. Andrew Henderson, of the firm of D. and W. Henderson, whose brother John was president of the joint association that year, was appointed to organise the engineers into a separate association, which was formally constituted as the Glasgow District Engineers' and Boilermakers' Association on 7 December 1892, Thomas (later Sir Thomas) Biggart was appointed secretary at forty guineas a year. In the next few years engineers in Greenock, Port Glasgow and Paisley dissolved their own local associations and joined that of Glasgow, which then became the North-West Engineering Trade Employers' Association. They considered joining the ITEA but turned the idea down.

Engineering firms elsewhere were much slower to leave the new federation, which at one time had tentative talks on the possibility of a merger with the newly-formed and extremely aggressive Shipping Federation. A 'separation committee' was appointed to arrange the split between the shipbuilders and engineers, but in 1892 and 1893, with Colonel Dyer now president, the federation was preoccupied with a long argument with the Boilermakers' Society on apprentice ratios which ended in a negotiated agreement. In September 1893, the separation committee was reappointed but the federation now became preoccupied with a demarcation dispute in Barrow and restrictions on caulking work by shipwrights. In 1895 the separation committee was once more reappointed.

In August 1897, with the engineering federation formed and the great lock-out begun, the shipbuilders finally lost patience with the engineers who had not resigned. It was 'resolved expedient that this Federation should be confined to shipbuilders and remitted to the secretary to arrange with the firms in question for their immediate retiral'. The secretary seems to have acted promptly and in November the title of the organisation was changed to The National Federation of Shipbuilding Employers. But that disappeared, to be replaced in August 1889, by the Shipbuilding Employers' Federation. There must have been some slip-up in the financial arrangements because in 1935 surviving members of The National Federation of Shipbuilding Employers signed a document dissolving the organisation in view of the formation of the Shipbuilding Employers' Federation and arranging for assets of £4828 3s. 1d. to be transferred to the SEF.

The final successful attempt to form a national engineering employers' federation was initiated in 1895. Movements to extend common action beyond the level of a single district had developed in both the North-east and on the Clyde–Belfast axis. A visit by Colonel Dyer to the Tees and Hartlepool employers during the 1884 dispute, with a warning that workmen's associations were 'becoming every day more powerful and aggressive', resulted in the establishment of a Tees and Hartlepool association, which agreed to work with the Tyne and Wear associations on all future trade disputes, and a joint committee was set up to co-ordinate their action. Since they acted together the three associations were often referred to as the North-east Coast association.

The following year came the Clyde–Belfast link-up. The Belfast association had also had its troubles arising from the inability of shipbuilding and engineering firms to sit down happily together. A breakaway association of shipbuilders and marine engineers had been set up in 1884, partly because of dislike of the promissory note system, under the chairmanship of W. J. (later Lord) Pirrie, of Harland and Wolff, a contentious character who was a frequent centre of dissension when he could not get his own way. They rejoined the old association when it changed its rules 'to withdraw the money responsibility' and became the Belfast Employers' Association for Engineers, Shipbuilders, Founders, Machine Makers and other Trades. Harland and Wolff resigned and went back again in 1888, and in 1891 there was a new crisis when Pirrie insisted on conceding a 1s. increase to the ASE although an association meeting had been unanimously in favour of resisting. The association met the difficulty of composing the different interests of various groups of employers by holding section meetings and in 1896 altered the rules to provide for seven sections – boilermakers, brass founders and finishers, engineers, iron founders, machine makers, shipbuilders and smiths.

In Scotland there were separate associations for iron and steel founders, brass founders and finishers and coppersmiths. The last two established close associations with the engineers and boilermakers by adopting similar rules and appointing Biggart as their secretary.

The temper of the employers in the North-east, on the Clyde and in Belfast was now such, in the face of growing aggression by the unions, particularly the ASE, that in spite of their fierce trade rivalries they were ready to take the final step to national collective action. In September 1895, with trade rapidly improving, the ASE put forward claims for wage increases in a number of districts. The Tyneside employers promptly suggested to those of Glasgow that they should exchange information so that if a strike occurred it could run concurrently. The Glasgow men agreed. A more formal proposal from Belfast resulted in representatives from Belfast, the Clyde and the Greenock association, about to merge with Glasgow, signing an agreement for combined action and mutual support. If there was a strike by ASE men in either district, the other would discharge 25 per cent of the society's men in their employment each week.

> From the date of the signing of this agreement [it said] all future negotiations with the Amalgamated Society of Engineers, and the arrangements which may arise out of the present demand, shall be entrusted to a joint committee consisting of representatives from the Clyde associations, viz. 2 from the upper reaches and 2 from the lower reaches of the river, and 2 representatives from the Belfast association.

A conference at Carlisle having failed to bring about a settlement, the Belfast men struck and the Clyde employers carried out their promise to lock out 25 per cent of their men. The Clyde ASE members immediately came out in a body.

Thus began the Clyde–Lagan (or Clyde–Belfast) dispute which affected 3000 ASE members and about 1300 non-society men, lasted three months and had an important effect on the organisations on both sides of the industry. It aroused national interest.

The Times took the side of the employers but the *Manchester Guardian* said: 'Public opinion has pretty generally condemned the Clyde employers for locking out a very large number of workmen with whom they had little or no quarrel in order that a far smaller number of workmen in Ireland might be forced to forgo an advance in wages.' A compromise settlement was finally accepted at the end of January 1896, the Belfast men being outvoted by those of the Clyde. Under pressure from the ASE, they reluctantly returned to work but an ASE delegate meeting condemned the action of their executive. The episode added to mounting dissatisfaction in the society which led later in the year to the dismissal of the general secretary, John Anderson, for 'wilful neglect of duty', and to his defeat by George Barnes, socialist and militant, in the election which followed.

The employers, on the other hand, were greatly strengthened by their experiment in concerted action. During the stoppage, a meeting at the County and Station Hotel, Carlisle, attended by eleven representatives from the North-east, nine from the joint Glasgow, Greenock and Belfast committee, and one from Barrow, expressed themselves unanimously in favour of forming a federation. On 24 April 1896, there was formally established the Employers' Federation of Engineering Associations, now the Engineering Employers' Federation. Dyer was made president and the headquarters were set up in Glasgow, with Biggart and James Robinson, from Newcastle, as joint secretaries.

Among the objects were to protect and defend the interests of members against combinations seeking by strikes or other action to impose unduly restrictive conditions; to secure mutual support in dealing with demands affecting their general interests, including 'interference with foremen, unreasonable demands for wages, minimum rates of wages, employment of apprentices, hours of labour, overtime, limitation of work, piece-work, demarcation of work, machine work and the employment of men and boys on machines'; to give all assistance to members, pecuniary, legal or otherwise, as appeared proper to the executive board; to promote the formation of conciliation boards; and to watch over legislative measures affecting the industry.

The one subject on which there was some debate was the extent to which the Federation should be concerned with wages. Dyer said at the first meeting that local matters would remain with local associations, including rises and falls in wages, while matters of principle would be dealt with by the Federation. Others argued that any issue could be a matter for the Federation and the reference to 'unreasonable demands for wages' was added to the objects at the inaugural meeting.

The story of the national organisation of engineering employers from 1872 to 1896 leaves some unanswered questions. Why, when the ITEA had been active for nearly a quarter of a century, was it necessary to form a new federation? While we do not know the number of member firms, the ITEA in 1895 had some membership in at least seventeen engineering centres – Barrow-in-Furness, Barnsley and Wakefield, Bolton, Bradford, Bristol, Halifax, Huddersfield, Hull, Keighley, Leeds, Leicester, Liverpool and Birkenhead, London, Manchester, Newcastle-on-Tyne, Nottingham and Sunderland. Yet both nationally and in Scotland, the possibility of joining the ITEA was considered by engineering firms, when they separated from joint shipbuilding and engineering organisations, and turned down. Perhaps it would have been difficult for the Scottish firms, having stood apart for so long, to have come in at that stage. The great marine engineering and armaments concerns generally may have felt that the ITEA was dominated by the numerous firms of the inland towns.

There may also have been a feeling that the ITEA had not kept pace with the times. In the period since its formation, there had been a good deal of progress with arbitration and conciliation boards in other industries in order to find some other method than force for settling disputes. Some arbitration boards had come into existence as early as the fifties and the first lasting joint board of importance, in the hosiery industry, in 1860. They spread a good deal after that time. The TUC passed a resolution advocating the formation of joint boards in 1888 and in the early nineties the Royal Commission on Labour was hearing evidence which was to lead to the Conciliation Act, 1896. No doubt many local engineering employers' organisations had their accepted joint procedures with the unions. In a major dispute the local Mayor or his equivalent would often intervene, as happened in the Newcastle 54-hours dispute and the 1895 Clyde–Belfast dispute. A number of shipbuilding conciliation boards had been formed as well as the iron founding board of conciliation.

All this seems to have passed the ITEA by. It remained what it

had been in the days of John Robinson and Sidney Smith – pre-
dominantly a union-fighting and strike-breaking organisation. It
is noticeable that the Federation of Shipbuilding and Engineering
Employers laid great stress on boards of conciliation at their first
meeting, and the Employers' Federation of Engineering Associations included their promotion among its objectives. The ITEA
Record says that their promotion of district associations of
employers did much to educate both parties as to the mutuality
of their interests and the advantages to be derived from the
friendly discussion of matters in dispute, but the year by year
record of their activities gives no sign that this kind of consideration was in their minds.

It is easier to concede the ITEA's more limited claim that

> the Association has been a valuable educational instrument to
> the employers, by showing the requirements necessary for a
> strong workable combination, particularly in two respects, (a)
> the sacrifice of individual opinion for the sake of securing
> united action as a whole and (b) rendering aid by subsidy, or
> otherwise, to members who, but for such aid, would be obliged
> to concede the unreasonable demands of the men.

The ITEA was an association composed of local branches,
which suggests more central control than in a federation of associations and perhaps more than the big marine engineering firms
wanted to accept, even in theory. It did not work like that in
practice and the common will of the big local associations in the
Federation proved much more effective.

Two of the Manchester employers' leaders, John West and J.
W. Hulse, explained the reasons for replacing the Manchester
ITEA branch by a federated association in a report to members
at the time. They recalled how they were 'out-manoeuvred and
defeated' by the ASE on the only two occasions the local
employers had been called together for years. After the surrender
of 2s. a week in September 1896, it began to dawn on some of
them, the report said, that if that sort of thing went on it could
not be long before they would be in complete subjection to trade
unionism. So they elected a new and more energetic ITEA executive, which sent a deputation to Glasgow to try and find out why
the organisations in Scotland and the North-east always seemed
'to win their battles or get peace with honour'. This deputation

found that the main weakness of the ITEA lay in the scattered nature of its membership and in the absence of strong local associations subservient to it for dealing with matters of principle affecting the whole engineering trade, but independent of it for dealing with wages and other minor questions which only affect localities. To bring up to date the ITEA, even if their ruling body had taken to it *con amore*, it was considered, would have been, if not an impossible task, one that must have taken a very long period and probably years to accomplish.

The impression given here is reinforced by a letter written during the 1897 lock-out by Major A. H. Hope, who succeeded Hutchings as ITEA secretary:

Biggart (the Federation joint secretary) is trying to rush me along at the same pace that the Federation travels. That is impossible in our case. Biggart's organisation consists of local associations with properly organised and paid staff in each. They can meet at a day's notice and say Biggart can have a free hand. The ITEA in many districts has only honorary secretaries, being employers themselves, and the whole organisation is much looser. Our committee cannot order any action but can recommend a course.

Nevertheless the association's branches were an invaluable nucleus for the development of local associations during the lock-out. When it was wound up, the Federation executive recorded that it had made possible in great measure the resistance of 1897.

Another puzzle of the period was the inability of shipbuilding and engineering employers to settle down in the same organisation. Since many of the big firms had both shipbuilding and marine engineering departments, with men often working side by side and moving from one to another, it would seem obviously desirable. Yet they always broke apart and all through the years of this century have remained apart. As late as 1964 the Shipbuilding Employers' Federation successfully resisted a merger bid from the engineers. There are important differences. Trade has always been subject to more extreme fluctuations in shipbuilding. Sometimes in the last century wage rates in shipbuilding would be varied several times a year. The system of payment by results is quite different. An important factor in the nineties was that the

Amalgamated Society of Boilermakers was the dominant union in shipbuilding and the ASE the dominant union in engineering. The boilermakers were still following the traditions of the craft societies, with which the employers had learned to live, if not always very happily. They had an exceptionally able and thoughtful secretary named Robert Knight. The ASE, on the other hand, had become 'tainted' with socialism and were behaving with an arrogance, as it seemed to the employers, which threatened the industry's future. The shipbuilders would want to avoid being involved with that.

The Great Lock-out 1896-1898

Seeds of Conflict – Men and Machines – The Eight-
hour Day – Battle is Joined – The Federation
Triumphs

When the Federation was formed in 1896, every circumstance
was leading towards the clash of forces which both sides felt to be
inevitable and which erupted in the great lock-out only fifteen
months later. In this brief interval the Federation twice threatened a national lock-out and the ASE held back only because
they were looking for more favourable ground on which to fight.

Over a period of years tempers on both sides had been raised
by a continuous succession of disputes which had their ultimate
origin in changes in the industry itself. The ASE, a proud craft
union, found the status and employment of craftsmen threatened
by technical change. New machines, operated by labourers or
apprentices, were doing work which their members had done. In
self-defence they tried to insist that skilled men should operate
machines where craft skill was no longer required or, failing that,
that each machine should carry a fixed rate so that the employer
gained nothing by training labourers to work them.

The number employed in the industry had grown steadily to
over a million. Britain was making 80 per cent of the merchant
ships of the world, and a large proportion of the warships. The
making of textile, agricultural and mining machinery and of
locomotives continued to grow while marine engineering expanded
even more rapidly and the new electrical engineering section was
making big strides. Yet even at the top of the trade cycles there was
appreciable unemployment in the industry while at the bottom
there was widespread distress. The employers argued that the number of craftsmen in the industry was continually growing, but
the unions replied that there was not enough work for them all.

It was understandable, even if it could be argued that it was short-sighted, to cling to work that had once been done by crafts-men, to demand a shorter working week, to limit the amount of overtime worked, to restrict the number of apprentices, to struggle against the introduction of piece-work, to refuse to work with non-unionists. It was no less natural that, when technical change blurred the division between their crafts and those of other societies, they should fight each other for the jobs. To strengthen their position in these struggles, they tried to insist that members promoted to be foremen should retain their membership of the union and make sure that those who left lost substantial social benefits.

The employers, on their side, were facing more intense foreign competition than they had ever known. The United States and Germany and to some extent other European countries were challenging their supremacy all over the world. The industry was growing but its share of world trade was falling. Foreign competitors were working longer hours and often paying lower wages. It was a matter of survival to make the most economical use of new machines, to start enough apprentices to provide the skilled men of the future, to introduce piece-work where it would raise output, to make sure that their foremen gave them undivided loyalty. They found it infuriating to be thwarted at every turn by the aggressive district organisations of the ASE and other craft unions.

And the ASE was growing increasingly militant. The social unrest of the previous decade, culminating in the formation of the general unions, had left its mark on the society. Socialist members of the ASE, such as Tom Mann and John Burns, had been prominent leaders in the struggle of the dockers and gas workers but remained active members of the ASE. In 1891 Tom Mann gave up his job as organiser of the Dockers' Union and stood for the general secretaryship of the ASE against Anderson, an advocate of the traditional conservative policy. He got 17,152 votes to Anderson's 18,102, but his vigorous campaign had its influence on ASE attitudes. The following year the delegate meeting reformed the ASE's structure. They established a full-time executive council of officials elected by eight districts in addition to six full-time organising district delegates. Instead of four full-time officials for a union of 70,000, there were now to be seventeen. In 1896, George Barnes, a member of the London committee which supported Tom Mann in 1891, was elected general secretary. After the recession of 1892–4, trade improved. District committees all over the country made new demands on the employers.

Even before these changes employers were showing signs of intense exasperation. Colonel Dyer, at Armstrong's Elswick works, reflected their growing irritation in a series of letters to Miss Potter (shortly to become Mrs Sidney Webb) who had written to him for some statistics comparing wages with twenty years earlier. There had been a decrease in employment at the Elswick works, he wrote, because owing to the interference of the ASE a considerable number of men had been suspended. The Society had made all their men give notice because some others, not belonging to the Society, worked machines overtime to provide metal to keep another department going. Because of their action, the men in the other department had to be suspended.

A beautiful illustration of Christian charity [commented Dyer]. It is indeed glorious to be a Briton and able to say with pride, 'Britons never shall be slaves.' It is proposed to alter that old song and add 'except to trade unions': it will, every one must admit, tend to raise the independence of character which has hitherto distinguished Englishmen . . . I hear so constantly that the working man is always right and the employer always wrong that I am almost ready to concur in the wisdom of their action although I fail to understand it – will wives and children who find no wages brought home be equally easy to convince? Don't fancy because I feel bitter at this arbitary action that I condemn unions – quite the contrary. I only condemn the abuse of their power.

The arrival on the scene of the Federation meant that at one stroke the area of potential conflict in the industry was raised from the district to the national level. During the era of the ITEA, the employers' structure had followed that of the unions, which so far as trade activity was concerned was based on their district organisations. In the old days the district committees would work not through collective bargaining but by unilateral trade regulations. In some areas they still did. They would periodically send to employers a circular listing the conditions under which their members were prepared to work – covering hours, minimum rates, overtime and night shift premia, dirt money, holidays and so on. They then tried to ensure that their regulations were carried out by every firm in the district.

Where no employers' organisation existed, or where they were unwilling to bargain, the unions had no other course open to them. Where employers' organisations were set up, often as a result of strikes, a collective bargain might be reached. Where permanent employers' associations were established, there was a tendency towards regular district bargaining, which would often include a rise or fall in wages. In a number of areas the ASE had also succeeded by the nineties in establishing district minimum rates, though employers generally were strongly opposed to this. It was for the workers, not the employers, to decide the amount for which they were prepared to sell their labour, Colonel Dyer would argue. There were no national agreements. When the employers extended their organisation to cover more than one district, as in the North-east or the Clyde–Belfast arrangement, the ASE found some difficulty in adjusting themselves to it. The jump to a national employers' organisation was a much bigger one. The strain on union funds of challenging a district association was multiplied many times if they had to deal with a national Federation.

From their first meeting, the Federation had to consider complaints of trade union 'interference'. The Naval Construction and Armaments Company at Barrow reported an attempt by the Plumbers' Society to 'interfere' with two foremen. The meeting was also told of an attempt by Clyde engineers to limit the employment of men on machines. 'The meeting was of opinion that the employers could not be too much alive to the importance of such action' – according to the minutes – 'and were agreed that every opportunity should be taken to impress this upon employers and against allowing such encroachments.' The first meeting also discussed a foremen's benefit scheme drawn up by Colonel Dyer the object of which was to get foremen out of the unions by offering them pension and other benefits to replace the union benefits they would sacrifice by leaving.

In August 1896, four months after the Federation's inaugural meeting, they first threatened a national lock-out. It arose out of an unofficial strike at Dunsmuir and Jackson's at Govan in protest against the employment on a lathe of a man who was not an ASE member. The Federation agreed to subsidise the firm and make this known to the press, and a telegram was sent to the ASE asking them to compel the men to resume work in four days or supply other men to take their places. On 24 August the strike was still going on and the Federation sent the following telegram to the ASE: 'The Federation is pledged to preserve freedom of employment both as regards society and non-society men and must now insist that the strike should at once cease or the responsibility for the consequences must rest with you.' Associations were recommended, if the strike was not settled that week, to give notices of a reduction of members of the ASE in their employment by 25 per cent per week.

With the endorsement of the associations – except that Belfast did not want extreme measures until every other means to settlement was exhausted – it was agreed to give notices on 2 September but before they could take effect the man went to another job, for which he was said to have applied six months earlier, and the strike was called off. Both sides claimed a victory. Dunsmuir and Jackson said that they did not want to take a subsidy but were pressed by the executive to do so. They were granted £500 and in addition grants of £100 and £25 respectively were made to William Cook and Andrew MacLeay, two workmen who stayed at work, 'as a recognition of their faithfulness to their employers and their support of the principle of freedom of employment'. The Naval Construction and Armaments Company protested because the rules said a subsidy should be paid 'if members so require'. So the rules were changed to make compensation automatic.

In the next few months troubles multiplied. From every association came reports of efforts by the ASE to control machines. The Board passed a resolution, endorsed by the associations, that in the event of any dispute arising through any trade society insisting that their members alone be employed on any given machines, the Federation should strenuously resist all such demands and the associations should support such action. Complaints were being made from the Clyde and Barrow that the ASE were demanding excessive wages and allowances for engineering workers on trial trips of warships and merchant vessels. Reports were also being received of restrictions on overtime.

In February 1897, a special general meeting was called and told of disputes over the manning and rating of machines at Sunderland, Barrow and Elswick and of ASE claims to machines in Glasgow and Belfast. The Board wrote to the ASE on the 26th referring to the 'aggressive action' of the Society for some months past, including the three disputes over the machine question, trial trip wages, arbitrary stoppages of overtime at Sunderland and the Hartlepools and arbitrary restrictions on overtime on the Clyde and at Belfast and at Barrow. They were anxious to avoid strife, the employers said, and offered a joint conference if the strikers at Sunderland and Barrow resumed work before 12 March. 'Failing this, the members of the Federation in defence of those firms whom you have attacked regret to say they will have no other alternative than to give notice to the members of your Society in their employment to terminate their engagements.'

The employers seem to have been generally agreed on this except for Pirrie, of Harland and Wolff. He had reserved his position at the special general meeting and when invited to a meeting of his own association and to one of the Federation Board, sent this telegram: 'See no use my attending either meeting, my view being so entirely ignored, and I have already made it clear we cannot join or take part in present dispute and it might only complicate other members' position by my attending.'

At the request of the Belfast delegates, the Board deferred the lock-out notices for a fortnight and in the meantime sent a renewed ultimatum to Barnes. The strike at Pallion Forge, Sunderland, had become the immediate issue. The Federation of Engineering and Shipbuilding Trades (FEST), of which the ASE was not a member, wrote to the Board on 23 March offering to take their man off the disputed machine for the time being if this would remove the block to the conference. The Board agreed on condition that all machines of that class at Pallion Forge stood idle during a joint conference. The ASE accepted this and called off the strikes at Barrow and Sunderland.

The conference, held at the Westminster Palace Hotel in Victoria Street, London, with Colonel Dyer in the chair, lasted for five days spread over two weeks. The atmosphere was generally friendly – certainly much more friendly than the tone of the preceding correspondence. Both sides began by expressing a desire for a settlement.

We are all most anxious for that [said Colonel Dyer]. These constant disputes are hurting you as much as they are hurting us. I think rather more; because if trade is driven out of the country it never comes back again. We think that the constant disputes we have had in the last few years have done more to upset the trade of England than a war would have done – a foreign war, I mean.

In the end provisional understandings were reached on trial trips, lodging allowances and overtime, but the greater part of the time was spent in arguing round and round the machine question without either side coming any nearer to the other's point of view.

It was the first ever conference between the leaders of a national engineering employers' organisation and leaders of the major engineering union, and both sides let their hair down and talked about their basic attitudes. Some of the pieces of dialogue are illuminating. For instance when the union suggested that the machine questions should be settled locally, on the basis of local custom, the exchange went like this:

Dyer: The difficulty I see in that is because of late years there has been a great number of aggressions made by your Society on the liberty of the employers. The employer had to give way to these aggressions because he stood alone and he could not resist them. That time, I am happy to say, has passed and the employer now meets you on equal terms, and therefore I don't think the local customs which are now existing could be taken as a rule for local customs in the future. Don't think for one moment that I am objecting to your Society in any way. I may be perfectly wrong and I may stand alone in my opinion, but I hope to see the day when every workman shall belong to some Trade Society, and when every employer shall also belong to an Employers' Trade Society. We shall then meet on equal terms and we shall be able to discuss questions on a broad and sensible basis. Up to the present time we have had to give way against our common sense and against our knowledge of trade and everything simply to save disputes. Therefore I don't think it would be possible to take the present custom as an established custom. We would have to go *de novo* into everything, not as to the custom, but as to what is the best thing to do – the best for the trade of the country and the best for everybody else.

Frank H. Rose [ASE District Delegate for Barrow and Belfast]: It only seems to me with reference to that, Colonel Dyer, that the fact of the disorganisation among the employers is not in any special sense our fault.

Dyer: No, but it is our misfortune, and we must not suffer now for the misfortunes of the past.

Rose: We don't want you to suffer, and we don't want to suffer ourselves. If we have gained any advantage, we have gained it fairly.

Dyer: You have gained that on account of the disorganisation of the employers.

Rose: That is perfectly fair.

Dyer: Perfectly fair, but there is no reason why we should always submit to it. We don't want to interfere with your rights in any way, but we also have rights, and we have given up those rights for an easy life. However, there is no reason why we should go on giving them up. If we can only come to an understanding we should find out that what is good for one is good for the other.

Again, the employers were arguing that a craftsman would not be satisfied with mere repetitive work on an automatic machine:

D. J. Dunlop [a Scottish employer]: It is only by the subdivision of labour with the self-acting machine that we get the man who is contented and willing to stay on. In time, three or four or six months, he becomes proficient. Beyond that he has no ambition, and he goes on working that machine constantly. He knows that as he improves he will get better wages. But the man who has got the general information will not be content.

Barnes: That is to say, the machine man himself becomes a machine.

Dunlop: He himself becomes a machine.

Barnes: Well, we are not going to have it in our Society if we can help it.

Dyer: In any society?

Barnes: In any society, and not in the trade if we can help it.

At another point Barnes quotes a letter from the employers saying: 'The machines are the property of the employers and they are solely responsible for the work turned out by them,' and commented:

If the employers say they have a property in the machines, we might just as well say we have a property in our skill and labour. We each of us have an interest in the trade. Each of us might say we have a property in something, and we would get no forwarder. We desire you to withdraw from that attitude altogether, and to discuss the matter fairly and squarely and in a good spirit.

Returning to the point a little later, Dyer said:

You say that the introduction of this machine is going to lower the wages of skilled men, and I think you are entirely mistaken. It is not the object of any one to lower the wages of skilled men; on the contrary, the higher the skill of the men the higher the wages, but what we do say is that to employ a skilled man on a machine that does not require skill is throwing away good power. You may as well take a steam hammer to crack a nut.

During the conference the ASE, while reiterating their claim for 'the right to work at any machine made by our trade and used by our trade' and their refusal to believe 'that any machine can be as economically and successfully worked by unskilled and semi-skilled as by skilled labour' put forward a scheme to solve the problem. Their proposal was that local joint committees should be set up in each of the districts covered by the Federation. These committees would be composed of equal numbers of employers and ASE members, with an independent person from the Board of Trade to act, if need be, as a referee. In case of a dispute as to wages to be paid for any class of machine, either side would have a right of appeal to the joint committee, which would fix the rate. No change likely to lead to dispute would be made without a definite understanding with the committee and any new machine, which by reason of its construction was likely to lead to dispute through inter- or over-lapping existing customs, would be submitted to the committee for decision.

The Federation at once rejected the plea and made no counter-proposal.

The employers [they said] are at all times willing to meet the members of your council to discuss, and if possible to arrange, any questions which may arise, and they are willing to appoint members to serve on local boards to arrange general rises and falls of wages. They cannot, however, delegate any further authority to the boards you propose or invest them with the power to interfere with the internal management of their works.

Elaborating this at the close of the conference, they said the proposals amounted to a suggestion to supersede the Federation by committees practically controlled by outside referees and the whole existence of the Federation would be brought to an end. The proposals would introduce the principle of allowing outside arbitration to take control of the management of their works.

Finally, in May, the ASE told the Federation that they would be compelled, should occasion arise, to take such steps as might seem to them necessary to protect their trade interests. And the employers told their members who had machines standing idle that they were at liberty to restart them.

Meanwhile the Federation had received an important access of strength. Dyer's Newcastle firm, which had become Armstrong, Mitchell and Co., acquired Sir Joseph Whitworth's in Manchester to become Sir W. G. Armstrong, Whitworth and Co. Dyer moved to Manchester to take charge and immediately set to work to bring Manchester into the Federation. Supported by Andrew Henderson, from Glasgow, he addressed a meeting of Manchester engineering employers on the machine question. A year ago, he told them, he had received reliable information that the ASE intended making an organised attack on the employers in England. The specific object was to gain possession for their members solely of all the machine tools in every works and the machines were to be rated at certain amounts fixed by the Society. He went on to describe how the North-East Coast Association had developed into a powerful organisation which had defeated the ASE in a major strike.

The significance of the meeting was that Manchester had for a quarter of a century been the headquarters of the ITEA. Dyer argued that it was better to have local associations than one large association divided into branches because in every district there were local customs and practices which it was impossible to interfere with. But one large Federation was needed to deal with all general questions of principle. The meeting passed a resolution declaring their willingness to form an association with the object of joining the Federation and the committee of the Manchester branch of the ITEA, with power to add to their number, were empowered to carry out the resolution. The following month the Manchester District Engineering Trades Employers' Federation was set up, with Colonel Dyer as the first president, and immediately applied for federation. If there was ever any doubt that the Federation would supersede the ITEA, this ended it. One of the new association's first actions was to approve the foremen's benefit scheme drafted by Dyer.

Though the machine question had been left unsettled by the April conference, the ASE showed no inclination to start a major struggle over it. But the following month a new issue arose on which both sides were ready to fight. On 20 May a joint deputation from the ITEA and the London engineering employers asked the Federation executive for support in resisting demands in London for a 48-hour week without reduction in wages.

The eight-hour day (or 48-hour week) had become a highly emotive issue during the preceding decade. The new socialist organisations, such as the Social Democratic Federation, had made its introduction by legislation one of their main demands in the eighties, when the depression gave force to any proposal which would result in sharing the available work. Tom Mann, who was an SDF member, wrote a pamphlet in 1886 entitled 'What a Compulsory Eight-hour Day Means to the Workers' and the same year became secretary of the London section of an Eight Hours League.

The movement was international. Skilled workers in Melbourne had got it as long ago as 1856 and it had spread to other parts of Australia and to New Zealand. Americans had been campaigning for it since the sixties and pressure was growing in France and other European countries. An international socialist congress in Paris in 1889 decided on demonstrations in all countries on 1 May 1890, a date already fixed by the American Federation of Labour in the United States. The British trade unions preferred the first Sunday in May, to avoid loss of work, but succeeded in organising a massive demonstration in Hyde Park which a *Times* reporter described as 'the greatest of modern times'.

The TUC had been only slowly convinced of the desirability of a statutory eight hours. The issue was debated regularly at annual congresses from 1887 onwards, but there was a good deal of opposition, particularly from Northumberland and Durham miners, who already had seven hours, and from craft unions which preferred to pursue the objective by industrial action. There were two inconclusive plebiscites, but the Trades Union Congress of 1890, with an influx of delegates from the new unions of unskilled workers and of socialists, finally decided in favour. The ASE had previously voted against it. Robert Austin, their general secretary, explained that they had got the nine-hour day themselves and would get the eight hours when the proper time arrived. But in the meantime they had to consider the hours worked in America and on the Continent and try to end systematic overtime. This attitude was contested by John Burns and others and the ASE delegates were instructed to vote at the 1890 congress in favour of legislative action as an adjunct to voluntary efforts. Burns pointed out that only one-and-a-half of the country's seven million workers were in unions.

In the early nineties some employers began to experiment with the 48-hour week to see if they would lose by its introduction. The normal practice was for work to start at 6 a.m., with a break for breakfast and another for dinner, but productivity on the before-breakfast shift was notoriously low so that comparatively little was lost by letting the men have breakfast at home. The Thames Iron Works and Shipbuilding Company, the largest firm of engineers in the South of England, introduced the 48-hour week in 1892. A Sunderland marine engineer, Mr William Allen, told the Royal Commission on Labour that after a six months' experiment with it, with better time-keeping and little overtime, the cost of production had not increased. In March 1894, William Mather MP, published a report of a year's trial of the shorter week at Mather and Platt's ironworks in Salford, employing 1,200 workers. He found that production and turnover were about the same as the average of the preceding six years. There was an overall saving on overheads, and absenteeism went down from 2.46 to 0.26 per cent. Practically no overtime was worked.

Accounts of some of these experiments read like forerunners of the productivity agreements of the 1960s. The Mather and Platt management began by calling a mass meeting of the men to get their co-operation and closely consulted the ASE executive. They also made 'an earnest appeal to foremen to exercise forethought and vigilance in forwarding work from process to process, furnishing materials well in advance and furnishing such simple facilities and workshop conveniences as might be suggested by the men'.

Mather told the Liberal Government what they were doing on 5 January 1894, Campbell-Bannerman announced in the House of Commons, in reply to a question by John Burns, that the 48-hour week was to be introduced in all the War Office arsenals and factories. The Admiralty followed suit and then the Post Office. The ASE reported that it had been introduced by companies in Sunderland, Manchester, Birmingham, Woolwich, Enfield Lock, Sheffield, Plymouth and Newcastle and that the movement was spreading.

The ITEA devoted 'very considerable sums of money' to trying to check the movement. They urged its dangers on the Government and issued to employers throughout the country a pamphlet arguing that, whatever the results to an individual firm in a short trial in a limited area, once the movement was general it would result in a very large increase in the cost of production and enable foreign competitors to secure control of the market. The spread seems to have slowed down in 1895 and 1896, perhaps because, with an improvement in trade, workers were turning their attention to wage increases. Unemployment was falling and overtime increasing. Nevertheless, the unions might well be excused for believing that they were well on the way to success. The concession of the 48-hour week by the Port of London Shiprepairers' Association in January 1897, was an important gain.

The demand when it was made to the London employers in 1897 came not from the ASE alone. They had set up a joint committee consisting of representatives of the ASE, the boiler-makers and five other sectional societies. After taking a vote of London district members, the joint committee sent a circular to the employers individually requesting an eight-hour day and asking for replies on 26 May. On 27 May a joint reply was received from a number of employers saying that the matter was receiving careful attention, but the time for reply was too short. The joint committee, Barnes recorded afterwards, were prepared to extend the time for reply, but found that some employers were introducing excessive overtime and rushing out work, apparently with a view to a stoppage. So the unions stopped all overtime from 28 May.

In the meantime, as has been said, the London employers had asked for support from the Federation, who arranged a meeting with the ITEA, the London employers and the shipbuilders' federation at which it was agreed to resist if they could get the support of all three organisations. This support was confirmed to a meeting of the Board on 5 June, when the London association, with 50 firms employing 20,000 men, was admitted to membership. Resolutions of support were received from all the other member associations except Belfast. It was decided to inform the joint committee of trades that the Federation could not concede a reduction in hours.

On 17 June, the Bolton association was admitted, and the ITEA reported on meetings of their branches in Bradford, Halifax, Liverpool, Leeds, Hull, Keighley and elsewhere. No reply had been received from the joint trades and a letter was sent to the seven unions requesting that overtime be at once resumed. On 1 July it was reported that the joint trades had threatened a strike against three London firms on Saturday, 3 July, and the employers decided that immediately there was a strike against any member, notices would be given to 25 per cent of employees in the unions involved at all federated firms. A joint committee of the employers' organisations was set up, with ITEA nominees from Hull, Birkenhead, Leicester and Leeds. Colonel Dyer was made chairman, with power to appoint a small emergency committee. It was decided that managers of railway companies, manufacturers, shipowners and others employing workmen of the classes involved, should be communicated with to persuade them not to give work to men locked out.

On 5 July, Federation leaders waited in the Glasgow office for news from London. The first telegram came at 11.28 a.m. from one of the threatened firms, Messrs Middleton: 'Amalgamated Society, Steam Engine, United Smiths, London Society Hammermen struck on Saturday.' Telegrams announcing that the strike had begun followed at 12.16 from Messrs Humphreys and at 1.42 from Messrs Thorneycroft. Letters were immediately sent to Federation members all over the country to post notices of discharge of 25 per cent of men each week beginning on 13 July. Notices were to be posted in non-union shops with an addendum that as the workers were not society members they would not be affected. Immediately the first notices took effect, all the members of the societies involved left work. The great lock-out had begun.

On the face of it, the ASE had chosen favourable ground for their challenge and timed it well. In ten years their membership had risen from 52,000 to 92,000. The Society's funds for the first time were above £300,000. The reform of the union's structure in 1892 had given it a new vitality. George Barnes, a future Cabinet Minister, was an able as well as a militant general secretary, only 38 years old, and he had the energetic support of John Burns and Tom Mann and other leaders of a new generation of trade unionists. The economy was moving forward as it had not done since the early seventies and engineering was sharing in the advance. Moreover the struggle for the eight-hour day in London was already more than half won – they were concentrating on the weakest point in the employers' line. In the preceding years the unions had been in frequent bitter conflict with each other over questions of demarcation, but they seemed to have largely united to press for the 48-hour week and in any case the ASE had half the trade union membership in the industry. The Society had experienced men in district committees all over the country while the employers had a new and untried organisation which had to be built up as the struggle proceeded. There was much justification for the feeling in the union that, as George Barnes put it afterwards, 'there was as favourable a combination of circumstances on the side of the unions as was likely to be presented.'

Against all these advantages, the employers had little on their side but confidence in themselves and their power of leadership and their conviction that they must re-establish their managerial freedom if they were to hold their own in the increasingly cut-throat world of international competition. They believed that to concede the 48-hour week when men in other countries were working much longer would be disastrous. If they allowed it in London there would be difficulty in preventing it from spreading to other parts of the country. Moreover the association of 48-hour week demands with socialist activities made it emotionally repugnant to them. Above all they wanted to be able to do as they wished in their own works.

They were a remarkable group of men – tough, determined, self-reliant, energetic, most of them with a strong sense of duty to their workers in a world where standards were very different from those of today. They were engineers who prided themselves on their technical ability and respected the skill of the craftsmen who worked for them. Many accepted civic responsibilities Frequently they were accused of wanting to smash the ASE, and impatient remarks during the struggle may have given some grounds for this, but there is ample evidence, before and after the dispute as well as during it, that they accepted the existence of the unions – so long as they were kept in their proper place.

The remarks by Dyer on collective organisation during the machine question conference, quoted above, are a significant indication of this. Visits to America had made him envious of management's freedom from trade union interference there, but he did not attempt to emulate the strongarm tactics of the American bosses. When Sir Benjamin Browne, one of his colleagues in the North-east, was invited to preside at the opening of a new headquarters for the Boilermakers' Society in Newcastle in 1890, he told his audience that he had always believed in and upheld trade unionism. He very much doubted, he went on, if it would be possible for the enormous enterprises of the country to go on as they did if the workers were not organised so as to act with unanimity and system all through the country.

That did not mean he thought the 1897 struggle unnecessary. For seven or eight years, Browne said as it was coming to an end, the ASE had been adopting a different policy from that of other well-established unions.

> The new unionism taught the workmen to disregard the interests of both customers and employers and get all they could for themselves; it also taught them that employers were their enemies and must be distrusted accordingly . . . the old unions stood aloof from it, with the exception of the ASE, which for some reason adopted a great deal of its policy, and from that time began to interfere in the management of engineering works, and to encroach on the employers in a manner not done previously.

Colonel Dyer – Lt-Col Henry Clement Swinerton Dyer – conducted the struggle like a military campaign. Sixty-three years old at the time, and troubled by a bad heart, he worked indefatigably, travelling from one engineering centre to another, building up the morale of the troops. Coming from a military family, he had entered the Royal Artillery at the age of 18 and served in the Crimean War and the Indian Mutiny. In both campaigns, according to *The Times* obituary notice, his horse was shot from under him. When he left the service he became superintendent at the Royal Small Arms Factory at Enfield and then went to Sir Joseph Whitworth in Manchester before his talent for organisation brought him to the position of director of one of Armstrong's great departments at Elswick. Photographs show him as a handsome, round-faced man with dark moustache, greying whiskers and hair, and steady, unquestioning eyes. He was a man of integrity, calm under attack, who was trusted by his opponents. One imagines that as an officer he would impose strict discipline, but look after his men, as he tried to look after his workers, always ready to help a promising apprentice to pursue his technical education. He resented union interference with his efforts to do this.

A gentler form of paternalism, perhaps, was that of Sir Benjamin Browne, also from the North-east, who was not only active in the Federation leadership but also became president of the ITEA in 1897. The son of a colonel, he grew up in the Cotswolds and his relations were all quiet country gentlemen, clergymen or soldiers. According to a memoir by his daughters,

> He had in his blood the squire, to whom the people dependent on him were the first charge on his income and care, and the commanding officer, whose men were as his children, to be trained, fed and kept in the highest possible state of efficiency. The necessity of any antagonism between employer and employed was foreign to his ideas . . . For working men as a class he felt the warmest affection. There was no trouble he would not take to put their cause on a permanently better footing and it was always a singular pleasure to him to have a talk with one of his workmen.

The London employers' leader, Alexander Siemens, was paternalistic in a rougher, German mould. A native of Hanover, he was a private in the Franco-Prussian War, in which he was wounded and won the Iron Cross. Later he came to London to join the offshoot of the German firm of Siemens Brothers, making and laying electric cables and later developing electric light, and became managing director and a naturalised Englishman. Mr J. D. Scott, in a centenary history of Siemens Brothers in 1958, records that the firm was one of the first to institute an old age pension scheme and sick fund for employees and an endowment fund for widows and orphans.

The paternal relationship, however, was not a soft one; it was based both upon the ordinary industrial descipline of the period, and upon a more local and specialised discipline which owed something to Germany and something to the sea. . . . Work was casual and intermittent. . . . With the discipline and *laissez-faire* harshness, however, was a sense of comradeship and kindness. A boy who looked peaky was sent off by Alexander Siemens for a spell at his house in the country where there was a dormitory above the stables for this purpose.

Another London leader, Alfred Yarrow, was a philanthropist who owned a marine engineering works on the Isle of Dogs which had never experienced a strike or lock-out. His men, according to his wife's biography of him, struck with tears in their eyes. He bought the Royal Mail Steamer *Southampton*, just as she completed her final trip, and had her moored opposite the works. He then advertised for non-unionist fitters, etc., intelligent apprentices just out of their time, improvers and others, stating that new hands could be 'comfortably quartered out of reach and annoyance of pickets'. For six and a half months workers lived on the ship. A religious service was held every Sunday with Yarrow and his family present. They had a library of between 300 and 400 books and frequent entertainments. A doctor attended twice a week without charge. Ambulance classes were arranged and a number of men got certificates. Boxing gloves were asked for and provided and indoor games arranged.

From the Glasgow headquarters of the Federation, Andrew Henderson, the Clydeside leader, was scarcely less active than Dyer himself in visiting different parts of the country, though much less in the public eye. There was too Thomas Biggart, the joint secretary, with all the threads in his hands, shrewd, skilful and industrious. He belonged to the firm of solicitors which shortly afterwards became Biggart, Lumsden and Co., and which still occupies the same Glasgow building as the Scottish engineering and shipbuilding employers' associations. A full-

length portrait of him hangs in the firm's boardroom – a somewhat hard-faced man with sandy moustache and hair, pince-nez
and wing collar. He was abstemious, a teetotaller and non-smoker
whose frugal lunches became an office joke, always punctilious,
an exacting superior with no interests outside his work. He was
to remain secretary of the Federation until the headquarters
were moved to London in 1910, when he was replaced by Allan
Smith, of the same firm. Biggart was also secretary of the Shipbuilding Employers' Federation until they too moved to London
and he was succeeded by yet another member of the firm –
Andrew Duncan, later to become a member of the Government
in the Second World War. Biggart himself remained with the
Scottish association, first as secretary, then director, then consultant, until 1947 when he was 85.

When the lock-out began, both sides found themselves suffering
immediate defections. The most important was that of the Boilermakers' Society, the second largest in the industry, from the
union side. Their district committee had been represented on the
joint committee of trades and taken part in its decisions, but
when hostilities broke out the society's executive council refused
to sanction their participation. Robert Knight, their secretary,
believed that a shorter working week was obtainable without a
great frontal battle and that the precipitate action of the ASE was
in part an attempt to outdo the unions in the Federation of
Engineering and Shipbuilding Trades (FEST) of which the ASE
was not a member. Writing a few years later, D. C. Cummings,
who succeeded Knight as secretary, said their district committee
was represented on the joint committee 'upon the distinct understanding that the movement was to be a peaceful one'. Had the
ASE allowed the federated trades to continue their efforts, he
declared, 'a shorter working week than 53 or 54 hours would
have been an established fact.'

On the employers' side, Pirrie in Belfast kept Harland and
Wolff out of the struggle and on the Clyde the Fairfield Shipbuilding and Engineering Company, one of the biggest firms,
refused to post notices. The Belfast firms which signed an undertaking to support the Federation had meetings among themselves
and tried to persuade Pirrie to change his mind. Pirrie told them
that owing to his difference with the Federation on the last
occasion it would be derogatory to his dignity to sign the under-

taking or act with the Federation, but he undertook not to take on any workmen who had been locked out. Later, speaking as Lord Mayor of Belfast, Pirrie referred to 'the impossibility of satisfactorily and permanently adjusting matters by the recourse to measures that might have been well enough 50 years ago, but are utterly impractical at the end of the nineteenth century'. The Belfast association made an angry retort, contrasting his attitude to the 1895 Clyde–Belfast lock-out 'primarily for the protection of his own firm' with his attitude to the same measures adopted in 1897 'primarily for the protection of the London employers'.

The Fairfield company wrote to the North-west association:

> When the minority of London masters decided to use the North-west District Association to fight their dispute with the men, I felt sure we should get into difficulties. Conditions of labour there and on the Clyde are very different and I cannot but be of opinion that when your association was formed and certainly when the Fairfield company joined it, such a course of action was not contemplated.

They refused to take part in the lock-out and the name of Fairfield was duly removed from the roll of members at a special meeting of the association in August.

The course of the struggle can be clearly followed in the daily reports to the executive by the Emergency (or Urgency) Committee. From the beginning effort was concentrated on spreading the lock-out as widely as possible. Within two days of receiving instructions from the Federation, notices had been posted by 140 firms, 30 in London, 27 in the North-east, 25 in Scotland, 20 in Manchester and 8 in Belfast. Reports of more firms joining in arrived almost daily. By the end of July, 250 were involved.

Frequently, the committee made requests for help. For instance on 8 July: 'Sheffield firms – can any members assist in enlisting their support?' The following day the Leicester secretary asked if anything could be done to get the Birmingham trade to join in, as Leicester firms were anxious on this point. Often particular firms are named. On 10 July: 'Inquiry has been received today whether anything can be done with these firms – Darlington Forge Co., Kilmarnock Forge Co. and others.'

Efforts in Birmingham, incidentally, were fruitless. A Birmingham, Wolverhampton and District Association was formed in October and within a week was visited by a deputation from the Federation to urge them to join in. But they decided that, while sympathising, they would not advise their members that any general lock-out was necessary. They could take what action they wished. In the event, no Birmingham firm ever joined in though five from Wolverhampton did so. Sir Richard Tangye, of the Cornwall works in Birmingham, was particularly critical of the Federation policy.

Having no quarrel with our men [he wrote at the end], having received no demands from them, and after an unexampled record of 40 years of peaceful relations with them, we were asked to turn them – nearly 2500 persons – into the street. In speaking to one of the principal members of the Federation, I said that such an act on our part would be a crime.

When it was all over, Tangye sent a donation of £500 to the employers' funds for the benefit of the worst-hit small firms, but he also sent £500 to the ASE in aid of men out of work. The Federation returned his cheque.

The emergency committee made several appeals for facts from actual experience of the 48-hour week because the Press were asking for them. The *Daily Chronicle* had published a series of enthusiastic interviews with employers who had introduced the 48-hour week. 'The early glowing accounts can be got but not the later experience, which is understood to be unsatisfactory,' said the committee. Several firms obliged. Members soon began to press for a manifesto in reply to one issued by the ASE the day before the lock-out began. This had pointed to the success of the 48-hour experiments and claimed that 159 London firms had already conceded their demand. The real object of the lock-out, it contended, was to crush the ASE.

It is for you to decide [said the manifesto to the public] whether these pseudo Napoleons of Newcastle are to ruthlessly dislocate the whole trade of the country with impunity in the foolish attempt to cripple the ASE, or whether, on the other hand, the workman is to be allowed quietly, peaceably and calmly to work his way upward to increased leisure, fuller home life and greater freedom, with the unfailing concomitants of mental, moral and physical development, which are the true sources of a nation's greatness.

The committee thought an employers' manifesto might be delayed a little.

The committee learn on good authority that the ASE are staggered with the unanimity of the employers and the unexpected adverse criticisms of the Press. All the independent Press are writing the employers' case strongly. The method of resistance is criticised in some instances, but that is a detail. Later on, when the public has been more educated, a manifesto from the employers will come much better.

On 16 July, the Mayor of Hull asked if they would accept the mediation of the Lord Mayor of London, but the committee were unanimously of the opinion 'that no outside interference was necessary'. The next meeting of the executive instructed the committee to decline all mediation at the instance of third parties as against the employers' interests.

By now letters were arriving regularly from railway companies promising not to take on men locked out. The ITEA were holding meetings in all their branch areas but the Federation executive observed that the Shipbuilding Employers' Federation had not yet given active assistance.

The struggle had aroused immense public interest, probably more than any previous industrial conflict in the country's history, and the papers were giving it an enormous amount of space. But by the end of July the emergency committee were getting less happy about the Press, complaining that some representatives were giving news in a more favourable light to the men than circumstances warranted. The unions were making extravagant claims about successes – for instance that 200 firms had conceded the 48-hour week since the struggle began or that 15,000 more men in London had got it, which could be denied and ridiculed but which made some impact. And some of the claims were justified. Members were asked to get in touch with someone in authority on the newspapers concerned. Not only news paragraphs but leading articles, it was suggested, could be influenced by discussion with those in authority. But *The Times* and other newspapers were complaining of lack of adequate information from the employers.

The executive decided to delay the employers' manifesto no longer and it appeared on 4 August. It asserted that, so far from being devised to smash the engineers' society, the Federation was a purely defensive body, 'less an invention of the employers than of the Amalgamated Society of Engineers itself'. The leaders of that society had formerly relied on conciliatory methods but of late years they had favoured more irritating and more irrational tactics. They brought their full resources to bear, first upon one employer then upon another and acts of aggression were not confined to employers but also directed against weaker trade societies. The situation became so intolerable that the employers were compelled to combine in their own defence. If combination was right for everybody, as the society averred, it could not be wrong for the engineering employers. The history of the dispute was outlined to show that the Federation 'exerted itself to the utmost to obviate a conflict'. The cost of the 48-hour week and the dangers of foreign competition were described, and it was argued that the workman was receiving his fair share of the benefits of labour-saving appliances.

During August the struggle grew increasingly bitter. Incomplete returns on 11 August showed 25,000 men now out, including 3200 non-unionists. Pickets were said to be becoming 'somewhat desperate' and in some areas an arrangement for 'picketing the pickets' had been adopted. 'Retired soldiers, members of the police force and others,' said the committee, 'have been engaged to remain around the works gates, watching and noting every action of the pickets and providing evidence if this should prove necessary.' Some firms were making use of organisations which had been started in the nineties to provide non-unionists to replace strikers.

The best known of these was the National Free Labour Association, led by the son of a policeman named William Collison, who claimed to have kept twenty of London's largest firms going. During the lock-out, towards the end of July, Colonel Dyer attended a meeting presided over by the Earl of Wemyss and moved that the Free Labour Protection Association be formed. The motion was seconded by G. A. Laws, general manager of the Shipping Federation, an employers' organisation which kept three vessels to carry strike-breakers from one port to another. Dyer and Siemens were both appointed to the committee. The new association was not overtly a strike-breaking organisation. Its objects were to test the efficacy of the laws for the protection of non-unionists and if necessary get them amended, to ensure the observance of the law in all disputes, and to oppose all legislation injuriously affecting industry. However, Frederick Millar, the secretary, later wrote to Leslie Field, of the London association, agreeing to set up a labour bureau and register for workmen for the exclusive use of members of the association and claiming to have been sending men daily, in charge of a detective, to federated shops in London and the provinces. Millar told the Royal Commission on Trades Disputes that the association had a large force of police at their disposal who could be sent anywhere at a few hours' notice and sworn in as special constables where necessary. 'These men happen to be big, strong, powerful fellows and their presence is quite sufficient to ensure the men getting about without discomfort,' he added.

Complaints of intimidation by pickets were being made in a number of districts. The Manchester employers agreed 'that the terrorism and interference with freedom now destroying this district is a scandal which calls for immediate action' and referred to 'this disgraceful condition of affairs where trade union law has entirely superseded the law of England.' Sebastian Z de Ferranti, inventor and employer, said there were hundreds of men and their dependents 'starving because they dare not start work for fear of their lives'. At the same time he was urging employers to take on non-unionists from other districts. The association sent a deputation to urge the Lord Mayor to create a police intelligence department to find out in what parts of Manchester crowds were assembling and to post a proclamation saying that the assemblage of crowds for intimidation and annoyance was illegal and would be rigorously dealt with. It was the duty of the authorities to deal with these illegal acts, they told him, and not the citizens concerned. The Lord Mayor replied that he was with the employers in the matter and would do all in his power to preserve order. In Leeds the Chief Constable attended a meeting of the association committee to discuss reports of intimidation. He promised he would supply the fullest protection he could 'free of charge' and arrange to have several areas patrolled by mounted police at dinner time and closing time.

It became evident as August advanced that the result of the struggle was in the balance and that the key to victory or defeat lay in London. There was no sign of progress there. Union propaganda in the North was to the effect that northern firms were bearing the brunt of the struggle while those in London were offering little resistance, while in the South they suggested that London employers were being used by a few northern firms to aim a blow at the unions. John Burns asserted that their aim was to divert trade from the Thames to the five northern rivers.

'I know as a positive fact,' Yarrow wrote to Field, 'that many firms have not joined the Federation simply because they were under the impression from what they saw in the Press that the men were getting numerous converts and that the masters were being gradually weakened and would have to collapse ultimately.' Canvassing committees were set up by the associations and that in London reported that some London firms despaired of being able to resist the unions. They had no acquaintance with the big employers of the North and had a feeling of isolation.

On 20 August, Biggart wrote to Field urging upon him the importance of getting some of the firms that had conceded the 48-hour week to revert to 54 hours.

It is becoming more evident every day [he said] that for a completely successful result to the present struggle, something of this kind must be accomplished in London. London holds the key to complete victory. [Five days later he returned to the theme.] For weeks we have heard nothing but reports of concession after concession, that London was practically won, that there was a mere handful of men out and that they were being rapidly absorbed, that the London employers were going on comfortably while scores of other places, not attacked in the first instance, were suffering fully. You can understand that such statements repeated week after week, and our being unable to give some authoritative denial and actual figures to controvert the position, have had a depressing effect.

Pressure on London firms was intensified. Apart from general arguments about it being in the interest of all employers in the industry to defeat union aggression, there were more direct pressures that could be used, for instance warnings that those placing orders in the future would direct them so far as possible to firms which had joined in the struggle. A careful note was being kept of firms which posted discharge notices, and a full list was printed in a booklet after the struggle was over and circulated abroad as well as in this country. 'The members of the Federation recognise that it is the right when ordering tools to give preference to other firms in the Federation,' Biggart wrote to Field. Nor was this presure confined to the engineering industry. At the end of August the Colliery Owners' Association informed the Federation that colliery firms at a recent meeting had agreed they would 'regard it as their duty to place and influence future orders for machinery with those engineering firms which have determined to withstand this demand from their workmen'. The London firms were also warned that those in the North would not give way so that if those in London did so, they would be in a worse competitive position. The Federation publicised an examination of the ASE finances to show the strain being put upon them, suggesting they would be in a desperate plight by Christmas. Favourable Press cuttings were regularly circulated. The emergency committee made repeated requests for the help of members to influence named London firms.

At last, on 9 September, Biggart wrote once more to Field: 'It is splendid news regarding the repentant sinners in London.' He must have had foreknowledge for it was not until 22 September that the emergency committee issued a list of five London firms which had reverted to the 54-hour week, and also of five new firms to post notices. Three days later eighteen members of the newly-formed London Master Brassfounders' Association, who had also received a 48-hour week claim, posted notices. From the beginning of October there were frequent reports of London firms reverting to 54 hours. On 5 October, twenty London ship repairing firms posted notices.

The turning point had been passed and from this time onwards eventual victory for the employers was certain, but the ASE were to keep up their losing battle for a long time yet. The Board of Trade were now making informal approaches to both sides and early in October suggested a basis for settlement. The Federation executive were unanimous that it could not be entertained, that conditions in the industry did not admit of any reduction in hours and that the Federation was determined to secure for its members absolute freedom in the management of their works. Spelling this out on 11 October, they said that this freedom must include

(a) the right to employ either union or non-union men upon an equal footing;

(b) the right to employ upon machines or any other class of work such men as the employers select as most suitable and at such wages as the employers may agree upon;

(c) the right to employ any man upon piece-work in cases where both employer and individual workmen are agreeable to this system of work;

(d) the right of employers to afford to all men and boys in their employment such instruction in handicraft as they consider desirable to enable them to perform skilled work and thereby earn higher wages;

(e) the right to work such reasonable overtime at the rates of wages agreed upon as may be required, and a provision that overtime working shall not be interfered with except by mutual agreement;

(f) no recognition of a maximum, uniform or minimum rate of wage;

(g) no limitation on apprentices.

As the Board of Trade were to comment later: 'Though the immediate cause of the general dispute was the demand for the eight-hour day in London, the real questions at issue between the parties had become of a much more far-reaching kind and now involved questions of workshop control and the limits of trade union interference.'

The Board of Trade continued to make informal contacts and on 20 October Sir Courtenay Boyle, the secretary, made a formal proposal to both sides for a joint conference. He suggested as a basis for a meeting the formula:

The Employers' Federation, while disavowing any intention of interfering with the legitimate action of trade unions, will admit no right of interference with the management of their business. The trade unions, on their part, while maintaining their right of combination, disavow any intention of interfering with the management of the business of the employers [and] the demand for a 48-hour week made by the joint committee of the unions without previous request for a conference with the employers is withdrawn.

The Federation executive replied that on the basis proposed, relations between the employers and workmen would be practically the same as before, with all the consequent probabilities of industrial disturbances. However if the Board of Trade's letter was regarded not as an offer of mediation but as a suggestion for a meeting, they were prepared to meet the unions. They restated their position and added: 'In view of the persistent misrepresentations which have been put forward during the dispute, the Federated Employers take this opportunity of again repeating that they have not and never have had any desire to encroach upon the reasonable functions of trade unions or in any way to interfere with the right of combination among workmen.' The ASE said that if they were to withdraw their demand for a 48-hour week, lock-out notices should also be withdrawn and they asked for an independent chairman. Eventually the Board of Trade draft, with some additions, was accepted by both sides.

To prepare for the conference the Federation collected some hundreds of examples of union interference with management functions, some drawn from the ASE monthly reports and the remainder received from member firms, classed under the headings Restriction of Output, Working of Machines, Restriction of Overtime, and Interference in Shops. At a preliminary meeting on 17 November between Dyer, Henderson and Biggart for the employers and Barnes and Alfred Sellicks, the ASE chairman, for the unions, it was agreed that there should be an immediate truce until the end of the conference under which the employers would suspend any notices that had not been carried into effect and the unions would not interfere with men working.

The conference opened at the Westminster Palace Hotel on 24 November and sittings took place on seven days between then and 3 December. The question of the 48-hour week was left to the last day of the fortnight. From the very beginning the employers were pre-occupied with the establishment of the right to manage their works. 'The free management of our own works we must have, or else we cannot work, and that is the reason of the lock-out,' said Colonel Dyer. He declined to allow discussion on other questions, or even to say what the employers' other proposals were, until that main issue had been thrashed out. It took the whole of the first week. The basis of their proposals was the formula suggested by the Board of Trade on the freedom to manage. To this they added 'Any condition of labour which prevails in

any of the workshops of the Federated employers shall be adopted
in any other Federated workshop at the option of the employer' –
this covered the introduction of piece-work – and 'The Federated
Employers affirm their right and duty to maintain freedom of
employment and to support freedom of action for themselves and
for those they employ.'

Other proposed clauses followed the principles adopted on
18 October. The Federation were prepared to recommend that
no man should be required to work more than 40 hours overtime
in any four weeks except in special circumstances, but all existing restrictions were to be removed. There was also provision
for machinery to deal with disputes arising out of the operation
of the proposals. The 48-hour claim was brusquely turned
down.

> It seems to us that the whole principle running through the
> whole of these proposals is the employer dealing with the indi-
> vidual workman [commented Barnes]. You concede no right
> at all to an individual workman making his bargain collectively
> if he thinks it proper. You ask us, as trade unions, to sign our
> death warrant, that we shall have no further opportunity of
> having anything to do with the conditions under which our
> men work.

The clause about pay seemed to rule out the negotiation of
minimum rates, although district agreements on rates already
existed in a number of areas, but the negotiation of rises and falls
in wages was to be permissible. The ASE, Colonel Dyer kept
insisting, had every right to fix any rate of wages that they pleased
for their own members and to say they would not work at a lower
rate. Dyer argued they were not doing away with collective bargaining but extending it. The employers had yielded little when
the conference was adjourned until 14 December so that the men
could vote on the proposals.

The conflict on the principle of collective bargaining provoked
public controversy during the ten days of the adjournment. The
Daily Chronicle published a letter from fifteen Oxford dons who
described the employers' terms as 'a deliberate attempt to over-
throw the principle of collective bargaining' and 'an absolute
denial of the legitimate action of trade unionism as such'. But
Robert Knight, of the boilermakers, was on the side of Dyer in

this. 'My society has never asked employers in any district to fix a standard wage for us,' he stated.

> The society has done this itself, in each district, and by doing this we have striven to make the cost of labour the same in all districts as far as possible so that no employer may have an advantage over another in taking contracts. Employers know our rates and do not attempt to pay our members less, but if they thought they could get men outside our society who would do the work cheaper, they would have a perfect right to do so.

A group of eminent authorities, including Sidney and Beatrice Webb, were asked for their views, and replied that it was 'a fundamental principle of trade unionism to replace individual bargaining between the wage-earner and the employer by collective bargaining between the whole body of organised workmen and their employers'. They quoted as examples agreed standard piece-work lists in cotton, a joint pay committee of the coalowners in Northumberland and Durham and the local miners' unions, and working rules made in most towns between local master builders and unions of building operatives.

When the conference reassembled on 14 December, Barnes reported that the men had turned down the employers' terms by 68,966 votes to 752 after the heaviest vote in the history of his society. Three more days of discussion followed, much of it in a three-a-side sub-committee. The employers had prepared notes and explanations of the proposed clauses in the agreement which were of a somewhat reassuring character and a good deal of time was spent on textual details in the proposals. When they came to the 48-hour week, the union leaders made determined pleas for a reduction to at least 51 hours and were obviously deeply disappointed when the employers refused any concession. The negotiations broke down with mutual expressions of regret.

> Dyer: We don't like it. We believe that we are fighting in a good cause. We are fighting for you as well as for ourselves.
> Sellicks: The difficulty is to get us to believe that. When you hit a fellow in the face and you say it is for his good it is difficult to make him believe it.
> Dyer: But we don't hit you in the face. We have been on the defensive and will always be.

During the long negotiations, some modifications of the original proposals had been made. The first clause on management rights had added to it a reference to the rights of any trade union to raise any question arising from the management decision. To the clause of freedom of employment was added a reference to the possibility of collective action against the employment of non-unionists (after going through the provisions for avoiding disputes) and advice by the Federation to their members not to object to union workmen or give preference to non-union workmen. On piece-work, it was stated that the Federation would not countenance any piece-work conditions which would not allow a workman of average efficiency to earn at least the wage at which he was rated. Existing practices regarding overtime could be continued if mutually satisfactory to the local employers' association and the workmen concerned.

After the breakdown of negotiations, there was another ballot, the ASE this time attempting to widen their support by taking a vote on the idea of a 51-hour week compromise as well as on the employers' terms. The terms were rejected by 54,933 votes to 1041 and the 51-hour week by 42,082 to 8515. The Federation executive met on 30 December and declared the truce at an end. Suspended discharge notices were put into effect and efforts to spread the lock-out still further were resumed. One of the new firms to post notices was the Fairfield Shipbuilding and Engineering Company.

Colonel Dyer had been obstinate but calm and patient at the conference but his suspicions of socialist influences in the unions were evidently preying on his mind.

The whole question [he said in his report to the Manchester association] was the socialistic element which had, most unfortunately for the country, got the power among the trade unions now. It was socialism which had caused the whole of the dispute – the new militant trade unionism which wanted to force upon the country and the employers at large a socialist propaganda which could not fail to ruin the country if it was allowed to persist. The hours question, the machine question and the variety of questions which had been raised, were merely the thin veil of sophistry under which the socialistic course was being forced upon them. Unless they faced this socialist

element and faced it with determination, they might rest
assured that the country would be ruined, and it was the
strong feeling that every employer had that he was not fighting
the trade unions but the socialist element alone, which was
trying its best to destroy the real proper function of the trade
unions, and to bring the employer and capital down to their
knees. They were perfectly willing and ready and anxious,
when trade warranted it, to increase wages in a reasonable
manner, and they did not want the trade unions to help them
to do it. He believed – and he said it honestly – that the
Employers' Federation was the kindest friend that the British
workman had ever had.

The ASE were now in a desperate situation. Not only were the
calls on their funds by their own members growing steadily
heavier but they were having to support some of the smaller
unions such as the United Machine Workers. Help came from
the public and from abroad but it was inadequate. The TUC in
September had passed a resolution of support but the ASE were
disappointed by the tone of the motion and the TUC showed
little energy in circulating members with an appeal for moral
and financial support. The results were insubstantial. In November the society was encouraged to make an application for membership of the Engineering and Shipbuilding Trades Federation,
which would have brought support from the boilermakers and
other engineering unions not involved, but when they sent a delegation to a federation meeting it was 'humiliated'. The ASE
called a conference in December, to which the unions in the
Federated Trades sent representatives, to try to get them to join
in attempting to enforce a 51-hour week but were unsuccessful.
Another meeting was called by the London Trades Council at
the end of the month but produced little additional financial
support.

On 12 January 1898 the ASE executive decided to withdraw
the demand for a 48-hour week and this was endorsed by the
joint committee. By now employers who had previously refrained
from posting notices were streaming on to the bandwagon – a
list of them appeared in the emergency committee's reports
almost every day – and on 22 January the Federation decided
to close their list of resisting employers. The union had one last

meeting with the employers and persuaded them to incorporate in the terms of settlement the notes and explanations which they had provided of the various clauses and to agree that they should be as binding as the clauses themselves. With this face-saver they recommended their members to vote for the terms.

The notes did make the agreement sound less harsh. That on the initial clause, saying that neither employers nor unions would interfere with each other's functions, added, 'No new condition of labour is introduced or covered by this clause' and that was the general tenor. On piece-work, the note said that the clause contained just the conditions that had been in force for long in various shops, and on overtime that the conditions were precisely those in operation in various places, and on the limitation of apprentices that the clause merely put on record existing practice. Following the clause saying that employers would be free to employ workmen at rates of wages mutually satisfactory, but that there would be district negotiations on general alterations in rates, there was the comment, 'Collective bargaining between the unions and the employers' associations is here made the subject of distinct agreement.'

Members of the unions involved, now numbering ten, and three thousand 'non-society' men, took part in a final ballot which resulted in 28,588 votes in favour of acceptance and 13,297 against. Work was resumed on 31 January. The lock-out had lasted just over six and a half months. During this time the number of firms involved rose from 140 to 702 and the number of workers affected from 25,000 to 35,000 directly and 12,500 indirectly. The number of working days lost was 6,849,000. The funds of the ASE were reduced from £360,000 to £134,000. The cost to the employers was never estimated.

There had been numerically bigger disputes, but because of the implications and the principles involved, it was generally recognised at the time as the most important the country had known. The Federation had won an overwhelming victory and been built up into the most powerful employers' organisation in Britain's history by determined and skilful leaders among whom Colonel Dyer was pre-eminent.

Less than two months after the settlement, Dyer died suddenly at his home in Manchester. 'An amiable man of generous disposition who would do right according to his lights,' said George

Barnes. 'But he was one who believed in the mastery of the employers. His influence in the Federation, which was very great, would have been used in the direction of peace and goodwill if he had lived.'

CHAPTER 4

Federation Rule 1898–1914

Consolidation and Expansion – The Procedure Takes
Root – Watching the New Laws – A North-east Coast
Strike – Wages as an Issue – The York Memorandum

From the end of the lock-out until the beginning of the First
World War the Federation dominated the engineering scene.
They had acquired prestige and self-confidence such as probably
no previous employers' organisation had known, while the ASE
had suffered a blow to their morale from which they were slow to
recover. Their losses in membership and funds were restored in a
few years, but the effect of the terms of settlement resulted in a
continuing internal conflict. The union executive did their best to
enforce the terms, but the district committees grew more and
more restive and rebellious. In the past they had been largely
autonomous, making their own working rules, which differed
from district to district, and carrying on their own negotiations.
They found themselves suddenly in a strait jacket of national
control. Where they could not reach local agreement, their disputes had to go up through the Procedure to the national leaders.
Where they attempted to persevere with their old policies, for
instance by opposing piece-work or trying to limit the number of
apprentices or interfering with the manning of machines, they
found themselves ordered by their own national officials to stop
it. They found even their wage negotiations subject to central
conference rulings and national agreements were negotiated
which the men repudiated and resented. While the national
leaders soon came to accept the value of the Procedure as a means
of avoiding strikes, many of the district committees regarded the
whole of the terms as anathema.

The result was continuous tension between the executive
council and the districts which from time to time broke into open

conflict. Several times branches and district organisations were suspended. George Barnes was howled down in Glasgow during a dispute in 1903 which was followed by suspension of the Glasgow district committee. In 1908, after the men on the North-east coast had repudiated the executive's advice, Barnes resigned from the general secretaryship. The internal dissension reached its climax in 1912 and 1913 when there was a physical struggle to occupy the union headquarters, followed by a series of lawsuits. New and more militant leaders won the final battles and only then, in the midst of the pre-war boom did the Society begin to regain its confidence. The strike which resulted in Barnes' resignation was the only one in the whole of the period which came near to precipitating a national stoppage. The great struggles which took place in other industries from 1910 to 1914 largely passed engineering by.

The union had left the TUC in 1899, partly because of resentment of its lukewarm support during the lock-out, and apart from the years 1905–7 remained outside until 1918. It continued to quarrel with other engineering unions, though in 1905 it affiliated temporarily to the Federation of Engineering and Shipbuilding Trades. A union in this state, divided within and almost friendless without, was in no position to challenge the power of the Federation, whose position the ASE were still describing in 1910 as 'strong and almost impregnable'.

The Federation's first object at the turn of the century was to make sure they enforced and maintained the freedom of management which they had secured as a result of the lock-out. New associations and members had to be absorbed into a reconstructed organisation and they had to work out, learning by experience as they went along, how best to operate the Procedure. In addition to the seven associations which were members when the lock-out began, numerous others had been hurriedly set up during its course – some based on former ITEA branches – and had to be given proper constitutions and make formal applications for membership. By the end of 1898 the number of affiliated associations had risen to thirty-six.

In 1899 a new constitution and conditions of federation were approved. The name was changed to The Engineering Employers' Federation. No alteration was made in the objects except that the reference to the promotion of conciliation boards was replaced by a clause 'to make provision for the settlement of all differences between members of the federated associations and their workmen'. Associations applying for membership had to include a resolution signed by their members accepting the federation constitution and undertaking to abide by it. The power of expulsion was clearly set out. The controlling body was to be the Executive Board consisting of the president, ex-president, two vice-presidents and not more than fifty members. Vice-presidents were not to serve for more than two years. There were to be three standing committees – emergency, finance and parliamentary. No step of general importance to the engineering trade was to be taken by any federated association without previous consultation with the Board. No member was to employ any workman on strike or locked out and use of inquiry forms was compulsory. The entrance fee was 2s. for each £100 of the average wages bill for the previous three years for associations and the same for individual members. The annual subscription was fixed as 1s. for each £100. Subsidies were to be provided for members involved in disputes approved by the Board and for workmen 'suffering in the employer's interests from labour questions or disputes'.

The Foremen's Mutual Benefit Society, which had been very much Colonel Dyer's brainchild, was also established to compensate non-union foremen for the lack of union benefits. Member firms of the association could become contributory members and recommend foremen from any department as members so long as they were not members of a union. The society was a self-governing body with an executive committee including members elected by the contributors and the foremen. Pensions were initially to be paid at sixty-five, or earlier to those disabled. Progress was slower than hoped for and in the summer of 1899 Henderson reminded members of the Emergency Committee that the most difficult questions they had had to deal with had been 'those cases where the difficulties have been intensified through the action or influence of union foremen'. In 1900 new benefits were added but only 12 per cent of member firms had joined the scheme. During the following half century the Federation appealed at frequent intervals for more support for the society. In addition to the FMBS, the Federation established a Dyer Memorial Fund to make special grants to foremen – or their widows – who had been expelled from their unions for having discharged their duty to their employers during the 48-hour dispute or who might suffer similar disadvantages from refusing to join or resigning from a union in the future.

The death of Colonel Dyer had left a gap in the leadership. Sir Andrew Noble, who was elected the new president – and was to hold the office until his death in 1915 – was a different type of man. Like Dyer, he had been an artillery officer and later became a director of Armstrong Whitworth's. As Captain Noble, he had been active in the development of employers' organisations in the North-east and was chairman of the Tyne association when it was founded in 1883. Like many Victorian industrialists, he was a many-sided character but he was essentially an inventor rather than an organiser. He was an expert on explosives with an international reputation. As president, he was held in wide and continuing respect but tended to be above the battle rather than in it. The detailed, practical leadership devolved upon others who had played their part in the great victory. Among them were R. Sinclair Scott, of the Greenock Foundry Company, who was chairman of the employers' joint committee during the Clyde–Belfast strike of 1895–6, and G. R. Platt, of Platt Brothers, Oldham, Alexander Siemens, Benjamin Browne and Andrew Henderson. Thomas Biggart and James Robinson continued as joint secretaries, with Biggart as the man who pulled most of the strings. Scott was the first chairman of the EC and Siemens of the parliamentary committee.

During the talks which preceded the end of the lock-out, there were probably few on either side of the industry who realised the importance of the procedure for avoiding disputes which was part of the terms of settlement. Yet its main principles were to remain unchanged for nearly three-quarters of a century and it was taken as a model by many other industries. When grievances arose, a worker or a deputation of workers was to be received by their employers. If they failed to agree then local associations or employers would negotiate with local officials of trade unions. Questions could also be raised directly by any trade union with the local employers' association. Failing settlement, the matter was referred to the Federation Board and the union's central authority. No stoppage of work was to take place before the Procedure had been exhausted.

The Procedure was preferred to the conciliation board system

as a method of dealing with disputes because the boards usually
had independent chairmen and the events of the nineties had left
the employers determined not to allow any interference by outsiders on matters of principle affecting managerial rights. Conciliation boards in practice concerned themselves chiefly with
wages and, in shipbuilding especially, with demarcation disputes.

The Procedure did not in itself provide for national bargaining,
which had begun in engineering with the machine question and
48-hour conferences in 1897. It was simply a means of trying to
find a peaceful solution to disputes which could not be resolved on
the spot. It was natural for a national organisation, which might
be asked to support a member in dispute, to assume the authority
to examine the rights and wrongs of the dispute before committing itself. But it was soon found that a local dispute or group of
disputes raised issues which could be best dealt with by a
national agreement. There were national negotiations from 1900
to 1902 on a number of subjects, of which the most important
concerned revision of the terms of setlement, allowances for men
on trial trips on warships, the introduction by a number of
employers of the 'one-break' duty system and the premium
bonus system of payment by results.

How to deal with wage questions was a subject that kept cropping up throughout the period. The terms of settlement said that
general alterations in the rates of wages in any district would be
negotiated between the employers' local association and local
representatives of the workers. But disputes over wage claims
began to come up through the Procedure before the end of 1898.
In October that year the ASE referred a dispute in Leeds arising
out of a demand for a 2s. a week increase. After much hesitation
the EC decided to hear the appeal provided the local association
would abide by their views and on the understanding that the
Federation would not be committed to any active support failing
an amicable settlement. The local association agreed and an
increase of 1s. was recommended and accepted by both sides.
After this the Federation handled a good many disputes over proposals to increase or decrease wage rates and the Board began to
divide central conferences into three kinds – first those dealing
with 'appeals' on questions of principle after failure to agree at
local conference, second 'wage references' which had previously

been discussed locally, and third 'general questions and complaints' which became in effect national negotiations on working conditions.

The work of the Central Conference grew steadily, partly because the ASE leaders, as least by 1900, had accepted the value of the Procedure. It dealt with 8 cases in 1898, 8 in 1899, 17 in 1900 and 18 in 1901. In the year 1901–2, the number of cases rose to 24, of which 10 were appeals, 5 wage references and 9 general questions. Apart from the year 1907, when there were 46 cases, the number did not rise to 30 until 1911, after which there were between 30 and 40 a year until 1914. At first cases were dealt with by the EC, but in 1905 a special conference committee was established.

The Federation from the beginning insisted on strict observance of the terms of settlement, by their own members and by the workers. The employers were given so much power by the imposed conditions that there might seem to have been little need to infringe them but some did. In August 1898, we find the EC ruling that the unions were right in their contention at a local conference on a wage issue and deputing Sinclair Scott to explain to a Belfast representative 'the desirability of local associations carefully and fairly following the procedure'. In October the same year the EC wrote to the Bolton association informing them that members ought not to discharge men for refusing to leave their union and deprecating the use of threats. The Manchester association was told that a proposed lock-out would be against the terms of settlement.

Such cases were comparatively rare, however. Where interpretation of the settlement was in doubt, the ruling was usually in the employer's favour. One important one affected the *Status Quo* argument which was seldom out of the minds of the two sides from 1897 to 1971. The settlement said that while a question was going through the Procedure 'work shall proceed meantime on current conditions'. This was held to mean conditions after the change that was being challenged, not before it.

The majority of disputes arose out of 'encroachments' by the unions on the terms of settlement. Local branches and district committees who for years had been struggling against piece-work, for stricter overtime limitation, for maximum proportions of apprentices, for the right of craftsmen to man machines, for the union shop, did not suddenly stop the struggle. Where they offended, the Federation would ask the union to bring them into line, which they did when they could.

The local ASE committees found it the more exasperating because other unions, not involved in the lock-out, were not bound by the terms of settlement and continued to make demands which would have infringed it, particularly the boilermakers' society and the foundry unions. The Federation encouraged firms to resist and subsidised them but were in no hurry to precipitate a new major struggle. Associations pressed from time to time for these other unions to be brought into the settlement terms, and informal efforts were made, but by 1912 only three additional small unions had accepted the terms as a whole, while three others were parties to the Procedure. The boilermakers' and the foundry unions were still out. From time to time ASE members became temporarily involved in joint movements with these unions.

This happened particularly in claims to reduce working hours, which was a particularly troublesome issue because a 54-hour week was being worked in some districts and a 53-hour week in others. Unions in 1898 and 1899 pressed in a number of localities for a reduction from 54 to 53. 'If we cannot get a uniform 53 hours now, we may as well hang the question up,' said the United Paternmakers' Association, whose members were in much demand at the time, partly because of the Boer War. 'It will be many a long year before we have such another golden opportunity.' There were strikes in Barnsley and Sheffield and one by sixteen unions in Barrow which the Federation considered the 'first major challenge' to the 1898 settlement. All failed, but because of 'special circumstances' the Federation did concede the 53-hour week in Barrow in 1905.

Facing growing restlessness among their members, the ASE accompanied by the Steam Engine Makers and the United Machine Workers, asked in August 1900, that the terms of settlement should be revised. They said there had been some difficulty in getting the men to conform strictly to the terms because they felt they were in certain respects unfair and unduly interfered with the men's freedom. The provisions for avoiding disputes, while preventing stoppages with consequent loss, had been slow in operation. They asked for the piece-work provisions to be amended so as to include the consent of the men concerned or recast so as to give real effect to the note in the agreement disclaiming any intention of interfering with the prevailing practice of paying for extra effort. They thought the clauses restricting overtime had been generally evaded and should be drawn up in more binding form and that there should be a declaration in regard to the manning of new machinery which would allay the fear of the men that their interests might be jeopardised.

Presenting a formal request for a central conference in October, Barnes started by saying that the unions wanted to maintain the procedure for settling difficulties.

> If it is possible to settle our difficulties over a table in this way instead of having to resort to more barbarous methods it is to our mutual advantage to have that done [he continued], and I think you will give us credit for having made a strenuous endeavour to maintain that method. We have done that at times in the teeth of our own men, and at considerable risk personally in regard to ourselves and to our own position. We have come to believe that peace may be in some cases bought rather too dearly. We think we have got very near to the border line, and that we have assented to certain things that we ought never to have assented to, and the feeling is getting so strong that in our mutual interest – both in your interest and our own interest to maintain continuity of work – it is absolutely necessary that we should meet together and re-discuss the Terms of Settlement.

The Board declined to accept the unions' proposals as they stood, which they considered would have been tantamount to abandoning the position established in 1898. But they recognised that after three years' experience of their working the terms might be improved and decided to do what was possible to smooth out 'asperities', as it would be valuable to have a mutually arranged agreement made 'not in hot blood but under calm, dispassionate conditions'. They met the unions at a conference extending over four days and hammered out a revised agreement, but the union members turned it down on a ballot vote.

It was not until March 1907, that the unions succeeded in getting a revised agreement which was accepted. It resembled closely the rejected version of 1901. The freedom of management clause was simplified and now read: 'The federated employers shall not interfere with the proper functions of the trade unions, and the trade unions shall not interfere with the employers in the management of their business.'

The clause on piece-work said clearly that each workman's day rate was to be guaranteed irrespective of piece-work earnings and there was a new concession that overtime and nightshift allowances were to be paid in addition to piece-work prices on the same condition as for time-work. (The Lincoln association resigned from the Federation because they would not accept the overtime addition and two firms in East Anglia and one in Leicester at first refused to pay it.) The recommended limit on overtime was reduced from 40 to 32 hours in any four weeks but the exception that it should not be restricted in cases of 'urgency and emergency', which the unions contended was some-times used by employers in such a way as to make the recommen-dation valueless, was retained. A new clause in the section on the rating of workmen said that 'in fixing the rates of skilled work-men, the employer shall have regard to the rates prevailing in the district for fully trained and skilled men' – a shift in the direction of accepting district rates. While there was still to be no recog-nised proportion of apprentices to journeymen, it was to be open to the unions to bring forward for discussion the proportion of apprentices generally employed in the whole federated area.

George Barnes told his members that the terms of settlement had been productive of some good and as amended embodied full recognition by each side of the rights of the other. If not perfect, they were 'moderately fair'. He accepted the *Status Quo* posi-tion – 'Pending settlement, somebody must say what must be done, and it seems to me that somebody must necessarily be the employers.'

Another agreement to be rejected by the union members dealt with the 'one-break' duty system. A good many employers, like those who introduced the 48-hour week in the nineties, were find-ing the before-breakfast shift unremunerative. So instead of starting work at 6 a.m., with a break for breakfast and another for dinner, they introduced a 7 a.m. start with only a single break during the day. The unions resisted the change unless it was accompanied by a reduction in hours and there was a long strike at Leeds after the issue had gone through Procedure. At a central conference in February 1902, the ASE claimed to have information on eighty-one firms working the one-break system whose hours averaged 51.

The Federation undertook to recommend their members not to introduce the system pending further discussion. At a special meeting of the Board, Sir Andrew Noble warned against giving the unions a lever for a demand of something like an 8-hour day, but opinion on the Board was divided. Siemens favoured a one-break system with some reduction in hours. He did not believe, he said, that hours were of such importance so long as they stuck to freedom of management. The Board were told that the system was being widely adopted, with a reduction of hours, by non-federated firms. But a majority of members, having fought for seven months to prevent a reduction of hours, did not intend to concede anything now. In April 1903, the Board ruled that the introduction of the system could be left to local associations – on condition that the hours worked in their district were not reduced.

Several firms accordingly introduced it, but were immediately taken through the Procedure and the ASE reminded the Federation of their agreement to recommend against its introduction until there had been further discussion. Associations were consulted again and there were more conferences and eventually in 1907 it was agreed that firms could introduce the system on a 51-hour basis. Firms already operating it would increase or reduce their hours to 51. But the union members turned the agreement down by 19,266 votes to 9466. So the Federation told firms they could introduce the system on any terms they could arrange, so long as the working week was not less than 51.

Yet another agreement which would almost certainly have been rejected if it had been submitted to the union membership, which it was not, was on the premium bonus system of payment. With ever-increasing mechanisation and standardisation, helped by the terms of settlement, payment by results had been growing rapidly and some British employers introduced from the United States a new form of it known as the premium bonus system. It had many variations, of which the best known were the Rowan and Halsey, but all were based on establishing a fixed time for a worker, or group of workers, to do a job. However long he took, he would get the time rate for the hours worked, but if he did the job in less than the fixed time, the saving would be divided between the worker and the employer.

This was attractive in two main ways. Firstly, there were still many operations for which ordinary piece-work was not suitable but which could be timed. Secondly, the way the earnings were calculated made it impossible under some variations of the system for a man to get twice as much as his time rate, however badly the job was timed and however hard he worked. Consequently there was in theory less temptation to cut the rate, a practice against which the unions were constantly protesting and was the main cause of their dislike of piece-work.

One reason the men objected to the premium bonus system was that the terms of settlement provided for 'mutuality' – 'the prices to be paid for piece-work shall be fixed by mutual arrangement between the employer and the workman or workmen' – but the fixing of bonus times was a job for experts whose decisions the workman was seldom equipped to dispute. Moreover its use became increasingly associated in their minds with the introduction of 'speed and feed' men or progress chasers, rate-fixers, operational inspectors or whatever they might be called, against the use of whom at Elswick the unions were already protesting at the April 1897 conference. Foremen, who found their authority taken over by these newcomers, were also unhappy about it and ready to join with the men in opposing it.

In February 1902, the ASE complained that the bonus system was being worked in so many different ways that it was not understood by the men, thus causing a want of confidence in it. They suggested that, for mutual satisfaction, a general system should be introduced. The suggestion was not pursued at the time but complaints against the working of the system at Armstrong Whitworth's in Newcastle and three other factories came before a central conference at Carlisle the following August when a general agreement was reached. It provided that the Federation would convey a memorandum – which became known as the Carlisle Memorandum – to their members and that the ASE in return would remove all restrictions on the working of the system. The memorandum said the employers' representatives had not the power to settle the conditions which should be observed in the working of the system, without previously having obtained authority, but they would advise employers to adopt the following suggestions: the time rate of wages for each job should in all cases be paid; overtime and nightshift would be paid on the same conditions as for time-work; a time allowance, after it had been established, should only be changed if the method or means of manufacture were changed; no firm should establish the system without intending to adhere to it. In discussion it was stated that the time allowance was not considered 'established' until it had been tried and found to be suitable.

There were immediate protests from the ASE districts at the signing of the agreement on the grounds that it meant the union was giving approval to a system which their members detested. The union refused to submit it to a ballot vote because, they argued, it was already in operation in a number of factories and management's right to introduce payment by results was in the terms of settlement. They were merely trying to ensure the system was not abused. Not only the ASE executive but some other unions saw merit in the agreement. In 1906, for instance, the Electrical Trades Union accepted it.

Vickers had trouble over the system at Barrow and there was a bitter strike at the firm's gun-making plant at Erith. The ASE, Toolmakers, Steam Engine Makers and United Machine Workers struck against the system in June 1907, and within a few days were joined by the pattern-makers, boilermakers, the tin-smiths and carpenters. The ASE gave the strike official support but when the Federation pointed out that this was in breach of the terms of settlement, they recommended a return to work. During the strike, which lasted six weeks, the company built a bridge from the railway into the works, so that strike-breakers would not have to pass through picket lines. It was intended to board them at the works, but the Labour-dominated Erith urban district council decided the works did not comply with their by-laws for sleeping accommodation and threatened legal proceedings. Eventually the men returned on day rates and the firm undertook that any points in dispute would be taken up through the Procedure, but they came back to the system later.

Engineering was not the only industry in which the bonus system was being introduced and in 1909 the TUC set up a committee which reported that the system destroyed the principle of collective bargaining, that the Carlisle Memorandum was persistently evaded, that it was destructive of trade unionism and a cause of unemployment and of the scamping of work, that it prevented proper training of apprentices and that it promoted selfishness and workshop favouritism.

The following year the EC received reports that unions were systematically establishing shop committees in firms adopting the system. They opposed this on the grounds that the function of such committees would soon extend to the negotiation of basic hours. There was no provision for this in the Procedure.

According to a Board of Trade inquiry, only 4–5 per cent of male operatives in engineering were working the system in 1907, but it must have spread widely after that. Payment by results generally increased rapidly throughout the period. The percentage of turners on piece-work, including the bonus system, was estimated to have risen from 6 in 1886 to 39 in 1913 and of machine men from 11 to 47. A Federation inquiry suggested that in 1914 nearly a third of the men employed by federated firms were on payment by results, the majority on piece-work, not premium systems.

Partly because of defeats in engineering and other industries in the nineties, and partly because of the Taff Vale and other legal judgements which restricted their rights, the unions turned from industrial to political action as a means of achieving their aims. It was the period of the formation of the Labour Party, of the Trade Disputes Act and of the Liberals' social legislation and in these developments the ASE played an active part. George Barnes himself was returned to the House of Commons in the 1906 election and argued that labour's strength should be focused on Parliament. 'We shall probably find that we do not need to strike at all except through the ballot box,' he wrote.

As a result of this shift in the direction of attack, the Parliamentary Committee of the Federation found themselves very busy, for the most part fighting a series of rearguard actions. They record constant meetings with Ministers and canvassing of MPs. One of the first questions that arose was the possibility of alliances with employers in other industries. At the end of 1898, Biggart called a meeting of officials of employers' organisations who set up a committee to meet quarterly for an exchange of views. Officials from the coal mining, steel, building, boot and shoe, shipping, furniture-making and cotton spinning industries were among those who took part.

They began by discussing how they could best get united action when it seemed desirable. William Tattersall, of the cotton spinners, advocated the establishment of a permanent committee representing industry generally, but most of the others, including Biggart, preferred that each trade should have its own parliamentary committee and work together only for specific purposes. There was in existence at this time an Employers' Parliamentary Council but in 1902 the Federation rejected an invitation to join it. In later years they expressed disfavour when the body attempted to recruit associations and members and advised them not to join. Experience had shown, the Federation said, that the interests of different industries were not always identical, and sometimes conflicted, but they were always prepared to co-operate with others on specific issues.

Biggart's committee gradually faded out after he had gone down with a long illness in 1903. It was revived in 1913 and had a final meeting in 1916 to discuss relations between employers and the Government on wartime labour matters. Among subjects taken up in its early days, on Biggart's suggestion, was the possibility of concerted opposition to trade union clauses in county council and municipal contracts, on which the Federation felt very strongly. A Fair Wages Resolution had been adopted by the House of Commons in 1891, following disclosures of conditions in sweated trades, which said all government contracts should secure the payment of such wages as were generally accepted as current in each trade for competent workmen. This was superseded by a more elaborate resolution in 1909. Many local authorities introduced similar conditions in their contracts, which the Federation considered an infringement of management rights. Throughout the period covered by this chapter they were constantly encouraging members to refuse to accept local authority contracts containing such conditions.

But it was proposed trade union legislation which most preoccupied the Parliamentary Committee at the beginning of the century. The Taff Vale judgement by the House of Lords in 1901, which made unions liable for damages for their own actions and those of their agents during a strike, had shaken the unions to their foundations and repeated efforts were made to restore their immunity. In 1903 a Royal Commission was set up to report on the position. Sir Andrew Noble, giving evidence on behalf of the Federation, said the Taff Vale and other judgements had largely stopped intimidation by pickets during strikes. 'There does not appear to be any reason,' he asserted, 'why trade unions should be placed above the common law, which imposes responsibility for wrongful acts on all corporations and all individuals all over the country and in all classes of life.' Noble went on to contend that the way to improve industrial relations was not to pass new laws, but to extend conciliation on the principles of the Procedure until the desire for legislation on the conduct of trade disputes disappeared. 'It is not probable, of course, that strikes will be entirely prevented,' he added, 'but a feeling of friendly co-operation between employers and workmen could be so developed as to reduce warfare to insignificant proportions.'

In 1904 the Parliamentary Committee considered how to increase its own usefulness and efficiency and advised associations to set up local committees to bring before Members of Parliament the views of the Federation. However, in spite of the opposition of the Federation and others, the Government's Trade Disputes Bill of 1906 conceded to the unions the immunities from legal action which they were demanding. In 1914 there was a move to secure amendment of the Trade Disputes Act but the Federation declined to take part 'in view of the fact that any amendment restricting the power of the unions to picket might be accompanied by a restriction of the employers' power to blacklist'.

Because industrial questions were increasingly becoming the subject of legislation and departmental regulations, the Federation moved their headquarters from Glasgow to London in 1910. 'While the tendency is all in the direction of the Federation having in future fewer strikes,' said the EC, 'special endeavours will be necessary to cope with the increased labour influence in Parliament.' Biggart did not want to leave Glasgow and the Federation decided to appoint as sole secretary and treasurer Allan MacGregor Smith, a man in his early thirties from the same firm of Glasgow solicitors as Biggart. Smith's name first appeared in the Federation's records in 1903, when he acted for Biggart during the latter's illness, and he had been appointed a secretary in 1908. For a quarter of a century Smith, later Sir Allan Smith, was to play a leading part in the counsels of the Federation. He was a man in something the same mould as Biggart – dour, abstemious, indefatigable and supremely efficient.

Throughout the decade from 1898 to 1908 the Federation seems to have been satisfied that the Terms of Settlement, with minor adjustments, were all they needed as a basis for their labour relations. The revision of 1907 made changes only in detail. Peace had been largely maintained. Disputes were generally settled as the employers wished. The EC recorded that in the year 1902–3 (after Taff Vale) there was not a single strike against a federated firm and only two 'minor stoppages of work' described as trivial matters. No other year had a record quite as good as that but the few strikes were rarely successful, many of them ending when the places of the strikers were filled by other workers. The solution of the problem of managerial control seemed to have been found.

But from 1908 onwards there were signs of change. Workers were growing increasingly restive. In 1904 the ASE had altered their rules in a way which gave increased power to the districts as against the executive council. Real wages were not rising and a new depression increased the men's resentment at the strait jacket by which they were bound. The Carlisle Memorandum rankled, particularly after the Erith struggle. Demarcation disputes increased in number. And gradually the old conflicts over the manning of machines, overtime, the closed shop and so on mounted again. The effect of the immunities provided by the Trade Disputes Act was making itself felt. Perhaps the chief indication that new thinking was needed was the North-east coast strike of 1908 which nearly precipitated a national lock-out and suggested that simply leaving changes to the associations, with Central Conference acting as a sort of conciliation board, was not enough.

The strike was to resist a proposed wage reduction of 1s. a week following a falling off in trade. The men demanded that the existing rate of 36s. should be maintained because it represented a minimum living standard and in February went on strike. David Lloyd George, the President of the Board of Trade, immediately stepped in – 'interference rather than intervention,' Allan Smith commented later – and got an agreement that work should be resumed on the understanding that the rates should be unchanged until Easter while the proposed reduction was submitted to a referee. A ballot of the men rejected this by a majority of 5842 to 2699. Lloyd George brought the leaders together again and they agreed that the ballot paper should be amended to explain that the referee would be chosen, with the concurrence of Barnes and Andrew Noble, from a list of impartial persons drawn up by the Board of Trade, and another ballot held. This time the plan was rejected by a majority of 4356 votes to 3693. When his executive council refused to support him in withdrawing the strikers' benefit, George Barnes resigned his position as ASE general secretary rather than be a party to the strike against the recommendation of the union executive. He said the men by their votes had negated the principle of collective bargaining.

The Board were still reluctant to regard a local wage dispute as a national issue but the North-east Coast association now argued that it was a matter of principle because the men were attempting to establish a minimum wage. After much argument, and consultation with the associations, the Board decided to call a national lock-out on 26 September, with Sheffield the only major association to dissent, unless there was an immediate settlement.

If the men succeed in establishing in so large a district as the North-east coast the principle they now contend for [said a Federation circular to members], their success cannot fail to have an effect on all other federated districts where a similar stand may be taken and the possibility of securing a reduction in wages seriously affected. The action of the men in discarding the advice of their leaders will tend to greatly weaken all the arrangements that have been made with the unions for the amicable settlement of labour questions.

After further meetings with Lloyd George, the men finally accepted the reduction on condition that there would be no further alteration in wages for six months and that there would be a conference between the two sides to consider how the procedure for dealing with wages could be amended to avoid stoppages of work and in October they returned to work. About 10,000 men had been out for seven months.

It is difficult in an era when national wage disputes have long been a normal part of the collective bargaining process to realise the shock which the events in the North-east caused to both sides – simply because they had nearly come to a national battle over wages. Major disputes of the past – with the exception of the

Clyde–Belfast lock-out of 1895 – had been over overtime and piece-work, hours and apprentice limitation and the machine question and other aspects of management functions. It was generally accepted that wages were bound to go up and down with trade conditions. In some industries there were sliding scales under which wages varied with the price of the product. There were often disputes as to the state of trade in a locality, which the unions measured mainly by the number of their unemployed and the employers by reports from members, but it was local conditions with which they were concerned and the Terms of Settlement had laid it down that rises and falls in wages should be negotiated locally. It has been noted that the Federation hesitated before accepting that wage disputes could suitably be referred to the Central Conference, and they hesitated even longer before intervening in the North-east coast affair. They would never accept outside intervention on questions involving the rights of management, but on a wage dispute they approved a reference to arbitration by the mid-Lancashire employers in 1899.

The Federation attitude was set out most succinctly by Alex. Siemens in 1913:

> Industrial agreements may cover two sets of questions – questions of principle and questions of fact. Questions of principle arise out of the rights and privileges of the employers and workpeople, either maintained by the party concerned or acknowledged in an agreement. Questions of fact, on the other hand, are questions which are determinable by circumstances which may be readily ascertained and which vary from day to day. A notable question of fact is the question of general alterations of wages.

This distinction led the Federation to concede that arbitration might be useful on wage questions though they would have no outside interference on anything which they regarded as affecting the management prerogative.

> The manner of dealing with questions of principle and with questions of fact necessarily differs [said Siemens]. On questions of fact it may be desirable to have a final settlement by negotiation which would preclude a stoppage of work. This

could be achieved by invoking the intervention of an outside impartial authority who would have a determining voice in the event of the parties failing to agree. In questions of principle it is difficult for an outside authority to be of assistance. The solution of such questions does not depend on the ascertainment of facts.

This analysis was part of a dissenting memorandum by Siemens to a report by the Industrial Council on an inquiry into the best way of securing the fulfilment of industrial agreements. The council, consisting of employers and union leaders, was set up by the Board of Trade primarily as a top level conciliation and arbitration body but was little used and the report on industrial agreements, for which it took evidence like a Royal Commission, was its main achievement. Incidentally, it is interesting to find Allan Smith, in his evidence, arguing in favour of the legal enforceability of agreements – because he thought this was needed in other industries rather than in engineering – and for a cooling off period of thirty days after failing to agree in the last stage of the Procedure.

To return to wages, one result of the North-east coast affair was that a number of associations, including those in Hull, Sheffield, Barnsley, Barrow and London in 1909, made long term agreements. In most of them the employers agreed to drop proposals for reductions of 1s. a week on condition that existing rates remained unaltered for five years. In Manchester a similar local agreement for five years was rejected by a ballot but a three-year agreement accepted. These agreements turned out to be of value to the employers during the trade boom of the pre-war years.

Meanwhile on the suggestion of the North-west (Glasgow) association the Federation began to plan a national wages board. After long consideration a scheme was finalised and approved by associations in April 1913. In the event of failure to agree at local conference a case would be referred to a Central Board representing employers and unions presided over by a High Court judge, who would have power to give a binding decision. The bargaining and the judge's decision were to be based on the state and prospects of trade. No new claim could be made for a year after the previous settlement. In the midst of other preoccupations, however, the plan never came to anything. It will be noticed that even now the Federation were not thinking of national negotiations, though in 1909 the Shipbuilding Employers' Federation had made an agreement with seventeen unions for national negotiations on general fluctuations in trade in addition to district negotiations.

The Federation were also seeking some new way of dealing with demarcation disputes, which were continuing to cause trouble, particularly in shipbuilding areas. As early as 1903, the North-east Coast association asked the Federation to devise some means of preventing them. The matter was raised again by the North-west association in 1907, when a sub-committee was set up in conjunction with the shipbuilding employers. The discussions and negotiations had a chequered history but an agreement was finally reached in 1912 between the two employers' federations and twenty-three unions providing that if agreement could not be reached in a works, the recognised practice of the works was to be continued pending settlement by a committee consisting of three representatives nominated by the local employers' association and three by the societies concerned. Because it was found that the majority of questions arose between shipyard unions and engineering unions, it was initially confined to the marine engineering branch of the industry. Its value was much reduced because the boilermakers' union declined to adhere to it, but some use of it was made in engineering and it continued to be used in shipbuilding for many years.

During the North-east strike, the Board formally adopted the principle of mutual business help between members in a recommendation dated 7 July 1908: 'Wherever possible the claims of federated firms to preferential treatment when orders are being given out should be recognised and also special consideration should be shown to federated firms who may be unable to fulfil their obligations as to delivery during the currency of a strike or lock-out.' Members were frequently reminded of this recommendation, especially during strikes and lock-outs after the First World War. To help members to observe it, lists of federated firms were circulated regularly.

Another indirect result of the North-east strike was that the Federation put on a formal basis the arrangements for paying subsidies to firms involved in approved disputes. For some years after the 1897 lock-out, payments were authorised by a special finance committee out of funds accumulated from outside sympathisers during the lock-out. Each case was treated on its merits but from 1901 onwards the committee appear to have worked on a recommendation from the EC that except in special cases the limit of compensation should be 45 per cent of the wages the men would have received had there been no interruption of work. But the North-east strike, followed by several manning disputes, made it necessary to call for a special levy in 1912.

There had been periodic talk about formalising the arrangements and in 1914 a Subsidy Fund was set up with a capital of £250,000. For each of the three years after becoming subscribers to the fund, members were to pay one half per cent of their average wages bill for the preceding three years and for another three years they were liable to a further call if the fund fell below £250,000. Payments were to be made, after the first fourteen days of any strike, at the rate of 30s. a week for each man on strike and 12s. a week for each apprentice or female.

In 1912 and 1913 the long wrangling in the ASE produced a more militant leadership with a full-time chairman named J. T. Brownlie, a socialist who was to be Allan Smith's opposite number for seventeen years. The old major issues were now formally revived – the manning of machines, the closed shop, the 48-hour week, the premium bonus agreement and the terms of settlement generally. The EC reported that there were 69 strikes in 1913, of which 20 were by members of unions who were parties to the Procedure – and 16 of those were unconstitutional in that they took place before the Procedure was exhausted.

Several of the strikes were against the employment of unskilled men on machines and six manning disputes were brought to Central Conference. The Federation formed the impression that this was the result of a pre-arranged plan. The unions suggested that the relevant clause in the terms of settlement was being interpreted to cover more than was intended so that the proportion of skilled men was being lowered and there were fewer opportunities for apprentices. A special conference, at which the Federation representatives were given power to modify the clause so long as the principle underlying it was maintained, resulted in failure to agree. Strikes followed at two firms, one of them lasting five weeks and the other sixteen weeks, but were unsuccessful. The Federation considered a lock-out but decided instead to support the

firms concerned. Individual cases continued to be brought before
Central Conference.

There were also several strikes against the employment of non-
unionists, though mostly by boilermakers and foundry unions
who were not parties to the terms of settlement. But in July 1914,
the ASE maintained at Central Conference, where a Scottish
case was being considered, that the obligation in the 1898 and
1907 agreements to work with non-union labour was not satisfactory to the society. Non-unionists, they said, were a danger to their
employers and their presence constituted a danger to the
society. In recent cases there had been striking evidence of the
unanimity amongst members of the society and their readiness, if
necessary, to come out on strike in order to force non-unionists to
join the society. Clyde members in particular were 'very much
inflamed'. The ASE had held them back in federated firms but
extreme action was taken against non-federated firms.

The employers pointed out that, if there was failure to agree, it
was open to the society to take what action they pleased, but it
was also open to the Federation to take what action it considered
necessary to assist any firm or district that was attacked. It was
explained 'in a friendly way' the exact risk that was being run in
attacking a district. The society accepted that the question was
'of much greater magnitude than was anticipated' and said they
would not take any action for the time being.

Towards the end of 1913, the unions gave notice to end the
terms of settlement as revised in the 1907 agreement and also the
Carlisle Memorandum on the premium bonus system. This action
was adopted after demands from ASE members with a supporting vote of 26,335 to 5156. The unions had also succeeded in per-
suading the employers, after trying for two years, to listen to a
renewal of their case for a 48-hour week. The Federation agreed
to discuss a new general agreement if in the meantime a truce was
observed on matters covered by the agreement and on the bonus
system. The unions would not accept the latter, but when they
asked for a reply to their claim for shorter hours, the EC replied
that a meeting would be facilitated by acceptance of a truce on
the bonus system.

However, the two sides came together at a conference in York
in April 1914, and the employers submitted a modified form of
the Procedure to operate while negotiations on the general agree-

ment and the premium bonus took place. A month later the new variation of the Procedure, which became known as the York Memorandum, was signed. It dealt with the *Status Quo* difficulty by leaving it out. There was no longer a reference to work proceeding on 'current conditions' while the provisions were carried out. But, the Federation informed their members, this did not imply any departure from the existing practice as this was covered by the clause about there being no stoppage of work until the Procedure was exhausted. Apart from that, the main change was the introduction of what became known as the works conference before the local conference stage, and the time within which a local conference had to be arranged was reduced from twelve to seven days from the receipt of an application.

The Federation then told the unions that they could not see any further reason for a reduction in hours beyond those advanced in 1897, but they would consult their constituents if the trade unions would explain what security they could offer that a reduction in hours would not result in a reduction of output and how a shorter working week could be arranged with regard to overtime, nightshift, continuous working, etc. The unions could not offer any security but instanced cases where employers who had introduced the 48-hour week had said output had not suffered. They thought arrangements on overtime and so on could be made when the reduction was agreed. And they offered to recommend members to work the one-break system, to agree to arrangements to ensure better timekeeping and to make special arrangements for continuous working.

The Federation consulted members, who voted by 3426 to 454 to resist a 48-hour week, even to the extent of a stoppage of work, but by 3020 to 754 not to resist some reduction. On 29 July, the unions prepared to recommend constituents to give them power to negotiate on a lesser reduction, and on 30 July the Federation set up a sub-committee to draft a *quid pro quo*. But on 4 August the First World War broke out and all the various negotiations came to an abrupt standstill.

The Government Takes Over 1914-1919

Orders and Controls – Employers Remonstrate – Shop
Stewards Revolt – National Wage Negotiations – The
47-hour Week – Visions of a New World

Management rights, like most other rights, cease to exist in time
of war. In a strange new world, the Federation, which had
defended employers' prerogatives with such determination, had
in the national interest to surrender them without a struggle to a
new usurper. It was the Government more and more which decided who should work where, what they should be paid, how
workers' revolts should be dealt with. Not only could the Government insist that their interpretation of the national interest must
have priority over all else but they were the paymasters, the customers for most of the industry's products. Employers developed
a feeling of helplessness. The Federation made protests at the lack
of consultation which grew more and more frequent as the war
progressed, and from time to time the frustration of members
and local associations exploded into angry recriminations against
the Federation or the Government or both, caused not only by
the loss of authority but also by the muddle and lack of co-
ordination of government labour policy.

How employers felt about it all was summed up in the report
of one small association, that of Huddersfield, as they entered the
last year of the war:

Employers have had imposed upon them conditions and restrictions which in normal times would be unthinkable. They
have been deprived of almost all freedom of action. Their
profits have been largely acquired by the Government. Their
own personal income from their businesses has been controlled.
Their men have to a large extent been spoiled not only by

wages awards which have been expedient rather than just, but by marked weakness on the part of the Government. In many other ways the just rights of the employer have been ruthlessly put aside for the purpose of maintaining industrial peace.

The Government paid more attention to the unions than they did to employers because whatever they did had to be tolerable to the men in the factories, and from the beginning of 1915 onwards unrest among the workers found leadership in the shop stewards' movement which grew until it presented a formidable challenge to the authority of the official union leadership. Official strikes were outlawed but the damage done by unofficial strikes steadily increased.

The abnormal pressures speeded new developments, some of lasting importance. As the war progressed, national wage settlements were inaugurated, shop stewards and works councils recognised, and immediately afterwards the 47-hour week conceded. Unions representing semi-skilled workers and labourers, already beginning to press on the Federation before the war, were brought into the Procedure. Provision had to be made for the army of women who flooded into the munitions factories. White collar unions began to make their presence felt. Faced with the new problems of war, and fearful of what peace might bring, the Federation played a leading part in the mobilisation of employers' organisations into new national bodies.

In the beginning both sides of industry were caught up in an upsurge of patriotism. In industry after industry domestic quarrels were abandoned. The engineering unions agreed to suspend their claim for a 48-hour week 'until a more favourable opportunity presented itself', and no more was said about the terms of settlement. At the beginning of August there were 100 disputes known to the Board of Trade. By the end of the month there were only 20. 'Disputes melted away as fast as the hours of the day, and often of the night, gave time for the hearing of difficulties,' recorded Sir George (later Lord) Askwith, the Chief Industrial Commissioner.

But in a few months the enthusiasm wasted away. Thousands of skilled engineers were allowed to volunteer for the forces and by December the shortage of craftsmen in the munitions factories was critical. The Federation found itself faced with the problem

of 'enticement' by its members which continued until 1918. 'In
their anxiety for labour, employers were bidding against each
other to entice skilled labour to their works, and bribing men to
remain in employment,' in Askwith's words. In response to
numerous complaints from members, the Federation in January
1915, sent a letter to all firms telling them to use inquiry notes
when engaging labour. Two months later they declared forcibly
that no firm should pay more than the district rates. But they
could not stop it. When they ordered the Coventry Ordnance
Works to discharge apprentices they were accused of enticing,
the company refused.

In April the North-west (Clyde) association complained to the
Admiralty about the evil of men moving from shop to shop from
one Admiralty job to another. The Director of Navy Contracts
ordered all contractors to recruit only men not already employed
on government work, but the association said the trouble was
growing worse. The Government issued an Order in Council to
prevent employers taking active steps – by canvassing, advertisement or otherwise – to induce workmen engaged on government
work to change their employment. But firms found ways round
this. A couple of months later the association pointed to the time-
keeping bonuses offered by some firms which were justified as an
encouragement to regular attendance but which acted as an
inducement to attract workmen from other shops where such
bonuses were not paid. 'The result has been a competition in all
sorts of illegitimate inducements,' they said. The Munitions of
War Act in July introduced a system whereby munition workers
could not leave their jobs without the consent of their employer
in the form of a leaving certificate.

Perhaps the most serious Federation dispute on this kind of
issue, however, occurred in June the following year. Coventry – a
problem association then as in later years – made an agreement
for a $12\frac{1}{2}$ per cent increase in the wages of day workers which was
approved by the Ministry of Munitions in spite of representations
by the Federation that it would seriously prejudice the position
of employers elsewhere. The EC told Coventry what they thought
about them but other associations were not satisfied with that. A
joint standing committee of the Birmingham, Leicester, Stoke
and Wolverhampon associations passed a resolution saying that
Coventry had broken the rules by conceding the advance without

reference to the Conference Committee and asked that the Coventry association should be expelled and the settlement repudiated. An interview with the Coventry office-bearers followed, but in the end the row blew over.

From the autumn of 1914, the major problem facing the Government was how to build up the labour force in the engineering and shipbuilding industries, on which war production largely depended, in spite of the scarcity of skilled workers. It soon became accepted that the main answer was 'dilution' – the employment of semi-skilled workers and labourers and even women on jobs formerly done by craftsmen, which often involved the breaking down of manufacturing processes to simplify them and doing away with trade union rules which hampered production. This was the old machine question writ large, and for all their anxiety to contribute to the war effort the unions found it hard to swallow the surrender of customs for which they had been fighting for generations. For one thing, most people at first expected the war to be a short one. Was it worth while to give up their rules for a little time with the risk that they would never be re-established? A series of conferences at the end of the year produced no result.

The Government got impatient. The shortage of munitions was becoming a national scandal. Both the War Office and the Admiralty wrote to the parties urging that temporary arrangements should be made to ease the labour shortage. Allan Smith suggested that Lord Kitchener, at the War Office, should make a personal appeal to the unions to suspend their restrictions. Kitchener refused on the grounds that the matter was in the hands of the Board of Trade, but continued to press for action.

The Government then set up, on 4 February, a three-man Committee on Production, consisting of Askwith and officials from the Admiralty and War Office, to report on the best ways of increasing output in engineering and shipbuilding. The committee rapidly produced a series of reports recommending that there should be no strike or lock-out on government work, that all restrictive trade practices should be suspended, with safeguards, during the period of the war, that demarcation disputes should be settled by arbitration and that greater use should be made of women. From then on the Committee on Production acted as a central arbitration tribunal. Following this, the Federation succeeded in making an agreement with the unions known as the Shells and Fuses Agreement, providing for some dilution on such work, but by now the Government had concluded that it must take the matter into its own hands.

Under heavy pressure by Ministers and public opinion, the unions signed on 19 March the Treasury agreement, embodying the recommendations of the Committee on Production, which was approved by a ballot vote of the membership. The Federation were not invited to take part in the negotiations which led to this agreement and did not do so. In June a Ministry of Munitions was set up under Lloyd George and the Munitions of War Act gave statutory effect to the proposals of the Committee on Production and the Treasury agreement. The Bill provided for the compulsory arbitration of disputes, the suspension of trade union practices on war work and limited the profits of firms concerned to one-fifth in excess of the pre-war rate.

The Federation kept up a running fire of complaints about lack of consultation and the Clyde employers became more exasperated than ever. They prepared a memorial to the Prime Minister, Herbert Asquith, and the Minister of Munitions. Measures to obtain full output from the shops were unavailing, it said. There was too much negotiation and compromise. The men believed that if there was a real need for a new state of affairs, the Government would not rely on moral persuasion but would enforce different conditions under the sanction of law. Rates of wages should be stabilised and employers on government work should not be free to pay more. Government powers should be extended.

The EC pointed out that to present a memorial without previous consultation with the Federation would be a breach of rules, to which one of the Scottish leaders on the EC, J. R. Richmond, of J. and G. Weir, Ltd., retorted indignantly that the Federation had given no lead to local associations on uniform wages policies or anything else. Firms in the North-west, he asserted, considered it extraordinary that the Federation should be inarticulate when important labour legislation was being prepared by the Ministry of Munitions. Smith explained to Richmond afterwards that the Federation had made suggestions to the Government but they were not well received because the employers were out of favour owing to serious delays in supplies. Though disappointed, the North-west association decided not to pursue the memorial but protested to the Federation that a most valuable opportunity had been lost.

The unions continued to extract concessions from the Government, who were anxious for increased efforts to make dilution effective. In October 1915, the Government conceded a guaranteed minimum wage of 20s. a week for women workers and in January 1916, amended the Munitions Act to impose a levy on profits made by government contractors, to oblige employers to consult workers before any changes in working conditions were made, to reinforce the assurances about the restoration of suspended practices after the war and to give the Government power to issue directions on the wages of semi-skilled and unskilled workers. All changes in working conditions had to be recorded so that the position could be restored afterwards, and the Federation warned members to be careful that nothing was recorded as a change that was not a departure from pre-war practice, even though the practice had been changed between the beginning of the war and the date of the control.

In August 1916, following reports that the Government intended to create a labour advisory department with at its head Arthur Henderson, the foundry workers' and Labour Party leader who had been brought into the coalition government, Richmond renewed his attack on the Federation for its 'supine and inactive' policy during the previous two years and 'its failure to educate the Government and public opinion in order to counter-act the activities of trade unionism' and urged that Allan Smith should sever his connection with the Government and make his entire services available for the advice and guidance of the Federation. The following month Richmond resigned from the EC.

Allan Smith was a member of about thirty government committees of one sort and another, and it was mainly through him that the Federation was able to exercise any influence on national policy. Not long after the Scottish complaint, however, the constitution was altered to allow for a full-time chairman of a management committee. Allan Smith was appointed the chairman. In future he was to preside at all meetings of the committee and be generally responsible for every aspect of the Federation's work, to which he was directed to devote 'all his time, attention and abilities'. Nevertheless he remained a member of many of the committees.

At this time a proposal further to increase women's pay provoked the most grave warning yet from the Federation. The Ministry of Munitions were told that 'the time had come when, owing to the nature of some of the proposals being made in regard to wages, it would not be possible for the employers to give effect to them if the Ministry were to continue their policy of cutting down contract prices'. The lack of co-ordination of government labour policies was increasingly a cause of confusion and unrest.

In March 1917, Allan Smith wrote to the Prime Minister, now Lloyd George, to press for immediate action to co-ordinate government policy. The danger of the situation was the greater, Smith told the management committee, because of the lack of any centralised control of labour questions and the overlapping and conflicting jurisdiction of the Admiralty, the Ministry of Munitions and the Ministry of Labour. Dilution had come almost to a standstill and the provisions of the order on the employment of women on skilled work were practically inoperative. Askwith reinforced Smith's letter to the Prime Minister but no action was taken.

Relations between the Government and the employers grew worse. The Ministry of Labour wrote to the Federation asking them to speed up the operation of the Procedure and suggesting that in each establishment a joint authority should be set up to settle minor differences and grievances. The Federation replied that there was no evidence of complaints by unions of delay in dealing with disputes.

In June 1917, the West of England association passed a resolution expressing 'bitter disappointment at the total disregard paid by the Government to the employers' point of view on every question affecting the industry' and saying 'that drastic action must be taken by the Federation at once to secure fair and equitable treatment of engineering employers'. A second resolution asked the Federation to refuse to put into operation any further advances in wages accorded by the Committee on Production unless they received an increase in prices to cover the extra cost. The Federation complained to the Government that the ASE had been given the opportunity to consult their members by ballot before that year's amending Bill to the Munitions of War Act was put before Parliament, whereas the employers had no opportunity to refer the proposed amendment to their constituents.

An important clause in the Bill gave the Government power to fix the wages of time-workers, which in many cases had fallen behind those of piece-workers. 'Much of the difficulty', complained the Federation, 'is due to the inflated earnings of piece-workers brought about by the action of the Ministry in refusing to allow employers to alter piecework prices or premium bonus basis times arranged under the stress of circumstances and manifestly unreasonable.' They wanted any directions on wages by the Government to be recorded as changes in working conditions to terminate at the end of the war and any payments made in accordance with such directions to be refunded by the Government.

After serious strikes in May 1917, Lloyd George set up commissions to inquire into the causes of industrial unrest and all stressed that two main causes of dissatisfaction were the leaving certificates which workers had to obtain before moving from a munitions firm and the fact that the earnings of many skilled time-workers compared unfavourably with those of production workers on piece-work. The Bill gave the Government power to deal with both of these.

Winston Churchill, who succeeded Dr Addison at the Ministry of Munitions when the latter went to the Ministry of Reconstruction, made an order giving a $12\frac{1}{2}$ per cent increase to certain categories of skilled time-workers in October and at the same time announced that leaving certificates would be abolished. The pay increase caused chaos. Many skilled time-workers already had lieu payments to meet the difficulty and there was a flood of demands for comparable increases from other time-workers of all kinds, and from piece-workers. A conference in York representing half a million unskilled workers demanded the bonus.

The Federation said the only logical course the Government could take in view of the threatened dislocation of industry was to extend the advance to all classes of time-workers and order an investigation into the position of piece-workers. At this late date the Cabinet appointed a labour committee under George Barnes, now a Cabinet member, to co-ordinate policy. The advance was extended to semi-skilled and unskilled time-workers and in January 1918, pieceworkers were given 7½ per cent.

The introduction of national wage bargaining was forced on the industry by the logic of war circumstances. In the first two years there had been two rounds of wage increases, mostly in the form of war bonuses, brought about by numbers of local claims dealt with through the Procedure or by reference to the Committee on Production or one of the other tribunals. The second round had to be completed with some rapidity because of the 12½ per cent concession in Coventry which caused so much annoyance to neighbouring associations. The main case for practically all the claims was the increase in the cost of living, with which the increases in rates failed to keep pace, but there was substantial upward drift in earnings, particularly of piece-workers. The Federation in 1916 was rejecting almost all further claims but the Committee on Production appeared to be starting on a third round.

The ASE said it took too long to go through the Procedure and then to arbitration and started sending cases direct from local conference to the Committee on Production. The Central Conference, they said, should cease to consider wage questions until the end of the war. On Askwith's suggestion, the two sides met to consider whether future applications could be dealt with on a uniform basis. The result was the National Wages Agreement at the beginning of 1917 which provided that the Committee on Production should have four-monthly hearings to consider what alterations in wages were required. The committee's awards were to be binding and nationally applicable. Similar agreements followed in other industries. 'The most far-extending single agreement which has ever been made or obtained force between employers and employed in this, or indeed in any country,' Askwith commented. The first award was of 5s. all round.

Since strikes were officially outlawed, militant leadership of the workers devolved upon shop stewards, who played an increasingly active part in the history of industrial relations throughout this period and stirred up some of its most dramatic industrial crises. The appointment of shop stewards had been provided for in the ASE rules in 1896. A first reference to them in Glasgow was a report by Biggart to the local association in that year that considerable trouble was arising in a number of shops in consequence of 'the newly-formed vigilance committee of the ASE known as shop stewards'. They seem to have been well-established in Belfast and Barrow, as well as Glasgow and some other centres in the early years of the century as representatives of the unions in the workshops either with the limited functions of recruiting new arrivals or to make sure that all union decisions were observed. They increased rapidly in numbers from 1909 onwards but had little collective significance before the war. The introduction of dilution necessarily increased their importance since it was only within the workshops that changes in pre-war practices could be discussed and recorded so that the position could be restored when hostilities ended, and later efforts to extend piece-work added to their responsibilities.

The first important strike led by shop stewards involved some 9000 men on the Clyde in February 1915. It occurred while talks about relaxation of peace-time practices were disturbing the workers, but it was primarily about wages. A three-year agreement ended in December 1914, and negotiations for an increase broke down. Prices were rising rapidly, rents were being put up as new labour crowded into the Clyde and there were widespread complaints of 'profiteering'. The strike was settled by arbitration, but when it was over the shop stewards who had led it formed the Clyde Workers Committee, the first of many formed in industrial areas. Unrest on the Clyde persisted and when Lloyd George and Arthur Henderson visited the area the following Christmas they were howled down. The following month four of the men's leaders were sent to prison for sedition and in March a new strike spread rapidly through the Clyde. When the ASE failed to get the men to resume work, the Government deported eight members of the workers' committee to Edinburgh.

After this there was an uneasy peace on the Clyde for a time but unrest was growing on the other side of the border. Industrial commissioners had been appointed to try to make dilution a reality and in many firms dilution committees, including shop stewards' representatives, were in operation. But the armed forces were demanding more men and from the autumn of 1916 the Government announced a number of measures which included an alteration in the basis of exemption from military service, the extension of dilution to private work and a campaign to extend payment by results. Dissatisfaction with these measures was intensified by the rapid rise in the cost of living which followed the unrestricted submarine warfare which the Germans proclaimed in February 1917, while the Russian revolution in March added to the restiveness of the workers. In April 1917, the management committee considered the spread of unofficial strikes and agreed to ask the Government to make a public pronouncement that further breaches of the Munitions of War Act would at once be followed by prosecutions.

Shortly afterwards the most serious of all the shop stewards' strikes began. Complaints that a Rochdale firm had extended dilution to private work without consultation led to a strike which brought out 60,000 men in Lancashire. Under the leadership of the shop stewards' committees, the strike spread rapidly to all the other main industrial centres except the Clyde and the Tyne. Within a few days, 10,000 men were out in Sheffield and 30,000 in the Midlands. The management committee decided that as the strike was against government proposals, the Government should deal with it. Action by the Federation, they thought, would be open to misinterpretation. Two firms asked if they were entitled to claim a subsidy but were told that as the disputes were between the workers and the Government, not the workers and employers, subsidies were not payable. On 18 May eight strike leaders were arrested and the stewards recommended a return to work on condition that their leaders should be released and that there should be no victimisation. Following the return to work, however, a meeting of representatives of shop stewards' committees set up a national administrative council.

Some of the associations were becoming alarmed. Birmingham foresaw the 'gravest possible dangers' and decided 'to oppose to the utmost any suggestion on the part of the Government or the Federation to institute shop committees or recognise shop stewards'. In June they called a joint meeting with representatives of the Bedstead Manufacturers' Association, the Brass Masters' Association and the Malleable Ironfounders' Association at which J. P. Chatwin, the chairman, said that recent strikes could have 'far-reaching and disastrous' results for manufacturers generally. 'The engineering trade has probably had to fight harder during the past 12 months and will have to fight harder in the future to uphold the rights of employers than was ever dreamed of in the past. Undesirable conditions may spread to other trades and become permanently established.' The four associations set up a joint committee and decided to contact other associations.

In November another dispute broke out in Coventry which had important results. The shop stewards' committee there accused an engineering firm, White & Poppe, of refusing to negotiate with shop stewards on the pay of toolmakers, and brought out some 50,000 workers. There were fears of a national strike for shop steward recognition unless quick action was taken. Allan Smith went to Coventry and, with the executive of the local association, had a meeting with the Mayor of Coventry and two Labour members of the city council. But before the proposals which emerged had been considered, the parties were summoned to London to see George Barnes, who promised to urge the conclusion of an immediate settlement covering the position of shop stewards. After three days of meetings with the fifteen trade unions who were now parties to the Procedure, the first agreement for the recognition of shop stewards was signed by all except the ASE, who came in later.

The shop stewards' movement continued to grow in power and militancy in the last year of the war. In January 1918, the Government announced they were going to call up skilled engineers between the ages of 18 and 25. There was strong opposition from the ASE and in March the National Council of Shop Stewards decided to call a nation-wide strike against the new Manpower Bill. The Germans' March offensive on the western front shocked the combatants into a temporary truce. Churchill wrote to Smith urging that every employer should cast about for means of releasing fit men for the fighting front. In terms which had the authentic ring of his utterances during the Second World War, he continued: 'Impose this moment and seize this hour to knot closer the bonds of common interest and of common sympathy which have often existed and must ever be preserved in this island between employers and employed.'

The danger over, strikes spread again in July to Coventry, Birmingham, Manchester, Leicester and elsewhere, this time against a Government order, known as the 'embargo', limiting the employment of skilled labour by some firms to a proportion of the total work force. Once again, the Federation had to complain that they had not been consulted.

As the war moved towards its close, the unions began to revive the claims they had suspended in 1914, and among the first was that for shorter hours which shop stewards were demanding locally. The engineering and shipbuilding federations agreed to negotiate jointly, an experiment which rapidly ran into trouble when Allan Smith and Sir George Carter, the SEF president, adopted divergent attitudes at a meeting with the unions in the Caxton Hall, London, in November 1918. One union representative present was Walter Citrine, later to become TUC general secretary.

Sir Allan Smith [according to an account Citrine gave later] displayed the usual dilatory tactics he resorted to whenever a union demand was under consideration. The indignation most of us felt was giving way to deep anger when Carter jumped up and in his outspoken manner completely repudiated the line taken by Smith, whose arguments he brushed aside peremptorily, greatly to the delight of all of us. It was the only occasion on which I have seen such open disagreement between the spokesmen of such influential employers' organisations.

The Federation called a special meeting of their management committee and drew up a pained letter to the SEF in which they complained of the 'wrong and unfortunate impression' given by their president's remarks and asked whether the shipbuilders' executive approved of what he said and if not what steps they would take to remove the impression created in the minds of the union representatives. The SEF eventually persuaded them to withdraw the letter and a common policy was agreed upon.

The unions rejected the first offer of a 48-hour week, pointing to the dangerous situation which existed owing to the activities of the rank-and-file movement and the desirability of supporting the executives in their efforts to maintain 'constitutionalism'. Eventually, with the war over, a 47-hour week on the one-break system was agreed, on condition that 'the unions shall take all possible steps to ensure that in the critical state through which the country has to pass, the greatest possible output will be secured and maintained' and 'the economic conditions and systems and basis of remuneration necessary in the interests of the industry shall be the subject of early consideration and the parties agree to

deal with these conditions from a broad national standpoint.'
Lloyd George sent the parties a letter of congratulation, referring
to the necessity of arranging industrial relations questions in a
friendly way in order to enable the nation to recover from the
effects of war.

But any hope that the concession would be gratefully received
was quickly dispelled. A ballot of union members endorsed the
agreement by 36,793 votes to 27,684 but in many districts the
shop stewards led a revolt. There were immediate strikes and bans
on piece-work and overtime in many parts of the country. Work
on the Clyde was stopped by a claim for a 40-hour week. The
unofficial movement represented by shop stewards from London,
Leeds, Sheffield, Belfast, Manchester, Southampton, York and
Crewe met and passed a resolution demanding a 44-hour week.
The ASE suspended the district committees on the Clyde and in
Belfast and in London. The Federation said the Clyde movement
was 'palpably revolutionary' and was being dealt with by the
Government as such. The strike there was followed by riots,
battles with the police, the calling in of the army and the arrest
of ten of the men's leaders, two of whom were sent to prison. The
men returned to work on 11 February.

Part of the trouble was that nothing was included in the
47-hour agreement to keep up the earnings of piece-workers, and
on 1 April 1919, an agreement was made that prices or times
should enable a worker of average ability to earn $33\frac{1}{3}$ per cent
above the time rate. A general agreement on piece-work arrangements had been made in 1917, when the Government was campaigning for the extension of payment by results, but this was the
first time that any national standard had been fixed for piece-
work earnings.

The ASE, meanwhile, conducted a new ballot which resulted
in a huge majority for a 44-hour week and in June 1919, put in a
new claim for 44 hours. 'The ink is not dry on the paper containing the agreement for the 47-hours week,' Allan Smith complained to the union. 'We have not yet completed that agreement.
And in the middle of the discussion we are now faced with a
demand for a 44-hours week.' He went on to say that they did not
yet know what the effect of the 47-hour week was going to be, but
output was going down very seriously and they were being under-
quoted in every market of the world. The unions referred to

'statements by politicians and other prominent individuals that after the war there would be a good time for everybody and the country would be "fit for heroes",' but the employers replied that increase in output must come before any further reduction. Eventually the unions suspended the 44-hour claim. A joint committee was set up to investigate the economic relation of production to hours of work and methods of manufacture in the shipbuilding and engineering industries in this and other countries.

The dispute over working hours was the last in which the shop stewards' movement of the period led a serious stoppage in the engineering industry. The employers in 1915 and 1916 had been inclined to wash their hands of such unofficial action, taking the view that it was the responsibility of the unions to get their men back to work and of the Government to ensure that production was maintained. But as the shop stewards strengthened their influence over the workers in the main industrial areas and built up a loose national organisation, some of the associations began to see them as a serious danger. On the one hand they were usurping the authority of the union executives and in doing so threatened the orderly system of collective bargaining and disputes procedure which had operated since 1898. On the other most of the committees were closely linked with one or other of the small revolutionary socialist sects which owed their origin to the wave of industrial unionism and syndicalist thinking which spread fairly widely through the union movement before the war, advocating the capture of power by the workers through industrial action.

Official ASE policy was little affected by this, even though Tom Mann was one of its major prophets before the war and during the war G. D. H. Cole, one of the leaders of the somewhat more moderate guild socialists, acted as an adviser to the union. The engineering union leaders shared the widespread hope for a new kind of society after the war, and believed that it should be a socialist society. Brownlie himself did so and public ownership became an objective of the ASE as it did of most unions at that time. But it was a very different thing to advocate the achievement of socialism by constitutional means and to advocate its achievement, as the shop stewards' movement did, by direct action. The movement's strength was not in its ideas so much as in the fact that it led the men in the workshops from within the

workshops and adopted militant policies to remedy their grievances when the unions could not do so because of wartime laws
and because they felt it their duty in the national interest not to
cause interruptions in production.

In these circumstances it was to the interest of the employers to
help the unions to re-establish their authority. The shop stewards'
agreement was not a surrender to irresponsible force but an
attempt to bring the stewards, accepting that they were there to
stay, within the framework of the industrial relations machinery.
The 47-hour week may also have been thought of as a concession
which would strengthen the unions. In after years Allan Smith
claimed that it was the employers who defeated the challenge to
union authority.

Once the war was over, the unions could resume their militant
leadership. The shop stewards played a part in the post-war
struggles but the formation of the Communist Party in 1920 provided a new focus of activity for extremists. Tom Mann was
elected general secretary of the Amalgamated Engineering Union
when it was formed in 1920 and regularly advocated workers'
control in the union journal but he was not the power he had
been and made little impact on union policy. With the slump of
1922 the shop stewards' movement faded out.

Not only trade unionists dreamed of a different kind of society
when the carnage was over. During the pains and discomforts of
war, many men and women find relief in planning for a better
world. Others, perhaps more realistic, make preparations for a
renewal of the rat race and the old bitter squabbles. Some hedge
their bets. But when there is common action against a common
enemy, it is easy to be persuaded that the co-operative effort will
be continued afterwards, that master and man will lie down
together, and Governments like to encourage such thoughts.

In 1916 Lloyd George established a Ministry of Reconstruction and there was a Reconstruction Committee with a sub-
committee to make suggestions for the permanent improvement
of relations between employers and employed, presided over by
J. H. Whitley, Deputy Speaker of the House of Commons. This
became famous as the Whitley Committee whose recommendations laid the basis of joint industrial councils in many industries
and of Whitleyism in the Civil Service. Allan Smith, it need
hardly be said, was a member.

'The circumstances of the present time are admitted on all sides to offer a great opportunity for securing a permanent improvement in the relations between employers and employed, while failure to utilise the opportunity may involve the nation in grave industrial difficulties at the end of the war,' the Whitley Committee said in their first report in March 1917. They recommended the establishment of joint standing industrial councils for each industry where the two sides were organised, to be followed by joint district councils and works committees. The object was 'to secure co-operation by granting to workpeople a greater share in the consideration of matters affecting their industry.'

Not all members of the Federation were pleased to see Allan Smith's name appended to these recommendations. The executive committee of the Birmingham association, much alarmed at this time by shop stewards' activities, noted it 'with indignation' and passed a resolution saying they had read with grave concern the report recommending works committees and considered it extremely unfortunate that Mr Allan Smith's name should be identified with this, especially as the majority of the Federation were strongly opposed to such institutions. They demanded an immediate explanation. Whether or not as a consequence of such reactions, Smith declined to sign a further report by the committee on conciliation and arbitration because, he stated, 'I consider that the subject dealt with is one which, unprejudiced by any pronouncement of the committee, should be left to the free discussion and consideration of the employers and workpeople in each industry.'

In a little over a year some fifty industries set up joint industrial councils, but, in spite of Smith's membership of the committee, the Federation did nothing at national or district level. The functions of national and local joint councils, they explained, were already provided for by the industry's machinery for local and central conferences. The Government had clearly indicated that there was no desire to interfere with existing procedures in so far as they covered the principle laid down in the report. This left the question of works committees.

The ASE were opposed to the Whitley reports in a general way but were in favour of works committees. It will be remembered that they were not parties to the shop stewards' agreement of 1917, but they now asked for a conference to discuss the recognition of their stewards and the setting up of works committees and in the meantime accepted the 1917 agreement. A new agreement for the appointment of works committees was then made, as an addition to that for shop stewards, in May 1919. Joint committees, it said, could be set up consisting of not more than seven representatives of management and seven shop stewards, nominated and elected by union members.

The place of shop stewards in the Procedure was clearly set out. After a worker had failed to agree with his foreman, the question could be taken to a higher level by a shop steward and one of the workers concerned, and if there was still no agreement could be considered by the works committee with a union official and a representative of the local employers' association present. Shop stewards were to be afforded facilities to deal with questions raised and might with the previous consent of the management (such consent not to be unreasonably withheld) visit any other shop in the establishment.

Employers in the last year or two of the war were also giving much thought to the future of their own organisations. They needed to get together so that they could speak to the Government with greater weight at the time but many of them also believed that their united strength would be needed to avert or deal with labour troubles after the war. Several new bodies were set up, with industrial, political and propaganda aims. Some proved ephemeral, but the Federation of British Industries in 1916 and the National Confederation of Employers' Organisations in 1919 established themselves as permanent parts of the industrial scene.

The Federation before the war had avoided any link-up with other employers' organisations except for temporary alliances for specific purposes, but we now find Allan Smith playing a leading part in the formation of several, while taking great pains to prevent the FBI and other new trade organisations from attempting to represent engineering firms in their capacity as employers. After a lot of hard work and persistence on his part, the FBI adopted a resolution in August 1917, saying that: 'In regard to labour matters, the FBI will not concern itself or interfere with any questions affecting working conditions or rates of pay except at the request of the employers' association or federation established to deal with such matters.' Somewhat similar resolutions were passed by several other bodies, including the British Engineering Association.

The activities of the FBI continued to cause the Federation anxiety, however. In January 1918, the FBI produced a report about relations between capital and labour after the war, covering such subjects as superannuation, unemployment, sickness and accident benefits, and profit-sharing, to which the Federation took strong exception. They decided that the time had come to further the formation of a federation of employers' organisations to deal with labour questions. The mutual interests of such a body and any national organisation dealing with commercial questions, they contended, could be dealt with by a liaison committee.

No such body had been established by the time of the National Industrial Conference which the Government called together just over a year later and difficulties were experienced in appointing a temporary committee to represent the employers' organisations. As a result, the Federation invited other organisations to a meeting at which a committee was set up under Allan Smith's chairmanship to work out plans for a confederation. The FBI became inquisitive and sent a circular letter to the organisations but it was agreed no action should be taken on this. The National Confederation of Employers' Organisations was duly established in the summer of 1919. One of its purposes was to discourage any organisations from acting without considering what the effect of their action would be on other industries.

While this was going on there were moves for joint parliamentary action by employers. In February 1918, Smith reported to the Federation management committee that

> various commercial, financial and parliamentary interests were moving in regard to the formation of an organisation to link up for the purposes of parliamentary action bodies of employers dealing with labour questions, manufacturing organisations dealing with commercial questions, of city interests, and a parliamentary party which would have for its object the development and maintenance of British commercial interests.

He added that political developments and the probable large increases in the strength of the Labour Party in the House of

Commons made such action a necessary development.

The outcome was the British Commonwealth Union with Allan Smith as chairman of its general purposes committee. When the Union appealed for funds, the Federation pointed out to members that a number of employers in different industries had agreed to contribute for three years 1s. for every £100 of their wages bill for the previous year – and others had given much more. The union declared itself to be political but non-party. Its primary purpose was that 'the essential experience of business men should be strongly represented in the next Parliament and should be fully brought to bear on all problems of reconstruction'. During the war, it pointed out, the country had shown increasing determination to place the organisation of the war effort in the hands of business men, whether employers or workmen. It advocated increased co-operation with organised labour.

The union sponsored some fifty candidates for the 'khaki' election of December 1919, including Allan Smith, who was elected the Member for the Croydon South constituency.

Allan Smith became one of the sponsors in 1919 of the National Propaganda Fund the objects of which were 'to diminish unrest and by positive propaganda to impress upon employer and employed the vital necessity of increasing production, and to correct economic and other mis-statements, to combat all activities directed against constitutional government, and to co-operate with and direct the activities of other non-political organisations having the like or similar objects'. Members were invited to subscribe to the fund through the Federation. The establishment of the fund was the outcome of a secret meeting of representatives of the Government and various propaganda organisations.

Associations were approached by numerous other new organisations towards the end of the war and in the immediate post-war period and frequently appealed to the Federation for advice. One which was commended was the Industrial Welfare Society (now the Industrial Society) because the Home Office were taking an interest in workers' welfare and the Federation thought better results would be obtained from a private organisation.

While all this was going on, the Federation were taking steps to expand their own domain. In February 1918, there was a meeting with representatives of the Shipbuilding Employers'

Federation and the National Employers' Federation at which a resolution was passed approving the principle of confederation and a sub-committee was appointed of three from each body. The shipbuilders soon dropped out, but the NEF entered into active negotiations for a merger.

The NEF began life as the Midlands Employers' Federation in 1913 to combat a 'prairie fire' of strikes which had swept through the Black Country and Birmingham to obtain minimum wage rates for lower-paid workers and women. The Black Country firms had previously been largely unorganised on both sides but the strikers were soon recruited into the rapidly expanding Workers' Union. The new employers' organisation, established for defensive purposes, included previously non-federated engineering firms and also a number in related trades.

The Federation was coming under pressure from general workers' unions at that time. Their membership had grown rapidly, partly as a result of the National Insurance Act. A dockyard agreement had been negotiated with some of them in 1911. Both the Birmingham and Wolverhampton associations became involved in the 'prairie fire' strikes and made settlements on the lines of those of the Midlands federation.

The Midlands federation developed effective negotiating arrangements for labourers and semi-skilled workers and there is little evidence of friction with the federated associations in the Midlands, though association members were advised not to join it. In 1917 it changed its name to the National Employers' Federation and expanded its activities outside the Midlands, setting up offices in Manchester, Leeds and Bristol. From January 1918, it published a monthly journal, *The Employer* – something the Federation never had. Sir Harris Spencer, its leader from the beginning, was a notable character.

At the time of the merger talks the NEF had between 700 and 800 member firms, mainly in trades closely allied to engineering, such as nut and bolt making, tube making, railway carriage and wagon building. Their total wages bill amounted to some £15m. a year. During the talks it was agreed that engineering should be seen as covering all processes connected with the manufacture of engineering products from the raw material stage. The structure of the NEF was somewhat different from that of the Federation, with districts divided into trade sections, which were autonomous in local matters, and national trade committees. A central council in London had responsibility for questions affecting more than one trade. This caused slight complications but it was agreed that the Federation constitution should be amended to provide for technical committees 'on a trade sectional basis' and special arrangements were made for the Midlands. All went smoothly and the merger took effect from 31 August 1918.

The enlarged body was given the title of Engineering and National Employers' Federations as a temporary measure because merger talks were going on with a number of other employers' organisations, for instance some of those for foundries. Not all the members of the NEF joined the new Federation. At the end of 1919, the Birmingham association listed about 100 resignations, of which 29 objected to the subsidy payment, 9 had refused to accept the obligations of membership, 30 had failed to pay their subscriptions and most of the remainder preferred other employers' organisations or Whitley councils. Nevertheless more than 650 NEF firms joined the Federation.

Partly to meet the additional demands on staff, the Federation acquired new premises at Broadway House, Tothill Street, Westminster, where they still remain in enlarged buildings. Very little had been paid out of the subsidy fund during the war. In fact some members had suggested in 1916 that payments should be discontinued, but the Federation rejected the idea because they 'viewed with some apprehension the position likely to arise after the war and felt that the existence of a strong subsidy fund would be a matter of great importance'. The trustees were now authorised to use the sum accumulated to pay the £75,000 required for Broadway House. *The Employer* was not taken over. There was a suggestion that it should be continued as an independent paper but this came to nothing.

When the war was over and industry was again becoming a battlefield, Lloyd George made another attempt to get the two sides together. He called a National Industrial Conference in the Central Hall, Westminster, on 27 February 1919, which was attended by about 500 representatives of workers and 300 of employers. Allan Smith, who played the leading part on the employers' side, said that if the Government would leave them alone, the employers and employed were far better able to settle their differences than any agency outside. Many employers, he declared 'with a full sense of responsibility', were prepared to go very much further in amelioration of conditions than any of the workers had any idea of. But there was to be no one-sided arrangement. If amelioration was to take place, if the work-people expected to have a greater say in the conditions under which they worked and lived, there was another part to the bargain – the State and the employers should receive from them an adequate output.

On his motion, amended by Arthur Henderson and adjusted by Lloyd George, a thirty-a-side committee was set up. The ASE and the 'triple alliance' – the miners, railwaymen and transport workers – would have nothing to do with it, Ernest Bevin remarking that the conference had been convened to side-track the efforts of men and women who were struggling for better conditions. However the committee, with Smith as chairman of the employers' side, prepared a report, accepted at a resumed conference in April, which recommended the establishment of a permanent National Industrial Council of 400 members, a statutory 48-hour week, statutory minimum time rates of wages, machinery for avoiding disputes in all industries, and systematic efforts to check unemployment, including organised short-time in periods of depression and restriction of overtime.

The conference members agreed to submit the recommendations to their constituent organisations immediately the Government officially declared its readiness to proceed at once by legislative and other steps to carry it into effect. Lloyd George wrote a letter to the provisional committee, which continued to meet, accepting the report in principle without committing the Government to all its details. The committee worked out proposals for Bills on the 48-hour week and minimum wages, legislation which was regarded as the touchstone of the Government's sincerity.

By June 1920, the Government were preparing a 48-hour Bill following the lines of an international convention adopted at Washington, but Smith objected that this was different from what the committee had proposed and therefore their function was terminated. However, there was one last meeting in July 1921, when it had become clear that the Government had no intention of introducing the legislation in the near future and Henderson and Smith were equally disillusioned. Smith said unions and employers were being 'used as pawns in a political game'. They had been asked to sit down together 'for the purpose of getting the Government out of difficulty'. It was 'a situation which no self-respecting organisation of employers or trade unions should for one moment submit itself to'.

The committee disbanded itself and that was the end of the matter.

CHAPTER 6

Power Regained 1920–1934

Boom and Slump – Wages Slashed – Managerial
Functions Restored – Mond–Turner Talks Killed –
Decay and Depression – Allan Smith Goes

Hopes of a new era in industrial relations after the war were soon
dispelled. Scarcely were the guns silenced before the great
struggles of the five pre-war years were resumed where they had
been left off. There were big strikes in the coal and cotton industries and on the railways. The triple alliance of miners, railway
workers and transport workers was reformed and involved in two
national crises before it collapsed. The TUC set up a general
council to co-ordinate industrial action. Labour mobilised to prevent war against the Soviet Union. In the boom period which
lasted until the second half of 1920 the Government and
employers were engaged in a holding action against massive and
aggressive trade unions, convinced that little or nothing was
being done to redeem wartime promises and stirred to a new
militancy by the shop stewards' movement and the impact of the
Russian revolution. The number of working days lost through
disputes in the five years from 1910 to 1914 averaged 16 million.
During the war the average dropped to 4 million. In the five
post-war years it exceeded 35 million. Before the war, engineering
was not in the front line. Now it was.

Both the Federation and the engineering unions emerged from
the war swollen in size but reduced in authority. With wartime
growth and the absorption of the National Employers' Federation
and some smaller organisations, the Federation had three times
as many member firms in 1920 as in 1913. The numbers they
employed reached a peak of nearly 700,000 in 1920 and the
number of firms a peak of 2690 in 1922, a figure not to be
exceeded until the Second World War. The aggregate annual

wage bill exceeded £60m. But the new members were a hetero-
geneous collection, including mushroom growths of the war years,
some on the periphery of the engineering industry, and some
engineering sections of companies outside the industry altogether.

The character of the industry was changing. Motor and aircraft and electrical manufacturing firms were growing in importance at the expense of the marine engineering aristocrats. The
production of motors, cycles and aircraft, which was less than
10 per cent of that of the industry, measured by value, in 1907,
rose to more than a quarter in 1924. Few of these new and
expanding firms shared in the traditions of 1897.

Moreover for four years, members old and new had been
allowed to go their own way, by a leadership deprived of power,
to an extent that would not have been tolerated in the old days.
At the same time the employers had been unable to enforce the
keeping of agreements by their workers, the observance of the
Procedure, the prerogatives of management. In some respects, for
instance the operation of dilution, the employers had been compelled to share control, and the workers were clamouring for a
greater share.

The responsibility for restoring internal and external discipline,
for welding the new Federation into a cohesive power and forcing
the unions back to the old frontiers, rested on one man, Allan
Smith, who had been knighted a few months before the war ended
and became an MP immediately afterwards. The circumstances of
the time and the remarkable attributes of the man himself had
made him the dominating personality in the Federation and the
natural leader of the nation's employers. The last of the 1897
leaders had faded from the scene during the war. Alexander
Siemens, the Board chairman, resigned on the outbreak of hostilities because of his German origin, though he had long been a
naturalised British subject. Sir Andrew Noble, the president, died
in October 1915, and Sir Benjamin Browne in March 1917.
Andrew Henderson, who followed Noble as president, retired in
1917. In the stress of war there were no strong figures ready to
take their places. Everywhere, whatever the issue, Smith became
the Federation spokesman and leader. His appointment as chairman of the Board in 1916 had given him the seat of power in
form as well as in fact.

Smith was a single-minded man of indefatigable energy and

rigid integrity whose work was his life. He had been a member of all the main war-time committees. He had been largely responsible for creating the Confederation of British Employers' Organisations whose small staff were housed in Broadway House, and the National Propaganda Fund, now the Federation's tenants in Abingdon Street. Without the financial support of the Federation, the Employers' Confederation would have found difficulty in surviving. He became a member of the Coal Commission in 1919 and of the Balfour Commission on Trade and Industry in 1924. He was taken as government adviser to international conferences. He had the ear of Prime Ministers and it was from him, through Clive Wigram, assistant secretary at Buckingham Palace, that the King informed himself about the industrial scene. As a debater and negotiator, he relied on a relentless marshalling of fact and argument, without variation in temper or tone, which tended to leave his adversaries stunned by the sheer weight of it. He could act ruthlessly in pursuit of his aims, whether dealing with resisting unions or erring employers.

Lord Citrine in his reminiscences describes Smith as 'an expert in procrastination, whose icy-cold speeches were enough to freeze to death any warm impulses towards progress which his members might feel,' and said Smith was 'loathed' by most of the trade union officials with whom he had to deal. Yet he was close enough to Brownlie, leader of the most important engineering union, to invite him to lunch at St Stephen's Club or to tea at his home. He was relentless in his conduct of the lock-out of 1922, but in the following year, in a bitter exchange of letters with Prime Minister Stanley Baldwin on the subject of unemployment, he referred to its disruptive effect on trade unions 'which are a safeguard of industrial peace' and showed an appreciation of its human effects: 'With regard to the workpeople it is a sad position to contemplate . . . age and infirmity and individual characteristics can stand a certain amount of demoralisation and distress owing to unemployment, but there is a time when the limit has arrived, and that time is apparently now.'

Smith was writing in his capacity as chairman of the industrial group in Parliament. The Minister of Labour had made a speech in the House expressing 'no doubt that the patience, the courage and the determination of our people will see us through as it has done in the past,' on which Smith commented that 'this pious belief' was an inadequate substitute for a strong, constructive policy in place of 'the present hard-hearted temporising and palliatives'. 'The patience, the courage and the determination of our people,' he wrote, 'might be strained beyond bearing.' What was lacking was foresight and imagination.

On behalf of the industrial group, Smith proposed that the whole question of the country's assets and their utilisation in the development of internal trade should be entrusted to a small committee of leading business men, with powers to report direct to the Cabinet. But Baldwin replied that he was not convinced there were good grounds for establishing a further committee of business men. Smith sent the letters to the newspapers, which disturbed the Conservatives of South Croydon. They withdrew their support from him with the result that he left the House of Commons when the next general election came at the end of the year.

The letters to Baldwin illustrate the deep distrust of politicians which was one of Smith's characteristics, no doubt a result of his experience of them during the war and on the National Industrial Conference provisional committee. He believed that industry should play a greater part in the conduct of the nation's affairs and was prepared to accept that employers and unions should do this in alliance. Hence his part in the recommendations of the Whitley Committee and the National Industrial Conference. All through the twenties he tried to get the unions to join the employers in forging a common economic policy for the engineering industry. But unemployment throughout the period was chronic. In only one year, 1927, did the overall percentage of unemployed workers fall below 10 after the slump of 1922 – a figure higher than that experienced in most pre-war depressions. With the state of trade as it was, the employers could not make the concessions that might have won the unions' confidence.

By most of his staff, Smith was regarded with a mixture of hate and awe. They were expected to stand when they spoke to him and address him as 'Sir'. He never looked at those to whom he was dictating. There were awful occasions when he would make an unheralded tour of the office, followed by a senior member of the staff and the caretaker, noting every detail, however small, whether it was a light left on unnecessarily or a switchboard girl looking over a comic paper in a moment of leisure. When he had gone up to his room again, the thunderbolts would descend. There was one legendary occasion when typeroom girls, found chatting about job vacant advertisements in a newspaper, were called in one by one and dismissed with a week's money.

Union membership also reached peaks not surpassed until the Second World War but the shop stewards' movement and later the Communist Party were constantly trying to undermine the authority of the official leadership. The ASE doubled in size during the war and in 1920 absorbed nine small sectional societies to form the Amalgamated Engineering Union with a membership of 460,000. But the important unions apart from the ASE, those of the boilermakers and foundry workers, did not join in. And the electricians and pattern-makers failed to get the 50 per cent necessary for amalgamation in ballot votes. Three of the foundry unions, however, merged to form the National Union of Foundry Workers.

The Federation's first major dispute, when the war was over and strikes and lock-outs became legal again, was not with the ASE but with these three foundry unions. It was the most damaging stoppage of work in the industry since 1898, the more so since it came at a time of hectic industrial activity, with an almost unlimited demand for castings by the railways, badly in need of new rolling stock, and by the motor firms. The strike lasted eighteen weeks, involved some 65,000 workers and resulted in the loss of 6,890,000 working days and much short time in other industries. It arose out of a claim by the three unions in August 1919, for a 15s. a week increase. The Federation pointed out that the unions were parties to the national wages agreement and that the claim, on behalf of all the engineering unions, had been rejected by the Industrial Court the previous month, and the next hearing would be in November.

The foundry unions then gave notice to withdraw from the agreement and called their members out on 20 September. They argued that there was great unrest because unskilled and semi-skilled men had benefited more than skilled during the war, to which the employers replied that this was due to the refusal of skilled foundrymen to accept payment by results. As the strike dragged on, the Federation asserted 'that the main-spring has become the eagerness of outside organisers to keep active every source of labour disturbance and to increase their hold over a key industry which might be valuable to them in any general programme of sabotage'. When the men returned to work on 16 January, all they got was 5s. a week already awarded to other engineering unions and a promise to discuss working conditions in the foundries and to fix minimum district standard rates. The Federation had treated the dispute as one of principle and demonstrated their determination to insist that unions kept to their agreements.

The Federation made the first post-war use of a lock-out threat at the end of 1919 against mid-Lancashire sheet metal workers, who were involved in a number of scattered disputes at that time over the rejection of a wage claim. More critical was the threat of a national lock-out of electricians in the summer of 1920. Members of the Electrical Trades Union at a Cammell Laird factory in Penistone, in the Sheffield area, struck because a worker had resigned from the union on becoming a foreman. When the union gave the strike official backing, lock-out notices were posted by federated firms throughout the country. The Minister of Labour proposed to set up a court of inquiry but was told by the Federation that there was a question of principle affecting the management of the industry and they would neither withdraw the notices nor be parties to an inquiry. The union gave in just before the notices were due to take effect. So 1920 ended with the Federation resuming their defence of the rights of management and rejecting outside interference, but Cammell Laird complained that their subsidy did not cover their losses.

Relations with the amalgamated engineers had so far been peaceful. In September 1920, the Federation concluded with them an Overtime and Night Shift Agreement which for the first time fixed national premium rates – time and a half for ordinary overtime, double time for Sunday work and time and a third for night shifts. The Double Day and Three Shift Agreement followed later the same year, partly in the hope of absorbing some of the unemployed, by then increasing in numbers.

The national wage agreement of 1917 was at first continued and in both 1919 and 1920 the engineering unions were awarded increases by the Industrial Court. But when in June 1920, a new claim for a rise of 6d. an hour was rejected by the court, the unions gave notice to end the national agreement and in October resubmitted the claim to the Federation. Before the employers gave their reply it became evident that the post-war boom was over. Business had turned downwards, prices were falling and unemployment was spreading. The Employers' Confederation set up a committee to discuss how wage policies in various industries could be co-ordinated and recommended that in the meantime no further advances should be conceded. The Federation agreed with the shipbuilding employers to reject the claim.

By the beginning of 1921 the Federation were thinking in terms of a cut in wages rather than an increase. They had an inconclusive meeting with the unions to discuss their conviction that costs would have to be brought down, either by reducing wages or increasing production or both. Finally they decided to propose the biggest cut in the industry's history. It was not only to reverse the increases of the previous year – 6s. on the pay of time-workers and 15 per cent on that of piece-workers – but in addition end the 'Churchill' bonuses of $12\frac{1}{2}$ per cent for time-workers and $7\frac{1}{2}$ per cent for those on payment by results.

There was some difference of opinion as to whether it would be best to continue with national negotiations or to replace them with local or trade negotiations, as the impact of the depression varied a good deal between one district and another and one section of the industry and another, but a special meeting of the Board decided in favour of continued national negotiations and a vote of the associations supported this.

Brownlie rejected the proposed cuts on behalf of 200 delegates from some 50 engineering unions in York on 12 May. 'Never in the history of trade unionism and of the engineering and ship-building industry in particular were we faced with such a demand,' he said. 'You are asking too much from us.' He suggested a court of inquiry but the employers would have none of that. They offered to make the cuts by instalments and when this too was rejected by the unions, decided to impose them unilaterally, the first stage on 16 June. A joint meeting of the unions decided to recommend a strike to begin the same day. The Minister of Labour persuaded the Federation to put the cuts back a fortnight to allow the unions to ballot on their proposal, but the union members rejected it by 257,532 votes to 125,014.

The unions were in a difficult position. Trade was still deteriorating rapidly and it would have been folly to embark on a national strike at such a time. They met the employers again and agreed that half the 6s. cut should take place in the middle of July and the other half in the middle of August, while the question of ending the Churchill bonuses would be reviewed at the end of September in the light of the trade position then. When the time came trade was worse, not better, and an agreement to end the Churchill bonuses in three stages in November, December, and in January 1922, was accepted by the men by 170,471 votes to 147,636. Before the operation was completed, the Federation decided that a further cut in the war bonus of 26s. 6d. a week was necessary. But they deferred action because another issue had brought them to the brink of the great Managerial Functions lock-out of 1922.

It will be remembered that the unions had withdrawn from the 1898 terms of settlement in 1913 and nothing had been put in their place except that the Procedure was maintained through the York memorandum. Many of the old issues had arisen again during the war and afterwards it was not long before there were signs that, on one issue or another, a new struggle over managerial rights was coming. The machine question, resistance to payment by results, the position of apprentices and foremen all caused local troubles. The question which sparked off the conflict, however, was whether employers should have the sole right to decide when overtime should be worked, subject to the overall limitation of thirty hours in four weeks provided for in the Overtime and Night Shift Agreement of 1920.

The AEU wrote to their district committees in December saying that the agreement implied that overtime should only be worked when it was considered necessary by both parties and advising them to have regard to the numbers of men unemployed when considering their attitude. Following this, embargoes were placed on overtime in several districts. The employers told the union they could not possibly accept this interpretation of the agreement.

The relevant clause read:

The Federation and the Trade Union agree that systematic overtime is deprecated as a method of production and that when overtime is necessary the following provisions shall apply, viz.:– No union workman shall be required to work more than 30 hours overtime in any four weeks after full shop hours have been worked, allowance being made for time lost through sickness, absence with leave, or enforced idleness.

There followed a list of circumstances in which overtime was not to be restricted – breakdowns, repairs, replacements, alterations, trial trips and completion of work against delivery dates. It is not apparent that this implies anything one way or another about who should decide when overtime should be worked.

The Federation met the union in February 1921, and demanded withdrawal of the embargoes and of the union insistence on prior consultation before overtime was worked. The AEU refused, pointing out that the embargoes were local and on production work only. 'It is not reasonable or humane,' they said, 'to insist that overtime should be worked by some if, instead, more men could be employed.' A special Board meeting was called and decided that if AEU members refused to work overtime they would be dismissed, and if a strike resulted there would be a general lock-out. They also suspended negotiations on working conditions until the embargoes were withdrawn.

At further joint meetings in April, other disputes came up. AEU members at the Bolton firm of Hick, Hargreaves & Co. had struck against the employment of apprentices on payment by results. And three cases about the manning of machines were coming up to Central Conference. Allan Smith told the unions that the employers would be obliged to impose a lock-out unless a solution could be found, and an AEU national conference decided that they would meet the threat by using the full strength of their organisation. However, the Hick, Hargreaves strike was called off and the lock-out threat was withdrawn for the time being. During the summer the parties were preoccupied with the dispute over wages, but in November they met again.

The Federation now formally raised the general principle of the rights of management to exercise its functions. The AEU, under heavy pressure, agreed on 18 November after 16½ hours of continuous negotiation to the following memorandum:

I. General
1. The trade union shall not interfere with the right of the employers to exercise managerial functions in their estab-

lishments and the Federation shall not interfere with the proper functions of the trade union.

2. In the exercise of these functions, the parties shall have regard to the provisions for avoiding disputes of April 17, 1914, which are amplified by the Shop Stewards and Works Committee Agreement of May 20, 1919, and to the terms of other national and local agreements between the parties.

3. Instructions of the management shall be observed pending any question in connection therewith being discussed in accordance with the provisions referred to.

II. Overtime

It is agreed that in terms of the Overtime and Night Shift Agreement of 29 and 30 September, 1920, the employers have the right to decide when overtime is necessary, the workpeople or their representatives being entitled to bring forward under the provisions referred to any cases of overtime they desire discussed. Meantime, the overtime required shall be proceeded with.

In the closing stages of the negotiations, the AEU reported to their members, the employers 'gravely and dispassionately' intimated that unless agreement was reached they would have to revert to a lock-out. The negotiators had accepted the memorandum 'having regard to the gravity of the situation and the fact that over 90,000 of our members are unemployed, industrial stagnation and the severe financial strain to which the organisation has been subjected and is likely to be for some time yet.' They recommended members to accept the memorandum in a ballot vote. But the members rejected it by 50,240 votes to 35,525.

The Federation then not only gave notice of a general lock-out of AEU members from Saturday, 11 March, but also decided that other unions should be asked to declare their policy. There followed what must surely be among the most high-handed operations in the history of industrial relations. From 1 March onwards a series of ultimatums was sent to some 50 other unions – none of which had been involved in the dispute – asking them to sign the first three paragraphs of the November memorandum. First came the National Federation of General Workers, representing 12 unions, then the Federation of Engineering and Ship-

building Trades (FEST) representing 35 including the boilermakers and electricians, then the National Union of Foundry
Workers, and finally five more little unions which were asked on
10 March to sign by 17 March.

There were indignant protests. FEST expressed surprise that
unions which had no quarrel with the employers on overtime and
working conditions should without provocation have an ultimatum thrust upon them. They considered it a violation of the
Procedure. They asked for time but the Federation management
committee agreed on 9 March that no time should be lost in
dealing with the other unions. Representatives of the two main
union federations and the foundry workers met them the following day and said that, while they could not recommend acceptance, they would ballot their members, to which the Federation
replied that they could not postpone notices. However, on the
intervention of Dr Macnamara, the Minister of Labour, Allan
Smith conceded that, while the AEU lock-out must go ahead, the
other unions would be allowed fourteen days for a ballot.

A final attempt was made to get an agreed formula with the
AEU but failed. 'The union representatives made it clear,' said
the Federation report, 'that they are determined that any restrictions they have been able to impose as a result of abnormal conditions during and since the war in relation to managerial acts shall
be maintained.' The members of the AEU were duly locked out
on 11 March.

In the following days, replies from some of the little unions
came in. 'We do not fully understand your letter,' wrote the
Amalgamated Machine, Engine and Iron Grinders' and Glaziers'
Society. 'We have loyally kept our contract with you. Will you
please give us more information. Overtime is working well in our
trade.' 'We cannot understand your reference to management
functions,' wrote the Amalgamated Moulders' and Kindred
Industries' Association. 'Can we have a conference?' 'We
strongly protest to being drawn into this dispute without any provocation on our part,' wrote the Amalgamated Society of Scale,
Beam and Weighing Machine Makers. 'We would like to discuss
the situation with you so that we can tell our members what it is
all about.' A few of the small unions signed the memorandum.

In the event, the members of the unions other than the AEU
were not locked out until 2 May, but from the beginning the

Federation were determined to make sure that this time the representatives of all their manual employees should accept the rights of management. A weakness of the 1898 settlement was that some important unions, including those of the boilermakers and foundry workers, were not parties to it and there were continuing difficulties with those unions in the ensuing years. The opportunity now was such as might not recur. The sudden slump had bitten very deeply, and more so in engineering than in other sections of industry. About a quarter of the AEU membership was out of work. There had been an unprecedented drain on union funds. The AEU paid out more than £2m. in unemployment benefit in 1921 and the burden was growing heavier. Widespread unemployment in other industries and a long miners' strike meant that they could hope for little outside help. The AEU leaders accepted the November memorandum because they knew they were in no position to face an all-out conflict. Its rejection by their members forced them reluctantly into battle and gave the Federation their opportunity. Other unions were mostly even worse off than the AEU. This was not, like the lock-out of 1897, a battle of equals. Victory for the employers was certain from the beginning.

The Federation's main anxieties were concerned with public opinion and government intervention. A few days after the lockout began the Federation issued a printed statement to be posted on notice boards and at factory gates and on public hoardings 'to correct misrepresentations'. There was no justification for the suggestion that the employers were out to smash the unions, it said. The issue was not one of overtime but the refusal by the trade unions to continue the recognition of the employer's right to exercise managerial functions except with the prior consent and approval of the unions. It was essential in the interests of the country, the workpeople and the employers that freedom of management should be maintained in the works, restrained only by agreements entered into mutually with the unions. It was only by this means that the pre-eminent position of British engineering would be restored in the markets of the world. 'In any organisation for the direction of human effort, it is necessary that there shall be one directional authority, and all experience has shown that dual control such as is now sought is incompatible with the proper working and efficiency of an industrial establishment.'

In a House of Commons debate on 20 March, J. R. Clynes, a general workers' leader, reminded Smith that he had signed the National Industrial Conference report which said that during periods of depression in an industry overtime should only be worked in special cases and should be determined in accordance with rules laid down by the industry's joint industrial council or other joint representative body. Smith stressed that the dispute was not over overtime, machine manning or workshop organisation but over a principle – whether the employers should have liberty to manage or whether there should be dual control with a veto on their liberty to manage. 'We, the engineering employers, have given the trade unions greater scope for representative discussions than any other employers,' he claimed. Arthur Henderson and other speakers criticised the employers for dragging other unions into the dispute and called for a court of inquiry. But Dr Macnamara said he was deferring a decision on this until he knew the result of the ballot by the two union federations and the foundry workers. This resulted in 164,759 votes to 49,503 against the memorandum.

Efforts at mediation followed. The National Joint Council of Labour, representing the Labour Party, the Parliamentary Labour Party and the TUC, intervened and Allan Smith and Arthur Henderson worked out a revision of the memorandum which was the subject of a fruitless conference. Lloyd George, the Prime Minister, then tried his hand and persuaded all the unions except the AEU to accept yet another formula as a basis for negotiation. Prolonged talks on this broke down after a final eighteen-hour session at a quarter to five in the morning on Good Friday, 15 April. Notices to lock out the members of the fifty unions, twice deferred, were posted to take effect on 2 May.

At this stage, seven weeks after the AEU lock-out had begun, Dr Macnamara set up a court of inquiry. Allan Smith had staved it off as long as he could. As a 'counter-stroke' to this, as Allan Smith reported to members, the Federation decided that the workshops would be opened to individual employees who signed a slip accepting that the employers had the right to issue instructions, to which workpeople undertook to conform. They did this, they explained to the AEU, because 'they have been forced to the conclusion that the difficulty they have to face at the moment is not one which has arisen owing to the action taken or opinions held by the workpeople in the shops, but is one in which political issues have been the motive, and in which outside and even international policy has been the real cause of the present unfortunate state of affairs'. This was a reference to Communist activities, about which a good deal had been said in the Press and to which Smith had referred in his House of Commons speech.

One or two members urged the Federation to call off the lock-out while the court was sitting, and a similar appeal was made at the first day of the hearings. Smith said the suggestion was irrelevant, as the court was merely a fact-finding body. 'We hope the inquiry will not be protracted,' he told the court. 'The effect is simply to prolong the agony and postpone the day of settlement.' The court consisting of one man, Sir William Mackenzie, reported on 10 May. It supported the employers' view that there must be freedom to the management to make decisions on over-time within the limits of the agreement and to put changes into effect while they were considered in the Procedure but put some emphasis on the importance of providing time for consultation, where possible, before a change was introduced.

The Federation submitted detailed proposals for a settlement at a three-day conference from 16 to 18 May. The AEU rejected them but the other unions, after consulting their executives, agreed to ballot their members and all but the Boilermakers' Society and the National Union of Foundry Workers accepted the terms on 2 June. Thus all but isolated, the AEU balloted their members. They and the foundry workers accepted the terms on 13 June and the boilermakers on 20 June. The lock-out of AEU members had lasted three months. At the end 250,000 workers were involved and about 15,000,000 working days were lost.

During and after the lock-out thirty-seven firms were expelled from the Federation for failing to post notices. Each time the names of such firms were circulated, associations were asked to remind members of the 1908 Board resolution that wherever possible federated firms should be given preference when orders were given out.

In the Managerial Functions Agreement the statement of principle was polished to its bare bones: 'The employers have the right to manage their establishments and the trade unions have the right to exercise their functions.' This formulation remained unchanged for half a century. Some concessions were made on the *Status Quo* issue. General alterations in wages, alterations in working conditions which were the subject of agreements and alterations in the general working week were not to be given effect until the Procedure had been exhausted. Where managements proposed an alteration in working conditions which would result in one class of workers being replaced by another, they would if possible give at least ten days' notice to afford opportunity for discussion. If no agreement was reached by the date fixed, the management would give a temporary decision pending the completion of the Procedure. On other questions the management decision would take effect while the Procedure was being operated.

The victory was quickly followed up. By the middle of June the Federation had made an agreement with the National Union of Foundry Workers and several smaller unions giving the employers freedom to introduce systems of payment by results, something which the foundry workers had previously obstinately resisted. They also put to the engineering unions their deferred proposal for a further reduction in pay of 16s. 6d. a week in three stages from July to September. A ballot of union members went against it but the unions advised them to remain at work and there were no strikes.

Some federated firms felt that the cuts were going too far. Members of the Burton-on-Trent association considered them too severe. Three Leicester firms and one Wakefield firm resigned. Other members urged that there should be no further reductions for the time being and the Federation decided to take no action on the 10s. of the war bonus which still remained.

By the 1922 settlements, the Federation established for the first time a complete industrial relations framework for the industry. All the unions primarily concerned with engineering were parties to the settlements and to the Procedure. In addition two white collar unions which had grown in strength during the war were being brought in. Provisions for avoiding disputes were agreed with the National Union of Clerks in 1920 and the Federation was preparing to give similar recognition, which they did in 1924, to the Association of Engineering and Shipbuilding Draughtsmen. But the Federation did not concede them the right to negotiate terms of employment for their members. A Staff Benefit

Society on the lines of the Foremen's Mutual Benefit Society, was set up.

Allan Smith now turned his attention to the structure of the Federation itself. Some changes had been made in 1916, when Smith became full-time chairman of the Board, and again in 1918, when the National Employers' Federation was absorbed. Smith worked out a new constitution, adopted in 1924, which changed the name of the organisation to the Engineering and Allied Employers' National Federation. It introduced as the supreme body a general council, replacing the former executive board, while executive action was entrusted to a management board, replacing the former management committee. The standing committees, in addition to the Board, were the conference committee, the finance committee and the administration committee. The president was chairman of the council and all office bearers had to be federated employers except the chairman of the Board, an office which Smith retained.

An important innovation was the establishment of ten regional committees, consisting of two representatives from each association and Board members in the area, taking the place of joint standing committees introduced during the war. They provided a medium for discussion of common problems between neighbouring associations. It was also hoped they would keep a watchful eye on the activities of local associations which were apt to make embarrasing agreements without submitting them to the Federation.

Simultaneously with these changes, the Subsidy Fund was revised and renamed the Indemnity Fund. Complaints were common that the obligation to pay contributions to the fund deterred firms from joining the Federation, particularly in times of bad trade, as the fund was made up of payments by new members. To help firms finding this difficult, it was agreed that the payments should be spread over five years instead of three but they continued in ensuing years to be regarded as a reason for declining membership.

Membership fell steadily from 1922 onwards, partly because of the difficulty of adapting the organisation to the numerous firms on the fringe of the engineering industry who had come in with the National Employers' Federation. Most were in the Birmingham area where two associations of about equal size had been set up – the Birmingham Association and the Allied Trades Employers' Association, linked together by a joint Birmingham Board.

Allied trades employers were reluctant to be involved in engineering disputes but vainly asked the Federation for freedom to decide what action they should take in the event of general lock-outs. Their agitation was resumed after the Federation came within an ace of a national lock-out in 1926. But a good many of the firms must have dropped out of the Federation during the twenties. Early in 1926, thirty-nine firms were lapsed, thirty-three of them in the Birmingham area, for failing to sign the new Indemnity Fund declaration form. Occasional suggestions that the fund should be optional were always firmly resisted.

The danger of getting involved in a lock-out over a dispute in which they were not involved was a real one, for the Federation never hesitated to use the threat. They did so several times in 1924, when trade had improved a little. The associations agreed to support the Scottish firm of Barclay Curle in a dispute with the boilermakers over a premium bonus question. About the same time they threatened a national lock-out against the Association of Engineering and Shipbuilding Draughtsmen who after going through the Procedure had struck for higher wages at three Kilmarnock firms. The plan was for all Scottish firms to lock out their draughtsmen first and if that was ineffective for members in other parts of Britain to join in a fortnight later. The Scottish associations at first demurred but eventually were persuaded, but in September the men returned to work. Also in 1924 the Federation got as far as preparing lock-out notices against members of the National Union of Vehicle Builders who had struck for higher wages at the Brush Electrical Engineering Company at Loughborough.

The most dramatic case, however, arose out of an unofficial strike in January 1926, by members of the AEU, patternmakers' union and General and Municipal Workers at the London firm of R. Hoe and Company, printing machine manufacturers. It was ostensibly about the employment of non-union labour, which had been an increasing cause of trouble since the 1922 slump, probably because large numbers of workers were dropping out of their unions. Membership of the AEU fell from 460,000 in 1920 to 235,000 in 1926. The Federation decided in 1924, and re-affirmed at the end of 1925, that members should maintain the principle of the open shop wherever possible. When the union leaders failed to get their men at Hoe back to work, and members of four other unions joined the strike, the Federation posted notices calling a national lock-out on 13 March but postponed the date to 18 March on hearing that the AEU had called a meeting of their national committee.

There followed a cliff-hanging situation which kept the country on tenterhooks for more than twenty-four hours. On the afternoon of 17 March representatives of the seven unions went to see Allan Smith and told him they had issued definite instructions to their members to resume work on 19 March and believed they would do so, or at latest on 22 March. To which Smith replied that notices could not be withdrawn on the mere hope of a resumption.

The strikers met again the next morning and at 2 p.m., with three hours to go before the industry was to be brought to a standstill, the executives again went to see Smith. The strikers had left the decision to their strike committee, the union leaders told him, and the strike committee were believed to have decided in favour of a return to work – but had agreed not to tell their executives until after the lock-out notices had expired. So they all waited, and it was not until after 5 p.m. that they got definite news the men would go back on 22 March. The employers stretched a point and called off the lock-out.

This was the last occasion on which the Federation has come near to imposing a national lock-out which could stop the whole industry. Fourteen firms, six in London, were reported to have failed to post notices and the Federation decided to leave it to associations to decide what action to take. The London Association was bitterly critical of this. They expelled their members – except one who resigned – and told the Federation that the failure to impose a uniform policy had strained the loyalty of members who had faithfully carried out their instructions.

The Federation believed that the complaint about non-unionists was a pretext and that what the Hoe strikers really wanted was a wage increase. There were at the time a number of local claims, arising mainly from dissatisfaction with national pay negotiations which had been going on since 1924. A little improvement in trade had coincided then with assumption of office by the first Labour government and the unions submitted a claim for a 20s. a week increase.

Allan Smith was deeply disturbed by the arrival of the Labour government and toured the country warning employers of the dangers ahead. He spoke of the promises of individual members of the Government to restore the recent wage cuts and by degrees to abolish private enterprise, of extremist forces operating behind Labour which might assume control and of successes of communists in the trade unions. The employers were the people to cope with this canker, he said, and the best way to do this was to introduce into the factories 'that element of satisfaction which would bring home to our workpeople the knowledge that there was now, as there used to be, a sympathetic management looking after their interests as far as possible.' At the same time he emphasised the importance of reducing costs and urged employers to stand together and fight for the interests of the industry and the country.

Smith's next step was to invite the unions to a meeting to discuss the position of the engineering industry. He gave the union leaders the results of surveys which the Federation had conducted into the financial position of the industry including the value of their orders, the turnover and the costs of production. The only thing to be done, he told them, was for the employers and the workpeople through their unions to sit down and find a way out of their difficulties by co-operation. He reminded them of the undertakings they gave in the 47-hour agreement and of discussions and joint investigations which had followed.

Brownlie was much impressed. 'I look upon this conference as marking an epoch in relations between the employers' federation and the workmen's unions,' he declared. On the other hand Will Thorne, a general workers' leader, described the meeting as 'the most farcical he had ever attended in his life' and at one point accused Allan Smith and Brownlie of collusion, but later withdrew this. The unions' £1 a week claim had been tabled at this time and both sides hired accountants to investigate the wage issue. In July the Board agreed, with only Sir Harris Spencer dissenting, that failing settlement the claim should go to the Industrial Court but the General Council rejected this and by 62 votes to 27 decided to turn the claim down.

A complex series of negotiations followed, with the Federation constantly stressing the problem of foreign competition. At one stage in 1925 the employers offered a 2s. a week increase if the unions would agree to a 50-hour week and other changes in conditions. When this was rejected, Smith and Brownlie first wrote to the Prime Minister and then went to see the Minister of Labour together to try to get the Government to induce other countries to observe the Washington international convention on the 48-hour week. (The Minister said he was in complete sympathy.) In January 1926, the unions said the national negotiations had gone on long enough and brought them to an end. This was the time of the Hoe dispute. Over forty-six local claims for £1 a week were on their way to Central Conference. The General Council decided to invite the unions to join in a small joint committee to explore future policy on wage fluctuations. But then the General Strike intervened. Finally, in July 1927, the unions accepted an offer of a 2s. a week increase for time-workers only.

The unions put in a new claim for an 8s. increase in 1928 which dragged on until 1930 when Smith, still clinging to his efforts to get an agreed assessment of the situation, suggested a joint fact-finding commission should visit the Continent. The unions declined and asked the Prime Minister, Ramsay MacDonald, (Labour was in office again), to order an inquiry into the industry. Smith went to see MacDonald and explained the difficulties of conducting an inquiry into such a complex industry. He suggested the transport industry, because of its basic character, was a much more suitable candidate for the next inquiry. The inquiry was refused but in any case the economic crisis was almost upon them all.

For ten years Allan Smith had tried, with determination and persistence, to find some agreed way of relating wage movements to the economic state of the industry. Brownlie had on occasion gone part of the way with him. But before 1930 both men must have realised that the quest was hopeless. In 1926 the Board set up a committee of their own to report on future fluctuations in wages. The committee tried to work out a scheme based on production cost returns. But in the last of several reports, in 1928, they confessed 'the committee has been unable to devise a formula capable of overcoming the tendency of the employers and of the trade unions to depend upon expediency'.

And in the same year, when Smith rejected the 8s. claim, Brownlie said: 'Notwithstanding the justice or efficacy of our case, notwithstanding the eloquence with which we state our case, or the cogency of our argument, a decision does not rest on the power of speech of those who address you on the question of an increase in wages. It is a matter of power.'

The General Strike of 1926, when the TUC stopped much of British industry for nine days in support of miners' resistance to wage cuts, resulted in forty-four engineering unions calling out their members. The Federation took it calmly, merely writing to the unions to point out that their action was a flagrant breach of agreement and procedure. 'There is now but one duty for all concerned,' they added, 'and that is by co-operation and reduction in costs to do what they can not only to overcome the effects of the recent dislocation and the resultant serious loss but also to revive our industry, at present so much depressed.'

The immediate public reaction was that something should be done to prevent it ever happening again, either by legislation or by a new initiative to bring about peace in industry. The Federation were anxious lest the Government should introduce punitive legislation.

> The Board felt there was a grave risk of the Government dealing with the matter from a political standpoint and without sufficient regard for the interests of industry [the minutes recorded]. They considered it of vital importance to the Federation, having regard to their agreements with the trade unions, and the large number of trade unions with whom they deal, and with whom they hope to work harmoniously in the future, that nothing should be done to interfere with the legitimate functions of the unions.

They were also conscious that any restrictions or obligations on trade unions would probably apply also to employers' organisations.

The Federation wrote to the Prime Minister urging that no decision on amending the law should be taken until the whole subject had been reported on by a Royal Commission. They also prepared a memorandum on the changes which they thought were required in the law. This advocated that unions should be liable for actions in tort and that inducing breach of contract should be actionable whether or not done in a trade dispute.

Suggestions for bringing peace to industry came from all sides. Sir Archibald Ross, the president, drew the Board's attention to a proposal that there should be a trial period of five years during which all disagreements between employers' organisations and unions should be referred to binding arbitration. But most of the Board members did not think this would achieve its purpose.

After the Trade Disputes and Trade Union Act had been passed, the Prime Minister, Stanley Baldwin, made a speech hinting at the possibility of bringing about peace in industry and this was taken up at the Trades Union Congress the following week by George Hicks, the president, who suggested a 'practical' conference between the TUC and the central employers' organisations. Leaders of the Employers' Confederation, including Allan Smith and Archibald Ross, responded with a statement that the most effective means of developing industrial goodwill was in the organisations and workshop contacts of individual industries.

Failing official encouragement from the employers' organisations, a group of industrialists, led by Sir Alfred Mond, later Lord Melchett, head of Imperial Chemical Industries, invited the TUC to a general conference. Before they met the Federation published a booklet, *Thirty Years of Industrial Conciliation*, which expressed in stronger terms the view put by the Confederation. There appeared to be a fixed impression, it said, that something had to be done to assist or even compel employers and employed to arrive at industrial peace. The whole idea seemed to be permeated by political rather than industrial considerations. If a general scheme could be arrived at, industry would serve as the plaything of politics and party politicians. Industrial prosperity under such an influence or control would become an absolute impossibility. Some of the phrases seem to echo Allan Smith's criticism of the Government after the National Industrial Conference nearly a decade earlier. Brownlie took a similar line. 'We, in an unassuming manner,' he said, 'have done more for a generation to maintain industrial peace in the industry than many of those who are advertising themselves in the public press and pulpits and platforms.'

Though the Federation was hostile, a number of well-known

engineering employers were in the Mond group, including heads of big companies in the expanding motor manufacturing and electrical sectors of the industry. The Mond–Turner talks (Ben Turner succeeded Hicks as TUC president) resulted in an interim report in July 1928, proposing the setting up of a National Industrial Council, equally representative of the Employers' Confederation and the FBI on one side and the TUC on the other, which would meet quarterly and could establish a joint conciliation board when asked. The Confederation asked for the views of their members and received from the Federation a damning reply. It referred to the close alliance of the TUC with the Labour Party, to its calling of the General Strike and to its aim to control industry. It noted that the most recent Trades Union Congress had set up a committee on the nationalisation of the engineering industry. So long as the TUC was the mouthpiece of the Labour Party, it said, it was impossible for it to meet the employers on the same basis. The document continued:

> The issue is whether or not a national movement of a destructive political character, instigated by the Labour Party, is to be helped on by capital either officially or unofficially. The principle underlying the discussions is a wrong one. If admitted it would result in industrial problems being handed over to politicians and sociologists. It would provide a public platform from which to preach hostility between employers and employed. It would not solve problems, it would make them more difficult of industrial solution because of the prominence it gave them. All such proceedings simply stand in the way of true co-operation between employers and employed who alone appreciate their industrial difficulties.

There followed a warning: 'The Federation cannot approve the interim report nor can they undertake to accept any obligations which further discussions may seek to place upon them.'

Why was Allan Smith so strongly opposed to the idea of a National Industrial Council now, when he had supported it at the National Industrial Conference? The Federation memorandum pointed to four differences in the position in 1919 – the National Industrial Conference was attended by representatives of the trade unions themselves, the national atmosphere then was so dissimilar as to make comparisons of little value, the General

Strike had not taken place, and the TUC had not allied itself so completely and effectively to the Labour Party.

The Board was unanimously against the proposed conciliation machinery. Smith toured the regions expounding their policy and reported that with the exception of two firms in London and two letters which had been received afterwards from the Birmingham association, there had been no opposition to the Board's attitude.

Opinion in the Employers' Confederation was divided and Smith fought with determination inside it to prevent acceptance of the interim report. At one point in February 1929, he warned the Confederation, with the backing of C. Laws, of the Shipping Federation, that it might disintegrate if it insisted on responding to the proposals. In the end the Confederation and the FBI rejected the report but took part in joint talks with the TUC and one or two joint memoranda were produced. But when the TUC wanted to meet the Confederation on the rationalisation of industry, the Federation produced yet another document protesting that discussion of labour displacement due to rationalisation or new techniques would constitute an invasion of management prerogative. They could not accept union claims that changes should only take place with union consent.

The talks petered out in 1931. Allan Smith (and the Federation) did as much as anybody to smother them.

By now the nation and the world were plunging into a major economic crisis following the Wall Street crash of October 1929. The number of unemployed in engineering, including vehicle building and repair, rose from 84,000 in 1929, the lowest figure for many years, to 280,000 in 1931. 'British engineering is in a very grave position,' said the Federation in a booklet, *Realities and Problems*. The booklet repeated previous criticisms of the high wages paid in sheltered industries, not affected by foreign competition, and attacked the burdens of taxation and social benefits.

For the last two decades, sentiment and sentimentalism rather than reason have been the mainspring of domestic policy. The industrial ignorance of political parties in this country, and the readiness with which they have from political motives added to the burden of industry, is illustrated by the fact that during the last 40 years social burdens have increased by about 1500 per cent . . . the conception of the State as a fairy godmother is a fundamental fallacy. The prosperity of people depends on their own exertions. . . . Industry as the patient beast of burden is on the verge of collapse.

The Federation appointed a crisis committee and set themselves to reduce costs, concentrating on working conditions – overtime and shift payments and the piece-work standard – 'heritages from the immediate post-war years'. Though warned that the alternative was to reduce wages, and once more weakened by loss of membership and the burden of unemployment benefit, the unions at first refused to accept the proposed cuts. But when the employers gave notice that they would impose them unilaterally on 6 July 1931, negotiations were resumed and the reductions were introduced on the date mentioned without provoking trouble. Overtime rates were cut from time and a half to time and a quarter for the first three hours, nightshift rates from time and a third to time and a sixth, and the basis for piece-work prices from $33\frac{1}{3}$ per cent above time rates to 25 per cent.

Implementation of the new working conditions disclosed that many members had got lax in observing agreements. 'In several districts,' reported the Board, 'practices or customs agreed or recognised have been allowed to remain in operation notwithstanding the fact that they have since become the subject of national agreements. In other cases objectionable practices have been allowed to grow up unknown to local associations.' These discoveries increased the anxieties which the office bearers were feeling at this time about the state of the Federation. The number of member firms had declined from its 1922 peak of 2690 to fewer than 2000, and the number of workers they employed, nearly 700,000 in 1920, was down to 378,500. These figures could partly be accounted for by the fact that many firms had been rationalised, merged or put out of business by the slump, while the remainder were working at far below their capacity.

But there were other factors. Employers no longer felt the need of mutual support against the weakened unions. They got lax in making their statistical returns to Broadway House. It was hard to get enough volunteers for Central Conference. Federation recommendations and policy statements, according to Allan Smith, seldom got beyond the association secretaries, often part-time and inefficient. Employers grudged having to pay contributions to the Federation at a time when they were cutting their costs to the bone to remain in business. A claim on the Indemnity Fund in September 1930, was the first for four years, but new firms still had to make their contributions and there were frequent complaints that this was preventing recruits from coming in.

The book value of the Indemnity Fund in 1932 stood at £644,000. Since it began, £807,000 had been paid in, while £124,000 had gone in indemnities and £132,000 in contributions to the Federation's administrative expenses. It was decided to make use of this fund, as well as the general funds, to make grants to relieve the financial pressure on associations, some of which had had to restrict their operations and cut their expenses and salaries, and to reduce the burden on new members joining in 1932 and 1933 by relieving them of half their contributions for the two years and extending the period allowed for the payment of instalments to the Indemnity Fund from five to ten years. Dr Alexander Campbell, who succeeded Sir Archibald Ross as president in 1930, toured the associations with Allan Smith and both were struck by the inefficiency of many of them, not all of it due to the crisis.

Dr Campbell, the head of a small Leeds firm, the Hunslet Engineering Company, brooded over what he had seen and compared it with the great days of 1897. On 21 September 1933, he sent a letter to Allan Smith which brought the accumulating uneasiness to a head and followed it up with a more detailed memorandum on the need to 'revitalise' the Federation. The old generation of employers, who were usually the actual heads of their businesses, was passing away, he said. Management had become in great measure the handmaiden of finance – not its master and not its equal. With the creation of ever larger industrial units, with the divorce between financial ownership and management, the controlling heads of the great concerns were no longer associated with the management of the Federation. The old generation was gone, the war generation was largely lost and the young men coming forward had no interest in the Federation and took its work for granted. Yet the Federation's power of discipline over employers and employed had never been so necessary.

There followed a passage which to some members of the Board seemed to be directed against Allan Smith himself:

> The effect of the changes is to throw ever greater onus and responsibility upon the permanent officials. A successor to the Chairman would find himself saddled with a burden of responsibility not to be borne. . . The whole process I have described has brought us within measurable distance of professionalising our institution. I should have thought the example of the trade unions would be quite sufficient to ward off any such lamentable occurrence. The founders of the Federation drafted a constitution that was democratic in its essence and expression, knowing full well that democratic institutions are only possible in intelligent bodies. If through supineness in business and affairs, the employers neglect the first essential of orderly existence, the training of themselves for defence, they are but repeating the mistake of Carthage, who founded her transient glory upon professional soldiery alone.

The Board had a special meeting at which Campbell's initiative was given a mixed reception. His positive proposals, vigorously supported by Allan Smith, had been mainly directed towards improving the efficiency of the associations, but his remarks about the lack of participation by the leaders of industry was taken by some as a criticism of the Board itself. Commander (later Sir Charles) Craven, of Vickers-Armstrong, a growingly influential Board member, said he could not see the reason for the sudden stir-up. However, a committee was set up which recommended that the associations should be re-grouped into larger units, all with full-time secretaries, that the limitation on the number of members who could be co-opted to the Board should be removed and that more information should be circulated to members by the Federation. But it was to be more than a generation before most of the associations consented to sacrifice their little sovereignties by merging into larger units.

The nub of Dr Campbell's letter was what he said about the danger of professionalising the Federation. If it was unwise to rely on a professional army, was it also unwise to have a professional commanding officer? At the special Board meeting, George Bailey, of Manchester, said the letter gave him the impression that they might have to revert to the old position where an employer was the Board chairman. 'That was never discussed,' interposed Allan Smith. And Dr Campbell repudiated suggestions that he had any individual in mind when he wrote the letter.

Whatever he intended, there is little doubt that Smith's domineering behaviour and conduct of affairs was causing increasing resentment. The opportunity to make a change was not long delayed. In the latter part of 1932 and 1933 Smith suffered several minor strokes. The other office-bearers got together and agreed that he should be persuaded to resign for the sake of his health. Sir John Siddeley, who followed Dr Campbell as president, had the job of putting it to him and Smith, now 64, reluctantly agreed. So in October 1934 Smith's long leadership of the Federation came to an end. 'He devoted his life-time with an extraordinary enthusiasm solely to one object – the building up of the Federation – and in the attainment of that object he has left a permanent mark on the industrial history of this country,' Dr Campbell said, a judgement that can hardly be gainsaid.

Smith wrote to Siddeley: 'My experience and knowledge may still be of advantage to the Federation and accordingly I would ask you to consider whether a re-arrangement can be made whereby I shall be relieved of the responsibility of administration of the Federation and my experience and knowledge still utilised.'

The office-bearers considered this among themselves. On their behalf, Siddeley recommended to the Board that Smith should be appointed 'Adviser to the President'. Members of the Board cautiously inquired what that involved. Siddeley explained that Smith would be available for consultation with the president for the time being 'if and when the president desired'. This did not entail attendance at Broadway House unless 'at the specific request of the President'. In other words, as adviser, Sir Allan's approach would be 'solely through the president'.

The Board were satisfied with that. Never afterwards was the chief executive officer of the Federation allowed to hold the office of chairman of the Board.

CHAPTER 7

New Men and a New War 1935-1947

Trade on the Mend – Apprentices Revolt – Holidays
with Pay – In the Shadow of Invasion – Problems of
the Blitz – White Collars on the Move

When Allan Smith departed, the Federation established a new
office, that of Director, and appointed Alexander Ramsay, a
one-time works manager in the engineering industry who had
been full-time chairman of the Birmingham association board
since 1921. A possible choice would have been General Baylay,
who had been Smith's principal assistant since just after the war,
but Baylay had been closely involved in Smith's policies and was
also a somewhat dominating though much less austere character.
Birmingham gave him the job of association chairman vacated by
Ramsay.

The Federation office-bearers were looking for, and found,
quite a different type of man. Thick-set, with black bushy eyebrows, Ramsay was formal but conciliatory in manner, ready to
listen to other people's points of view. His staff found him 'more
human' than Smith. He could work round the clock when necessary but could also ease off when things were slack. He liked a
round of golf at Guildford or a fishing holiday by Loch Leven.
He had been elected to Parliament for West Bromwich in 1931
and prided himself on his powers as an orator, which were considerable. He combined an ability to marshall clearly an economic
or industrial argument with a somewhat vague idealism (which
would hardly have commended itself to his predecessor), qualities
which he had displayed in several books. A Freemason and
Rotarian, he often made speeches, many of which he preserved,
at their functions and on Burns nights and at association dinners.

It was a great disappointment to him that the Board made it
a condition of his appointment that he should give up his par-

liamentary career, and he often paid nostalgic visits to the House
to look in on debates and meet his Ministerial friends.

Altogether his approach to life was less cold and hard than that
of Smith. 'The modern employer,' he said once, 'knows that a
contented worker is a good worker and that he must pay for this
contentment.' His attitude to the Mond–Turner talks was quite
different. In an address to the Sparkbrook Brotherhood Movement he described the first meeting between the Mond group and
the TUC as 'the most remarkable, the most significant the most
pregnant with good that has ever been held in the industrial
history of this country'. But he shared with Smith the belief that
industry should play a greater part in shaping national policy.
'Industry has been too long inarticulate,' he told the annual
dinner of the Birmingham association in 1930.

> We have had organisation, it is true, commercial and other,
> but so far it has been singularly ineffective as a factor in for-
> mulating national policy. We have all been so busy trying to
> preserve our own little prerogatives, and jealous of the other
> fellow's, that we have now reached a point when leadership is
> passing out of our hands and is being assumed by newspaper
> proprietors and an engine-driver turned politician. (No doubt
> J. H. Thomas.)

As a student of economic questions – he produced a book on *The
Safeguarding of Industry* in 1930 – he commanded attention at a
time when the Federation became unavoidably involved in discussions on trade policy in spite of its principle of leaving such
matters to others.

Ramsay contributed to a striking change in the industrial
atmosphere towards which many other factors were tending.
Unemployment began to fall in 1933. In that year Hitler came to
power in Germany and from then onwards, particularly after the
1935 election, steadily growing rearmament put new life into the
engineering industry. In 1939 unemployment in general engineering was still 6.6 per cent and in motor and aircraft manufacture
and electrical engineering 4.4 per cent, high by recent standards,
but the steady improvement was quite a different thing from the
almost unvarying gloom of the twenties. Trade union membership and confidence climbed again. The AEU had opened their
ranks to the semi-skilled in 1926 and from the middle thirties

recruited them in large numbers. The Federation was also expanding, the membership rising from a few more than 1800 to more than 2000 in 1939 and the number they employed from less than 400,000 to 860,000. From the wage reductions of 1922 to the cuts in working conditions in 1931, engineering workers got one increase of 2s. a week and no other important concession, though of course prices were falling all the time. (At its lowest point in the middle of 1933, the cost of living index was little more than half the peak figure at the end of 1920.) In the five years from 1934, the engineering workers got four wage increases and their first paid holidays. Relations between the employers and unions, which reached a peak of bitterness during the economic crisis, steadily improved.

This was partly due to a new spirit in the Central Conference at York, which more than anything else used to influence relations between employers and union leaders. From 1926 to 1935 the chairman of the Federation conference committee was an uncommunicative and antisocial Scot named William S. Watson, from a small company in Troon, who dressed in rough tweeds and big boots and treated the union representatives, it was suggested, as workmen with caps in their hands asking for a handout. He enjoyed technical arguments but seldom if ever conceded that the unions could be right. Some of the smaller societies decided that going to York was a waste of time and gave up using the final stages of the Procedure. From 1920 to 1925 the number of Central Conference hearings averaged 164 a year. After that they got steadily fewer until from 1929 to 1934 they average 52.

But in 1935, Watson was succeeded by Colonel (later General) Appleyard, an ex-regular from a firm in Birtley, Co. Durham, who had a pleasant, friendly manner, treated the union officials as human beings and when they had a good case acknowledged it. From 1936 until the Second World War, when he returned to the army, more than twice as many cases went to Central Conference as in the latter part of Watson's time. Even staff references, of which there had been only thirteen altogether up to 1937, began to get commoner.

The period after 1932 was the most peaceful in British industrial history up to that time. Days lost through stoppages averaged only 1,700,000 a year from 1933 to 1939. In engineer-

ing the only serious strikes were those of apprentices in 1937.
The threat of a national lock-out was never used.

Relations improved not only with the unions. One of the first
remits Ramsay got from the Board was to bring about closer and
more cordial relations with the Employers' Confederation. After
the Confederation had escaped from the tutelage of the Federation there had been many periods of strain between the two
bodies. General Baylay, who was a regular delegate to the ILO
at Geneva, engaged in a running war with John Forbes-Watson,
the Confederation director. Ramsay at once accepted appointment to the Confederation's general purposes committee as an
indication of the Federation's desire for closer co-operation.

One of the most recent causes of strain was among the issues
which Ramsay found waiting for him when he took over at
Broadway House, that of the 40-hour week. The TUC had
decided in 1931 that the time had come for a maximum week of
40 hours without loss of pay, mainly as a means of sharing work
among the unemployed, and the engineering unions mounted a
campaign as a preliminary to an approach to the employers. It
was argued that an important factor in the growth of unemployment was the speed of mechanisation which increased production
while demand was decreasing because men were being displaced.
The campaign would not have worried Allan Smith if the
question had not been taken up by the ILO, which early in 1933
passed a resolution saying that a reduction of hours would contribute to the reduction of unemployment and the maintenance
of working class standards of living. The Government invited the
Employers' Confederation and the TUC to discuss the resolution.
Smith declined to attend the meeting with the confederation and
afterwards told the confederation that the Federation would
dissociate itself from any discussions on the subject with the TUC.
He followed this up with another booklet, *Unemployment: Its
Realities and Problems*, which pointed out that work was already
being shared to the extent that more than a third of the workers
in the industry were on short time. To share employment while
refusing to share wages would increase costs which would have
the effect of diminishing trade and therefore employment.

When Ramsay took over, a new Minister of Labour, Oliver
Stanley, was initiating a new series of meetings, first with the
Confederation and then with individual industries. Ramsay

thought there was a danger that smaller industries might make concessions prejudicial to the bigger ones and tried to get the Confederation to come to a general conclusion, which would make it unnecessary for member organisations to deal with the issue individually. He told the Board there would probably be very serious pressure brought to bear on the Federation and other employers' organisations as the success of any political party depended upon their ability to deal with the unemployment problem. An election was coming soon and the Labour Party were expected to make unemployment a main issue. Once the election was over, the 40-hour week ceased to be a live question.

The first general wage claim after the crisis, for an increase of 2d. an hour and the restoration of the pre-1931 working conditions, came in December 1934, and resulted in agreement on a rise of 2s. a week. Further increases of 3s. came in 1936 and 1937 and 2s. in 1939. The last, which followed a minor recession, was the only one which caused difficulty. The unions immediately after the settlement demanded a further 10s. Every claim in this period and during the war was accompanied by a demand for the restoration of the pre-1931 working conditions. This produced minor concessions in 1937 but nothing more. Women, increasing in numbers in the industry but little organised, did not do so well as the men. Instead of four increases amounting to 10s. a week they got two of 1s. each – all they had had since immediately after the First World War.

While the national wage negotiations went fairly smoothly, the Federation from 1935 onwards was involved in prolonged and complex discussions on how to deal with district wage claims and with claims limited to one section of the industry. The pre-war system of district bargaining had left behind many anomalies. To take one example, firms in low-paid areas in the West of England were finding they could not get skilled workers. The rate for fitters in Yeovil was 3s. less than the rate in Bristol – but the rate for labourers in Yeovil was 1s. higher than the rate in Bristol. That kind of situation was not uncommon and made it hard to make adjustments without starting a general and costly levelling up.

When it was agreed after the war that general rises and falls in wages should be negotiated nationally it was accepted that local claims could go through the Procedure but if they were general claims for the district they were always rejected. Within a few months of the 1935 national settlement, however, four district claims were referred to Central Conference. It was clear that the unions were aiming at a general levelling up. The matter was given some urgency when the unions in Derby had a strike ballot on a claim to bring their rates up to those of towns of similar size and importance, by which they meant Coventry. But their rates could not be brought up to the level of Coventry without starting claims in Birmingham and other Midland towns whose rates were below those of Coventry. Eventually they were conceded 1s. to bring them to the Birmingham level, though the Derby rate for moulders was already higher than that in Birmingham.

The Federation meanwhile discussed the whole question with the unions. They pointed out that concessions made on such claims could vitiate the national negotiations and would be better dealt with by a negotiating rather than a conciliating body like Central Conference. So they suggested such questions should come before a national committee consisting of the Federation negotiators and representatives of the unions. This was accepted and in October 1937, a batch of five local claims were dealt with at the first hearing of the new body. It did not, however, become a permanent institution.

The principal sectional claims were in aircraft manufacture. Several claims for increased rates for workers in aircraft firms went through the Procedure about the same time that the local claims began to come in. The AEU argued that the aircraft industry was not part of engineering and should have separate wages and conditions. Sixteen unions other than the AEU formed a National Council of Aircraft Workers. There was also strong pressure from below. An Aircraft Shop Stewards' National Council was formed and in 1936 got a ballot majority for a strike but did not put it into effect. Ramsay wrote to Sir Thomas Inskip, Minister for the Co-ordination of Defence, regarding the circulation of subversive literature, particularly in aircraft factories. The policy of the Federation was that 'the aircraft section, like other sections, is part of the engineering industry and cannot be isolated therefrom for the purpose of wages and conditions' and they stuck to it.

The outstanding concession to the workers in this period was one week's paid holiday, included in the 1937 agreement. The unions had been intermittently pressing for this for a dozen years. A government committee was examining the question and in 1936 Ramsay reported that an increasing number of federated firms, including the Nuffield motor empire, were conceding it. The concession was hailed by the unions as a breach in the Federation principle of 'paying only for work done'. It spread quickly to other industries.

The year 1937 was also that of the apprentice rebellion. Apprentices had been important in many disputes in the nineteenth century, but this arose out of union attempts to limit their numbers, not out of their wages and conditions. The employers had always insisted that they had a special responsibility for apprentices (often a legal responsibility) with which they would brook no interference. If apprentices joined in a strike they might be penalised. The first mention in the Federation records of apprentice action on their own behalf was in 1912, when they struck in a number of districts for increases to compensate for the deduction from their wages of their contributions under the National Insurance Act. The Federation refused the increases but considered that the Act, in so far as it covered apprentices, was an injustice both to them and to their employers. During the First World War the Federation repeatedly refused requests to negotiate on apprentice pay, and told associations not to do so, though they did consent to talk about apprentices making up time lost on military service.

They maintained their attitude after the war, though at least from 1921 onwards associations were issuing their own scales of maximum rates for each apprenticeship year. In the middle thirties the shortage of skilled workers made an increase in the number of apprentices urgent, but many boys preferred the much higher earnings they could get on semi-skilled piece-work. The Federation pressed members to train more, and advised associations to revise their scales, but still, again and again, refused to talk to the unions about them, though the unions warned them that the boys were getting restless. At the end of 1936 they ruled out discussions even on selection and training – 'essentially matters within the province of management alone'.

In March 1937, the apprentices struck at one Clyde factory and by the middle of April 13,000 had walked out of the Clyde engineering works and shipyards. The local unions asked for a conference and formalised the boys' demands into a three-point 'charter' – uniform rates for all apprentices, recognition of the right of unions to represent them, and regulation of the numbers employed. When the conference was refused, the unions called a one-day strike of adult workers and imposed a ban on overtime. By now apprentices at Edinburgh and on the North-east coast were joining in. Employers in Glasgow and some other areas raised their scales and under pressure from the national union leaders the apprentices returned to work on 5 May.

But later in the year apprentices in Manchester and other Lancashire towns struck for the 3s. increase granted to adults, and for negotiating rights, and the trouble spread to other parts of England. Glasgow joined Manchester in sponsoring a meeting of representatives from all districts at which it was agreed that if negotiating rights had not been granted by 14 October, there would be a national strike on that day. But a national conference was held and provisional agreement reached and on 22 December 1937, the first Apprentice Procedure Agreement was signed. Apprentices under indentures were not covered but the Federation undertook to recommend that such apprentices should be placed in a not less favourable position than the others.

The change from peace to war in September 1939, produced nothing like the sudden transformation in industrial relations that had occurred in 1914. On the one hand, preparations for it had been slowly gathering pace since 1935, with a crisis in 1938, and on the other the war itself began with seven months of limited activity in western Europe. Instead of a violent mobilisation of forces, there was steady progression until May 1940. All the familiar labour problems for which solutions had to be hurriedly improvised in the First World War – enticement, dilution, the employment of women, reservation of essential workers – were being dealt with, albeit in a somewhat leisurely manner, before 1939.

Complaints about the enticement of skilled men began as early as 1934, although there were still more than 140,000 engineering workers unemployed, and became increasingly frequent. The Federation had urged firms to maintain apprentice training during the slump but evidently with inadequate response. The shortage of toolmakers in Coventry was already acute because their earnings were less than those of piece-workers on production. Competition for craftsmen for aircraft manufacture, on which the labour force was being doubled, soon became intense. By 1937, government departments were saying that large scale dilution was essential, but neither the Federation nor the unions were convinced. The following year Sir Charles Craven and Ramsay, now Sir Alexander, were summoned to Whitehall to be told that the Government were dissatisfied with the rate of rearmament. The Prime Minister, Neville Chamberlain, and other Ministers had numerous meetings with the two sides of industry. But they still left it to the parties to work out the necessary steps to speed things up. In August 1939, a week before war broke out, the Federation signed a relaxation agreement with the AEU which provided that, where it could be shown skilled men were not available and production was being prejudiced, an alternative class of worker could be employed.

When war was declared, immediate massive air raids were expected, with heavy civilian casualties, and a huge operation was mounted to evacuate children from danger areas. The Federation moved about half their staff to temporary premises in Guildford, including the statistical, legal and financial departments. But when nothing much happened, life soon settled down again. The Guildford office was closed early in December and the staff returned to Broadway House, where they remained for the rest of the war. Progress in dealing with manpower problems resumed its slow pace. An arrangement was made with the general unions for the replacement of men by women where it was agreed there were no suitable males in the district. The 10s. wage claim was settled with an increase of 5s. in February 1940. Complaints of enticement increased.

But the life of the nation was given a sudden new urgency by the German victories of April and May 1940, first against Denmark and Norway, then Belgium, Holland and France. Britain was left fighting for existence. Churchill replaced Chamberlain as Prime Minister and brought in Ernest Bevin, leader of the Transport and General Workers' Union, as Minister of Labour. On 22 May the Emergency Powers (Defence) Act was passed requiring all persons to place themselves and their property at the disposal of the State. The Minister of Labour was given power to use all labour for any services required, to proscribe pay and conditions and to move employees from one works or district to another. To prevent competition for labour, all workers were to be engaged through employment exchanges and would not be allowed to leave their employment without authority. The National Arbitration Order prohibited strikes and lock-outs unless disputes had first been reported to the Minister, who could refer them to a National Arbitration Tribunal for a binding award.

The Federation accepted it all as inevitable and promised Bevin their whole-hearted co-operation. They and the unions soon found themselves harried along at unaccustomed speed but showed no signs of resentment. First Bevin wrote to them urging that outstanding problems about the increased employment of women should be settled at once. So a new agreement for the extended employment of women was signed without delay. Next came the toolrooms, where men were dissatisfied and hard to find because they were earning less than production workers. Bevin wrote personally to Ramsay and Fred Smith, the AEU general secretary. 'I regard it as essential that this problem should be dealt with immediately,' he told Ramsay. 'I should like to ask you to arrange to meet the executive of the AEU not later than Tuesday next and to endeavour to reach an immediate decision.' Three days later, on 4 June 1940, the two sides met at Broadway House and late at night reached a settlement. It provided that the minimum earnings of skilled operatives in the toolroom should be not less than the average earnings of skilled production workers, defined as fitters, turners and machinists, in the same establishment.

This was all right for most districts, but not for Coventry. In spite of remonstrances from the employers, the Government had built five big shadow factories there and when war came these factories had to find labour, which they did by paying wages far above the district level mainly through easy piece-work prices. If toolroom workers' pay in each of these factories was to be based on what they paid their production workers, those in the new factories would have much higher earnings than those of established firms. The employers' angry protests brought Ramsay to Coventry to defend the signing of the agreement. 'What would you have done?' he demanded. 'Would you have said, "To hell with the country"?'

After a series of local conferences with the AEU, it was agreed that Coventry toolroom workers' pay should be based on the average earnings of skilled production workers in the district instead of the average in the firm where they worked. This put all the firms on the same level, but within six months the result was found to be devastating. Workers of all kinds were using the return made under the toolroom agreement to force up their own pay, and earnings in the town, already high, soared far beyond those elsewhere. Several attempts to control piece-work prices met little success.

The evacuation of the defeated armies from Dunkirk was completed by 3 June, but their equipment had gone. Under the threat of invasion, the need to rearm the land forces and build up the air force was urgent. The Government called for a seven-day week and for all holidays to be cancelled. The Federation advised members to observe the agreements on enhanced wages for week-end and holiday work for the time being but contacted the unions (unsuccessfully) to try to get them temporarily revised. Summer holidays were treated as postponed, not cancelled. Within a couple of months, however, it was realised, as Ramsay told the Board, that continuous working without rest was affecting productivity and the arrangements were modified.

Air raids became more frequent. When the warning sirens sounded it was normal practice to stop work and take refuge in shelters. But often the bombers did not come and valuable production was lost. To obviate this, the Government proposed that work should continue after the sirens sounded, with aircraft spotters on factory roofs to give warning of immediate danger. The Board disliked the idea of managements and workers taking on this responsibility but eventually had to accept it. 'All engaged on vital production are front line troops,' declared the Government.

The Federation recommended that workers should be paid the appropriate time rates when production was suspended because of raids. A man who arrived at work late because of a warning should be paid from the time he clocked on. But overtime should be paid as if he had started at the normal time. A man who left work for a shelter would be paid until his ordinary stopping time but not after that.

Firms were asked to make their own invasion plans. 'If the Germans land we can't, won't and shan't retreat,' wrote the Minister of Production, Oliver Lyttelton (later Lord Chandos) in a pamphlet of instructions, a fading copy of which is preserved in the London association archives. There was no question of stabilising a line within Britain, it said. The country was too small for two vast armies to sit down in. So the instructions were: 'Keep production going everywhere up to the last possible moment' and 'If your works are about to fall into enemy hands, don't destroy them. Rather take what steps you can to prevent him destroying whatever may be difficult to replace. But, at the same time, try to put out of his reach any facilities that may be of immediate military value to him.'

When the Battle of Britain had been won and the danger of invasion receded, industry became more and more immersed in manpower problems. The Board were unhappy about the Essential Work Order early in 1941 which said that no person on essential work should be dismissed except for serious and wilful misconduct and no worker should leave his employment without the permission of a national service officer. They thought this would undermine established practices but that because of the emergency they would have to accept it. However they set up a sub-committee of office-bearers to make representations to the Government 'on the desirability of safeguarding established principles'.

The air raids brought the Second World War much closer to the associations than the first, as it did to civilians generally. In some cases it came very close indeed. The offices of the Coventry and Liverpool associations were both destroyed by German bombs. Those of the London association were hit three times and for a period the staff took refuge in Broadway House but later were able to return.

Association records show them constantly dealing with tricky problems arising out of the blitz. For instance, when one factory was put out of action, the workers were employed on repairing the premises and claimed compensation for loss of piece-work earnings. The ruling was that they were not entitled to lieu payments as they would not have been able to work anyway. But when they were taken off normal work to help on repairs they did get a lieu bonus. The Liverpool association invited serving officers to visit factories to talk to workers about the nation's dangers and helped to arrange the staggering of working hours to ease transport problems after raids. We also find them relaying Government announcements, for instance informing firms that helmets for civilians could be bought for 5s. 6d. each, that permits to buy

alarm clocks could be obtained for workers rising between midnight and 5 a.m., that there were facilities to obtain patching
material for overalls coupon-free.

The Federation also found many unfamiliar tasks. When
'music-while-you-work' was encouraged in the factories, they
got involved in arguments about copyright with the Performing
Rights Society and the Attorney General. There was a rule that
shop stewards must be over 21, but the Federation sanctioned the
appointment of a girl of 19 in one London firm because all the
girls there were under 21. They were asked whether those who
stopped work to listen to a broadcast service on a national day
of prayer in 1943 should receive pay for the period and advised
firms to adopt their previous practice in such cases.

Preparations for Britain's invasion of the Continent in 1944
brought new problems. Ramsay and Greville Maginness, the
Federation president, discussed with Bevin the position which
would arise if troop and transport movements prevented people
from getting to work and employers from obtaining materials or
removing their finished products. Bevin decided that in so far as
labour could be quickly allocated, employers would be given
permission to discharge, with seven days' notice, workers made
surplus in this way. The Board were not satisfied with this and
tried to get an undertaking from the Treasury that guaranteed
wages, paid when work was thus held up, would be recoverable.

The Federation's relations with the Government were incom-
parably better than in the First World War, partly because the
lessons had been learned and partly because of Ernest Bevin. This
powerful, ponderous trade union leader made sure that there
was one labour policy, and he understood what he was doing.
Employers did not always like it but they knew where they were.
They were listened to, and when they were over-ruled they
accepted the inevitable. There were of course occasions when
they were upset by Bevin and by other Ministers, especially Lord
Beaverbrook, who was constantly at odds with Bevin, but it was
usually over some slight to their pride rather than over the nature
of the measures promulgated.

Early in 1941, for instance, Jack Tanner, the AEU president,
launched a series of attacks on the efficiency of the engineering
employers and they were not satisfied with Bevin's attitude when
these criticisms were repeated in a House of Commons debate.

After an angry meeting of Federation office-bearers, Ramsay wrote to Bevin:

> There is a feeling that you do not regard the employers as contributing their proper and efficient share to war production and to the solution of the many questions affecting labour. . . . The employers do not resent criticism as such. When public criticism, however, actual or implied, is directed against the management side in industry in general, there must be repercussions on the minds of the workers that cannot make for industrial unity and will ultimately have some considerable effect on industrial discipline and morale.

Ramsay contended that the output figures were evidence of reasonable efficiency and said that since Bevin took office, the Federation had rendered him every service and support possible. Bevin replied that he had repeatedly acknowledged this and knew nothing to justify the inference they had drawn about his attitude towards them.

Jack Tanner's charges of inefficiency, much publicised, aroused the interest of the Government Committee on National Expenditure, who invited him to give chapter and verse. The London association wanted the Federation to appoint a public relations officer to defend employers against 'injurious misrepresentations'. There were demands for a public statement but Ramsay preferred to meet Labour Correspondents of national newspapers at an off-the-record lunch to get the facts straight. A press campaign, he argued, would give greater publicity to the allegations. One suggestion was that the Federation should consider getting representation in the House of Commons. A committee was set up to go into this and Ramsay discussed it with the Employers' Confederation. The Board were inclined to favour the idea but nothing seems to have come of it.

More than two years later, another debate in the House provoked a pained protest. Bevin, discussing strikes in a debate on manpower, said some strikes were deliberately provoked for ulterior reasons by employers. Ramsay complained that this was a reflection on employers generally and promised the Federation would investigate any case, involving one of their members, which Bevin brought to their notice.

The trouble with Lord Beaverbrook, the irrepressible little

newspaper proprietor who had been made Minister of Aircraft Production, was due to his allowing his enthusiasm to run away with him and cutting corners at other people's expense. There was a storm when he received a deputation of unofficial workers' leaders from a factory at Speke which the Ministry of Labour had refused to see.

The growth of unofficial movements is a phase common to every period of industrial expansion and strain and constitutes one of the industry's greatest difficulties [protested Ramsay]. If such movements are countenanced by Ministers, thereby side-tracking the unions, the management and the recognised procedure of negotiation, the situation in our view can rapidly deteriorate and may get out of hand.

Beaverbrook was evidently attacking Bevin in the Government for insisting on conventional methods in handling labour problems. Frederick Leggett, Chief Industrial Commissioner at the Ministry of Labour, wrote to Ramsay: 'This department in counselling reference to constitutional authorities is often thought to be avoiding action and to be the victim of old-fashioned ideas out of keeping with present needs.'

Beaverbrook annoyed the Federation again in January 1941, by sending a telegram to aircraft firms urging them to continue Sunday working months after everybody else had agreed that continuous working on seven days a week did not help production. This was the practically universal view, Ramsay told Beaverbrook. The men got stale and nervy and absenteeism was encouraged.

Compared with the First World War, there was comparatively little time lost through strikes, though the number of small ones reached record levels from 1943 to 1945. One reason was that after the German invasion of Russia in June 1941, the Communist Party supported the war effort and opposed strikes. But probably the main factor was the effective control of prices by subsidies and other measures. Between 1914 and 1918 prices went up steadily all the time and by the end of the war had about doubled. From September 1939 until the end of 1940 they went up by nearly 30 per cent but after that they were kept practically stable.

All national wage claims for engineers, after the 5s. increase in

1940, went to the National Arbitration Tribunal. The unions got impatient about the time taken to go through the negotiating process before being referred to arbitration and suggested that, as in the previous war, they should go straight to the tribunal, but the Federation denied that there was undue delay and refused.

The Federation themselves were not entirely happy about the way things were being done. A special meeting of the General Council in January 1943, expressed the view that it was not consonant with the dignity and best interests of a great industry, accustomed to settling its own affairs with its workers, that it should regularly resort to arbitration. While that was the easy way out, they said, the more employers discarded their own responsibilities the more they would hasten the advent of bureaucratic intervention in industrial affairs, nor was it desirable to encourage in the minds of workers the idea that their interests were dissociated from the employers' views. But the current claim went to arbitration as usual. The unions always hoped they would get a little more from the tribunal.

That year's arbitration award – No. 326 – was not the simple addition to the war bonus which was usual. It transferred £1 from the bonus to basic rates and raised the minimum piece-work standard from 25 per cent to $27\frac{1}{2}$ per cent. The latter went part of the way to meet the demands of the unions who were still trying to get the 1931 cuts restored. It also awarded 6s. to time-workers only. There were disputes about the interpretation of this and some strikes, including an eighteen-day stoppage by 9000 workers at Vickers-Armstrong in Barrow. The tribunal was asked to elucidate eight specific points in the award, but problems continued to crop up.

The effect of the swollen piece-work prices in Coventry and elsewhere was accentuated after the Government adopted a policy of dispersing factories to avoid offering concentrated targets to German bombers. Men transferred to other areas expected to retain their high earnings, and lower-paid workers in the host areas grew restless. The Federation, to conserve the existing district rates, got an agreement that the men transferred should be paid their new district rate plus a 'dispersal bonus'.

Some firms were dispersed into South Wales, which led to the formation and affiliation of a South Wales Association. The new association refused to take part in a Central Conference in England and has never gone to York, but they were eventually persuaded by William Grant, when West of England chairman, to go as far into England as Bristol for the final stage of the Procedure for administrative convenience.

Other internal changes during the war were the suspension of the Administration Committee, the functions of which had never been clearly distinguished from those of the Board, and later the setting up of a smaller policy committee to avoid occupying the time of the large number of Board members. Initially the policy committee consisted of fourteen Board members, with others attending in rotation three or four at a time. The Dyer Memorial Fund, which had become inadequate for its purpose, was merged into a Benevolent and Dyer Memorial Fund. The Foremen's Mutual Benefit Society and the Staff Benefit Society were merged into the Foremen and Staff Mutual Benefit Society.

The pressures of war, as in 1914–18, brought about some changes in relations between engineering employers and employees which would have otherwise taken much longer to develop. Perhaps the most important, certainly the one which caused most uneasiness among members, was a movement towards collective bargaining between the Federation and white collar unions. The National Union of Clerks had been recognised for procedural purposes in 1920 and the Association of Engineering and Shipbuilding Draughtsmen in 1924, but both had been weakened by the drop in union membership between the wars. When the Second World War broke out, the Transport and General Workers' Union were negotiating for a similar type of recognition for their white collar section. The Federation said a manual workers' union was not appropriate for organising clerical and supervisory staffs. So the union reconstituted their white collar group as the National Association of Clerical and Supervisory Staffs which was granted recognition in April 1940, on the conditions that it should act independently of the transport union and that supervisors should be excluded from the agreement.

It remained the policy of the Federation that the terms and conditions of employment of staff workers were a matter for managements and their staff to deal with, and members were sensitive about this. In October 1940, when the Federation recommended that any balance of holidays due to staff should be paid for at the end of the year, there were immediate complaints that this was interference with the freedom of managements to deal with staff conditions as they thought fit. Early the following year the clerical workers made identical wage claims to a large number of firms and nine were referred to Central Conference. The Board decided that the Manchester claim should be made a test case. The 'Manchester Settlement' in July was the first to provide a scale for clerical workers up to 21 and served as a model for other areas. Draughtsmen were also pressing for war increases and members accused the Federation of interference.

After a year of controversy, a series of questions was put to the associations. They decided in favour of continuing the existing procedure agreements and favoured the negotiation of war bonuses up to the age of 21. But they were almost equally divided (49.4 per cent to 50.6 per cent) on the negotiation of war bonuses over 21 and also (47.8 per cent to 52.2 per cent) on the negotiation of district or national agreements on working conditions such as hours, overtime and holidays. In June 1942, the Federation offered the same war bonus as that of manual workers, 13s. 6d., which was accepted by the clerks but the draughtsmen rejected it and made firm by firm claims.

This was not the end of controversy. The Federation, now working through a staff committee, were handling the conditions of draughtsmen and clerical workers not by formal agreement but by recommendations to members, and in August 1943, British Thomson-Houston, of Rugby, refused to operate a recommendation on overtime. The London association proposed that in future there should be no more recommendations but that proposals for staff conditions should be subject to referenda to members and made binding. A statement of policy in January 1944, provided for the Federation to obtain the views of members on the basis of the number of staff they employed.

Meanwhile two other white collar unions, the Association of Scientific Workers and the Association of Supervisory Staffs, Executives and Technicians (formerly the National Foremen's Union) were pressing for recognition. In 1942 the TUC intervened in support of ASSET's claim and passed a resolution protesting against the non-union rule of the Foremen and Staff

Mutual Benefit Society. Ramsay had a talk with Sir Walter
Citrine, the TUC general secretary, but the TUC were threatening to make the recognition of ASSET a major policy issue and
the Government, notably Sir Stafford Cripps, now at the
Ministry of Aircraft Production, were sympathetic. ASSET also
submitted claims for each of its 280 members at the General
Electric Company plant at Witton to the National Arbitration
Tribunal. The Federation still held that no foreman ought to be a
trade union member, but in view of the pressures signed a procedure agreement at the beginning of 1944. However it applied
only where the union had a majority of a particular grade in a
plant and provided that the next step after failure to agree at
factory level was a meeting of executives at Broadway House,
thus omitting the works and local conference stages which would
have brought in local union officials.

The Association of Scientific Workers had been negotiating for
recognition from early in 1943. They agreed that managerial and
supervisory grades could be excluded from a procedural agreement, as they were with the draughtsmen, but there was much
argument as to exactly whom this would apply to. An agreement
was signed in May 1944.

The recognition of ASSET perturbed the Foremen and Staff
Mutual Benefit Society and in August 1944, the Board adopted
a fifteen-point document which said it was axiomatic that foremen are an essential part of management, made a number of
proposals to maintain and improve their status, and urged that
all foremen should be given the opportunity to become members
of the FSMBS. The unions complained that pressure was being
put on foremen to join the FSMBS so in September 1945, the
Federation issued a circular to remind firms that membership of
the society was voluntary and that there should be no coercion
but advising firms to join and bring in members of the staff who
wished to join.

As the war ended both draughtsmen and clerical workers were
pressing for wage-for-age scales up to 25 and the clerical workers
also wanted a job-grading scheme. The Board asked for authority
to negotiate on staff questions without restriction and were given
it by a big majority. The National Union of General and Municipal Workers were asking for recognition for their small number of
white collar members but were unwilling to make arrangements

similar to those of the transport workers and did not sign a procedure agreement until 1953.

The Federation also relaxed a little further their special relationship with apprentices. In March 1941, an agreement was reached on a scale for apprentices, boys and youths giving them for the first time fixed percentages of the skilled fitter's rate. This followed a strike of apprentices in Scotland which spread to Barrow, Belfast and Manchester, and involved altogether about 5000. One of the main complaints of the boys, who were said by the Board to have come under the influence of such subversive elements as the Young Communist League, was that their wages compared unfavourably with those of dilutees to whom, in some cases, they were giving instruction. The settlement was followed by further unofficial strikes in London and Lancashire because of dissatisfaction with the scale.

Another development which the Federation feared might affect management prerogatives was the establishment of joint production committees in the factories. These were first suggested by the AEU at the beginning of 1941 as a means of securing co-operation to increase output. Initially the Board merely reasserted the principle that the setting up of works committees by mutual consent was provided for under the 1922 settlement, but there was pressure from the Government and, after the invasion of Russia, shop stewards also became active in the matter. The TUC wanted to make joint production committees compulsory in essential undertakings. In January 1942, Ramsay told the Board there was a strong feeling in the Government that some definite procedure was necessary and the Board decided they had no objection so long as the new bodies 'did not prejudice the rights of employers to manage their establishments'. So in March 1942, an agreement was signed with the AEU and by 1944 it was estimated that 4000 of these committees had been established. The employers were constantly on their guard to prevent the committees being used in ways which they thought undesirable and to avoid their being made compulsory.

The agreement was for the period of hostilities and it was assumed would be ended when the war was over, but the unexpected return of a Labour government in 1945 placed the employers in a quandary. They would have liked to get rid of the agreement but were anxious lest the new Government introduce something less acceptable by statute. In February 1946, the Board decided after much cogitation that it would be unwise to approach the unions for its termination. In many federated establishments the JPCs had fallen into desuetude and it was felt better to allow this process to continue than to do anything that might revive interest in the subject. But the unions asked for a revised agreement. The Federation said a period of abnormal post-war conditions was not the time for fundamental changes but agreed to renew the 1942 agreement.

Sir Greville Maginness was president of the Employers' Confederation at this time and he succeeded in getting the TUC and Government representatives on the Minister of Labour's National Joint Advisory Council to agree on conditions for supporting the setting up of joint consultative machinery where none existed. It was to be purely voluntary and advisory and would not deal with terms and conditions of employment and each industry was to be free to adopt the form of machinery best suited to it. From time to time afterwards Labour Ministers made statements which caused the Federation renewed anxiety but they managed to stave off legislation until Labour lost power in 1951.

Many wartime controls were continued into the first years of peace. The National Arbitration Order, which made almost all strikes illegal, remained in force by mutual consent. Subsidies continued to be used to keep down the cost of living. In 1946 the Federation made their first negotiated wage settlement with the unions since 1940. In between, five increases had been awarded by the tribunal. The agreement provided for an addition of 6s. a week to the national bonus, pay for working on bank holidays and a guaranteed week of 34 hours. At the end of the year agreement was reached on a reduction in the working week from 47 to 44 hours, to be worked in five or five-and-a-half days. This concluded a long argument within the Federation as to whether their old rule that the week must be five-and-a-half days, relaxed during the war in some circumstances, should be reimposed. Joint talks with the unions took place on the revision of the wages structure.

The Federation were trying to get back to peace-time normality. The end of the Control of Engagement Order in 1945 left employers free to advertise vacancies, with the result that the Board found itself in one of its periodic discussions on 'enticement'. The Federation decided, with an association majority of 26 to 15, to make the inquiry form compulsory again. Its use had been discontinued because of the 1940 Restriction of Engagement Order, but the rule about it was still there. It might, it was thought, give a certain amount of protection against enticement.

Post-war demand stretched the economy tighter and tighter until the winter of 1946–7 power supplies broke down. While rationing and material controls had been retained, manpower controls had largely been dispensed with and had now to be partially restored. A new Control of Engagements Order was introduced in October and a Registration of Employment Order two months later to try to get labour shifted from inessential to essential industries. Men in the coal and engineering industries, which had just negotiated a five-day week, were asked to work longer hours. There was a campaign to bring back women who had dropped out after the war. Industry was called upon to stagger hours and introduce shift-working to spread the electricity load.

Engineering employers looked upon these difficulties as the sort of abnormalities to be expected immediately after a great war and awaited a resumption of peacetime conditions as they had known them in the past. But the old conditions did not return.

Inflation and Frustration 1948–1957

Wages and Prices Spiral Upwards – New Leaders at
Broadway House – Governments Urge Restraint –
Twice the Employers Throw Down the Gauntlet –
Twice the Government Persuade Them to Pick It Up
Again

The decade from 1948 to 1957 was the most frustrating in the
history of the Federation. Continuous full employment and
shortages of labour, particularly skilled workers, resulted in
annual demands for higher pay or shorter hours or both. The
Federation's history became a history of almost continuous wage
negotiations against a background of chronic inflation and
periodic economic crises, accompanied by Government appeals
for restraint and numerous efforts to stimulate higher productivity. Several times the Federation nerved itself to resist trade
union pressures, even at the cost of a national stoppage of work,
but each time the Government, unwilling to face the consequences of a major struggle, pulled the carpet from under their
feet at the last moment. The result was a series of humiliating
anticlimaxes.

None of this was foreseen. After the First World War there
had been a boom lasting barely two years and then a sudden
fall in prices followed by wage reductions. This time the physical
damage had been much greater, and it would presumably take
longer to replace the world's shattered and deteriorated capital, but many employers assumed that afterwards there would
be a return to something like the old order. After all, the country
had never experienced continuous full employment in peace-
time.

The Government during 1947 became increasingly preoccupied with the need to keep down wages and prices. At the

beginning of the year a White Paper on 'economic considerations affecting relations between employers and workers', drawing attention in general terms to the dangers of inflation, had little effect. An economic crisis in the summer made the Government's anxieties more acute, but a series of conferences with the TUC did not help much. On 4 February 1948, the Prime Minister read to the House of Commons a statement on 'Personal Incomes, Costs and Prices', also published as a White Paper, which said there should be no further increase in the level of personal incomes without at least a corresponding increase in the volume of production, except in certain circumstances.

1948 Wage Claim

Exactly a fortnight after the Prime Minister's statement, the Confederation of Shipbuilding and Engineering Unions submitted a new claim. The Federation president, Philip Johnson, of Hawthorn Leslie's, Newcastle, told the General Council that this was contrary to the Government's policy as stated in the White Paper. In fact the submission of the claim can be taken to mark the end of the honeymoon period between the two sides of the industry which had until then survived the war. The employers had yet to acclimatise themselves to the new peace-time era in which, come rain, come sun, they were bound to get a new claim almost every year, and the employers would be expected to concede something each time.

Johnson feared the claim would widen the gap between the Federation and the trade unions and result in disappointment for their workers.

During the war [he said], when we were all working for a common end, there was a big advance in mutual confidence and co-operation between employers and their workpeople, and between the Federation and the unions, and indeed this spirit was maintained throughout the wages advance in 1946 and the shorter working week negotiations at the end of that year. I feel that the spirit of mutual understanding is being undermined, partly by the influence of left-wing Communists, and partly by statements by members of the Government which, although they may not make definite assertions, certainly engender feelings of suspicion against employers as a class.

So the Federation tried to carry out government policy by rejecting the claim and had the first of numerous experiences of being let down by the Government when it came to the point. The claim was a comprehensive one arising partly from the wage structure joint talks, which had proved abortive, and included a request for a pay increase of about 13s. a week. The unions contended that it came within the qualifications of the White Paper because the basic wage in engineering was not sufficient to maintain a reasonable standard of living and was lower than those in other sections of industry.

The admittedly low basic rate was a constant embarrassment to the Federation. Average earnings were much higher, but there were some workers on the minimum rates and the figures could be used effectively against the employers in negotiations and in appeals to outside opinion. When the claim was rejected, the executives of the thirty-seven organisations in the Confederation of Shipbuilding and Engineering Unions considered the possibility of a strike ballot but instead decided by a majority to ask for a court of inquiry.

The court, under the chairmanship of Sir John Forster, recommended an all-round increase of 5s. a week on the bonus, a levelling up of the district minimum rates and that negotiations on a simplified wage structure should be reopened. The recommendations, which were accepted, established for the first time national minimum basic rates – 66s. for skilled workers and 51s. for unskilled. The Federation set up a special committee on the wages structure but made slow progress, partly because of the technical difficulty of consolidating the bonus without substantially raising the earnings of highly paid piece-workers, and partly because the unions regarded a new structure as a means of increasing wages.

1949 Wage Claim

Then, in September 1949, the Confederation submitted a new claim, with timing characteristic of the engineering unions, immediately after Sir Stafford Cripps had announced the devaluation of the £ and a month after the TUC reaffirmed their support for wage restraint. The claim was for £1 a week wage increase 'to be paid from profits instead of being added to the price of the industry's products'. Before arranging a conference, the Federation wrote to the unions suggesting that in view of the industrial and national circumstances, particularly devaluation, the unions should reconsider before seeking to proceed further. They also took the unusual course, for them, of explaining their reasons at a Press conference.

The Confederation executive passed a resolution deploring 'the action of the employers in breaking away from what has hitherto been regarded as traditional practice in these matters, which has provided for initial meetings between the parties in order that there might be mutual understanding of the issues involved', and regretted that the employers were 'endeavouring to negotiate through the public press' before the precise nature of the application was known. They called a conference of the executives of the thirty-seven member unions, which on 16 November decided by a majority to pursue the claim.

All through the autumn, while these exchanges were going on in the engineering industry, the special economic committee of the TUC was discussing a request by the Government for greater wage restraint than before in spite of the inevitable price increases following devaluation. Finally in December the TUC recommended that unions should reconsider their existing claims, that cost-of-living sliding scales should be suspended and that wage claims should not be pressed unless the price index rose five points or more. This was approved at a conference of union executives by 4,263,000 votes to 3,606,000. The big minority vote made it unlikely that the recommendations would prove effective. Nor did they. Certainly the engineering unions were not deflected.

After receiving discouraging reports on trade prospects in the aircraft, marine engineering and motor industries, the Board again followed government policy by rejecting the claim in February 1950. This time, owing to misjudgement on the part of the unions, they were able in the end almost to dictate the terms of settlement, with results which were, to say the least, disconcerting.

A conference of Confederation executives decided by a narrow majority to take a ballot of their members to choose between a strike and arbitration. The Transport and General Workers' Union and the General and Municipal Workers' Union, at that time the leaders of the right wing, were outvoted on this by the AEU, the boilermakers, the Communist-led Electrical Trades Union and smaller unions. A strike would have been illegal under the National Arbitration Order and the Ministry of Labour reminded the Confederation of this. The Federation took counsel's opinion as to whether the ballot was in itself illegal and were advised that it probably was not.

The Ministry considered a stoppage of work in the engineering industry could not be tolerated having regard to its position in the internal and external economy of the country and suggested to the Federation that if they were prepared to reopen negotiations on the wage structure, the ballot might be called off. But the Board took a firm line. They were opposed to any proposal involving increases in costs and felt it would not be dealing fairly with the unions to lead them to believe the employers would concede any increase through revisions of the wage structure:

> The only assurance that could be given to the unions was that the employers would meet them on the wages structure, but as a long-term policy only, entirely dissociated from the application for an increase of £1 a week out of profits. It would be necessary to stipulate before any negotiations were entered into that the strike ballot should be withdrawn; it was impossible to negotiate under duress.

The Confederation decided to proceed with their ballot. They did start informal talks with Federation officials on the basis of a revised wage structure, but when they allowed it to be known that they had in mind consolidated rates of 130s. for skilled men and 100s. for labourers, the Board said no useful purpose would be served by continuing. The Minister of Labour, George Isaacs, told the House of Commons that neither party had reported a dispute was reported. The unions were hopelessly divided. The two general unions tried until the last moment, but without success, to persuade the Confederation to withdraw the ballot and both advised their members to vote for arbitration.

The ballot resulted in 326,233 votes in favour of arbitration and 111,049 in favour of a strike. Even the AEU members were three to one against a strike. Having thus demonstrated that their members did not want to support the militant policies of their leaders, the Confederation had no course open to them but to report the dispute to the Minister of Labour. He persuaded the two sides to meet again and the employers now made an offer on the basis of which a settlement was reached on 28 November.

To explain the consequences it is necessary to outline the wage structure. Before the agreement the basic rate for skilled workers was 66s. in addition to which there was a national bonus of 41s. These were now merged, with an addition of 11s., making a consolidated time rate of 118s. for 44 hours. The pay of labourers was consolidated in the same way to make 100s. for 44 hours. But the increases were limited to time-workers paid within a range from the minimum district rate up to the minimum piece-work standard. Piece-workers received no straightforward monetary increase, but the minimum piece-work standard, still based on the old basic time rate, was raised from $27\frac{1}{2}$ per cent to 45 per cent. In addition their overtime and night shift premiums were in future to be based on the consolidated time rate. But piece-workers already getting more than 45 per cent were not supposed to get any increase on their piece-work standards. Consequently large numbers of the more highly paid piece-workers and many of the more highly paid time-workers got little benefit from the agreement.

The result justified some associations which had opposed increases for the lower paid only. Within a few weeks thousands of more highly paid piece-workers were demanding increases comparable to those for the lower paid and going on day work (a damaging form of go-slow) or banning overtime. The movement began in Manchester and quickly spread to the Clyde and the North-east Coast, and then to Sheffield, Leeds and London. The Federation made immediate protests to the Confederation and the Minister of Labour. After some delay, the unions met the Federation and agreed on a joint memorandum saying that piece-work times or prices had always been dealt with by individual managements and their workers. Normal working should be resumed and complaints of low piece-work earnings taken through the disputes Procedure. Altogether ninety-eight embargoes or threatened embargoes were reported to the Federation.

By the time of the February Board meeting seventy-two of

these had been lifted but only half in accordance with the national agreement. Trouble was now concentrated at Barrow and on the Tyne, where the AEU district committee issued instructions to go over to day work and twenty-three firms, including some of the largest, were affected. The Federation complained that the AEU sent no executive member to Barrow to deal with the trouble, an omission they attributed to the fact that a union election was going on at the time.

Vickers-Armstrong said that at both their Barrow and Elswick undertakings men were not even working at day work speed, so that in effect the company were subsidising a go-slow movement at 'vast increase' to their costs of production. They wanted to sack go-slow workers at Elswick and asked the Board to tell the unions they refused to accept the 'intolerable' position. The Board discouraged them from sacking men, because a stoppage might spread to other areas. At the same time it was reported that since the embargo had been lifted at Metropolitan-Vickers in Manchester, the firm had been discussing a form of 'super bonus' based on additional production. The Leeds association wanted to know whether firms affected by the go-slow were entitled to payments from the indemnity fund. The finance committee thought not, but a committee was set up to consider whether the payment of indemnities could be extended to forms of industrial action short of a strike.

All through April and May 1951, the struggle at Barrow and on the Tyne went on and the Board were finding increasing difficulty in restraining the employers from taking drastic action. At their meeting on 26 April, the Board were informed that the First Lord of the Admiralty was concerned about delay in the delivery of gun mountings and employers were asked not to post discharges until the Federation had further consulted the Government. It was also reported that the men at the Elswick works had reverted to normal working on the understanding that the firm would make an offer which went beyond the terms of the national agreement. A hurried telephone call to Newcastle established the truth of this. The offer had been rejected by the men but there was to be a further meeting that afternoon. There were more telephone calls and eventually the management agreed to withdraw the offer on condition that office bearers and the director of the Federation would go to Newcastle.

A national conference with the unions shortly afterwards produced no result, but by the time the Board met on 31 May, settlements had been reached by all the Tyne firms except three and there was to be a meeting at Barrow the following day. The members were congratulating themselves that the trouble was almost over when there was another phone call from Newcastle. Negotiations at C. A. Parsons & Co. had broken down and the firm wanted to post notices saying that normal conditions included piece-work and that employment would be available only to those willing to accept normal conditions. The company were told that the Board would think it unfortunate to take precipitate action when the issue seemed virtually resolved.

But it turned out the issue was not resolved at Barrow. The men decided to continue their action and Ramsay and Sir Robert Micklem, chairman and managing director of Vickers-Armstrong, went to see Alfred Robens, the Minister of Labour. Robens thought it doubtful if men could be compelled to do piece-work if they preferred time-work, but was told that the working rules of Vickers-Armstrong contained a provision that employees could be required to work piece-work or day work at the option of management. He was further told that the firm could not allow the position to go on indefinitely and might have to dismiss numbers of workers, even though they knew this might cause repercussions in other engineering centres and possibly throughout the country. The Minister said he would consult the Defence Committee of the Cabinet. That committee thought it a first priority that the new rearmament programme should not be damaged. In view of this, Micklem decided not to take action for the time being. Later that month the Barrow men agreed to accept a settlement similar to those reached in Newcastle.

The incident was over, but its repercussions continued for years. Partly because of pressure from the Government, preoccupied with the needs of the rearmament programme, the Federation had failed to enforce a national agreement, even with the half-hearted support of the unions, and had dissuaded individual employers from doing so. The men in the workshops had demonstrated their power irrespective of union action. Moreover, except in the Midlands and the West of England, which had come off almost scot-free, the experience had left the employers with a determination never again to attempt to restrict increases to the lower paid. Financial losses had been enormous and by the end of the year, many employers said, the old differentials had been restored almost everywhere. Defeat had been snatched out of the jaws of victory.

The workers' use of embargoes on a wider scale than ever before was a warning for the future. A sub-committee, under the chairmanship of Sir Percy (later Lord) Mills pointed out that the method had many advantages for the workers over the old strike weapon. There was no drain on union funds. The workers themselves were enjoying the new enhanced time rates throughout, so that the employer was paying them for taking part in a partial strike against him. Employers who gave notice that workers' services would be dispensed with unless they resumed normal working by a given date were successful in some cases but in others met with disastrous failure. The committee said it was essential the Federation should have a definite policy. They proposed that working conditions of shops should be carefully defined by notice or works rules and men who refused to operate them should immediately be given seven days' notice unless they observed the conditions. Any firm which dismissed men in these conditions, with the approval of their association, should be given financial support.

1951 Wage Claim

It was now nearly two years since the rejection of the claim which had caused so many complications, though only nine months after the settlement, and a new one was overdue. It duly arrived on 28 August – for £1 a week. A month or two earlier the unions had reopened their claim for two weeks' annual holiday with pay. They had also proposed amendments to the overtime and night shift agreement. The South Korean War and threatening international situation had resulted in rising prices, rearmament and a consequent intensification of manpower shortages, particularly in sections of the engineering industry. For once there was a general feeling among the employers that some all-round increase should be offered. The only question was how much and whether concessions should be made on the other claims. In contrast to the two-year struggle over the last claim, this was settled in three months with an increase of 11s. for men and a second week's paid holiday.

1952 Wage Claim

Less than five months later, the Confederation submitted a new claim for a substantial increase, which they later defined as £2 a week. But in the preceding year much had changed. The Labour Government had replaced the National Arbitration Order by the Industrial Disputes Order and strikes were once more legal. The electors had returned a Conservative Government to which the employers looked for greater support in resisting wage demands. International tensions had eased and there were hopes of a truce in Korea. The rearmament programme had slowed down and world prices were falling. There was still intense competition for labour and the new Government introduced a Notification of Vacancies Order to try to steer workers into essential industries. The new Chancellor, R. A. Butler, cut subsidies in his Budget, which was one reason for the size and early presentation of the engineering claim, fixed by the Communists and militants against the opposition of moderate union leaders. Butler warned the two sides of industry of the dangers of a wage–price spiral and asked them to turn their minds to a policy which would relate the national wage bill to production.

In this changed environment, the employers felt the size of the claim was provocative and determined once more to resist. The associations cast 97.4 per cent of their votes against granting any increase and 99.1 per cent said that in the event of a final failure to agree they were prepared to resist the claim even to the extent of a stoppage of work. Members of the Board said that for fourteen years the workers had benefited by a sellers' market and had not realised there was now a buyers' market, coupled with a fall in the prices of raw materials and a reduction in purchasing power abroad. Other main industries were looking to the engineering employers to give a lead against further increases in wages.

When the claim was rejected in August, the AEU national committee called on the Confederation to hold a ballot to choose between a strike and a national ban on overtime and piece-work. The Confederation asked for another conference to warn the employers of 'the serious industrial situation which had been created' and to ask whether they were rejecting any increase in principle. The Federation, after listening to the unions again, replied that they had no offer to make and prepared for a struggle. The Board set up an emergency committee consisting of the president, director and office-bearers, and produced a shortened version of their reply to the unions for distribution to workers.

The Confederation decided by 113 to 75 votes at a conference of executives to impose a ban on overtime and piece-work. The Federation then offered to accept arbitration, because they thought that if their attitude was purely negative the Government was certain to intervene, but the unions rejected this. Sir Robert Gould, the Chief Industrial Commissioner, called the two sides together and told them that the Government had no wish to interfere but viewed with concern a situation that might lead to a dislocation of production. The cost of living was rising and arbitration awards of about 7s. a week had been made in other industries.

The Board met on 8 October and found themselves divided but a majority favoured a new referendum of members to ask for authority to negotiate and this was endorsed by a special meeting of the General Council. The argument was that the Government would intervene in any case and nothing was to be gained by waiting until after serious damage had been done by the embargoes. The effect of the unofficial embargoes of the previous year was fresh in their minds. The voting by Federation members was 57.9 per cent in favour of negotiating an increase and 32.2 per cent against. Some Birmingham and Coventry members, with 9.9 per cent of the votes, were opposed to a general increase but willing to concede an increase on the minimum. Negotiations were resumed, and a general increase of 7s. 4d. finally agreed. The Federation's backdown caused restiveness in some areas. The West of England Association passed a resolution deploring the reversal of opinion among federated employers, not occasioned by commercial considerations, which was revealed in the voting.

The Federation had tried to prevent three of the last four wage increases. Each time they gave way in the end, twice because the Government and perhaps their own members could not face the struggle when the testing time came. But their most determined attempts were still to come under new and more aggressive leadership.

On 26 February 1953, Percy Mills became president in succession to Sir William Wallace, an industrious but somewhat colourless man who was head of Brown Brothers, of Edinburgh. Mills was hard and vigorous, reputed to have the ability to reduce to embarrassed silence any industrialist who made an ill-considered remark at a Board meeting simply by fixing his eye upon the man. Some members became reluctant to speak at all. Union negotiators often had the same sort of experience.

A 63-year-old Yorkshireman, Mills left school when he was 15 and studied accountancy in his spare time. He became an official of the National Employers' Federation but was not taken over when it merged with the engineers – a slight said to have caused him lasting resentment. He got a job with W. & T. Avery, Birmingham manufacturers of scales and weighing machines, and by the time he was 43 had become managing director. He also became a force in the Birmingham association, of which he was president in 1939–40. During the war he was controller-general of machine tools for four years, and earned the respect and friendship of Harold Macmillan when Macmillan was Parliamentary Secretary to the Ministry of Supply. Afterwards Mills was head of the British economic section of the Control Commission in Germany and was as tough in argument with Russians on the Commission as he was later to be with employers and union leaders. In 1951 Macmillan, as Housing Minister, called him in to help achieve his target of 300,000 new houses a year.

A man of Mills' stamp was badly needed by the Federation at this time. Membership had grown rapidly during the war. Between 1938 and 1949 the number of federated firms more than doubled and now exceeded 4000. But the staff had not kept pace. Moreover, because of war-time preoccupations, not many young men had joined the Board. Only a handful of leading industrialists were regular attenders.

Partly because of this Ramsay had established a dominating position – if not to the extent that Allan Smith had done, at least sufficiently to cause increasing irritation to the office-bearers. He and Alex Low, the secretary since 1939, had made a highly effective combination. Ramsay, more than ever imposing in appearance and manner, was not the hail-fellow-well-met type but Low was smooth and friendly with everybody, always ready to exchange chaff with union leaders and to pick up a useful word or hint in corridor or hotel lounge. He had been with the

Federation since 1920 and there was little about its working he
did not know. But on 4 January 1951 he died. E. C. Happold,
who took his place, was experienced, meticulous and conscien-
tious, but not the foil that Ramsay needed. The director seemed
lost without his old partner and became increasingly aloof, some
said pompous. He was also being accused of being 'too soft' with
the unions.

Mills set himself to revitalise the Federation. He got Kenneth
Hague, of Babcock & Wilcox, who was second vice-president, to
look round for half a dozen vigorous young industrialists who
could be brought on the Board. Hague, who was much closer to
Mills than 'Eric' Braby, the first vice-president, suggested six
names, of whom three later became presidents. Another step
Mills took was to reduce the period for which the president and
two vice-presidents held office from three years to two – he
himself was the last to serve the three-year period. Holding office
for three years had meant that a man had to give up part of his
time to the Federation for nine years, which few were ready to do,
and also that when he reached the top office he was unlikely to be
young. But perhaps Mills' main aim was to restore the authority
of the office-bearers in relation to that of the Director.

Ramsay was 66 and his health was uncertain. Mills and the
other office-bearers persuaded him to retire, reluctantly, and
agreed that the next director would not be a man who could or
would be allowed to dominate the Federation. Mills was out of
the country when the final choice was made but the others were
of like mind. The strongest candidates were St John Wilson, an
outstanding official of the Ministry of Labour, and Ben Macarty,
who for the previous five years had been director of the Manchester association, a choice suggested by Greville Maginness. It
was natural in the end for the office-bearers to prefer Macarty,
outspoken Lancastrian with practical engineering experience, to
St John Wilson whose manner, for all his wide knowledge of
labour matters, was apt to give the impression that he was an
intellectual.

So the office-bearers put Macarty's name to the Board, who
accepted it unanimously, but not everybody was happy about
the choice. When the recommendation was submitted to the
General Council – normally a formality – Vincent Everard, of the
Birmingham firm of Bellis and Morcom, a future president, moved

that the question be reopened and the appointment readvertised. He only got one supporter but it was an unusual thing to happen. Everard thought Macarty was too parochial in his attitude and argued that the Federation should offer a much higher salary and bring in a QC with a broad vision – a step taken a dozen years later, when Everard was still an office-bearer, with the appointment of Martin Jukes. There may also have been behind the incident an old rivalry between the Manchester and Birmingham associations.

However, Macarty was appointed and in time his critics accepted his positive qualities. For six months he had a running war with Mills, who was apt to ignore him and do things without his knowledge, but in the end they established a practical working partnership. Macarty did not then or later try to dominate the Federation as his predecessors had come to do but neither was he the sort of man to accept relegation to the status of office clerk. He had a practical knowledge of engineering at least the equal of that of most of the office-bearers. A native of Pendleton, he was articled to the Town Clerk of Salford but in 1938 left the local authority to join a firm of scientific instrument makers with two shadow factories and was responsible for personnel management for the whole group employing 11,000 workers. In 1944 he joined the Manchester association, becoming director four years later.

Macarty was above all an extrovert. The Federation, as he saw it, was there to do the practical job of helping its members in their industrial relations. He was impatient of the 'old washerwomen' at the British Employers' Confederation and of Ministry of Labour officials and of 'international talking shops', though he was an accomplished linguist, and would have no truck with such fancy ideas as a research department. The Federation had a first-rate statistical section which, as he saw it, could quickly provide any factual information needed. Extremely quick-witted, he was apt to say what came into his mind with a frankness which sometimes embarrassed his colleagues. As a negotiator he has been described by one of his colleagues as a master of the 'knock down, drag out' school. He was intolerant of those who strung together words for their own sake and union spokesman were seldom given their head. He was not interested in 'hob-nobbing' with union leaders.

Macarty was sometimes accused of being parsimonious in his

dealings with his staff. It was his job, as he saw it, to run Broadway House as efficiently as he could and give value for money but he could claim with justice that he had brought forward some able men. The staff respected him for his ability and his integrity, which no one ever questioned, and they found his direct man-to-man approach a relief from the pomposity of Ramsay's later years. He was always ready to give credit at Board meetings to those who had done a good job. Though contemptuous of the Press, and apt to infuriate industrial correspondents, he began to break down the barrier of secrecy which had previously stood between the Federation and the public. He sometimes disappointed members by the lack of serious content in the speeches he made at association dinners. But by and large he was the sort of director the members wanted at that time.

1953 Wage Claim

Macarty was not yet in the saddle (or at the stirrup) when in May 1953, a new claim arrived from the Confederation – for a 15 per cent increase. Earnings had more than kept pace with a small rise in the cost of living since the last settlement and a Federation survey showed that orders and profits were falling. In September the members voted by a huge majority against any concession and 98.8 per cent of those voting answered 'Yes' to the question, 'In the event of union actions against any or all employers are you prepared to co-operate in any action which may be necessary even if a stoppage of work is involved?' Mills tried to make sure that the Government would not let them down this time by taking some of his colleagues to see Sir Walter Monckton, the Minister of Labour, to appeal to him not to interefere. Monckton seems to have listened politely.

When the claim was rejected, the unions called a one-day strike on 2 December. It was generally observed, but since it had no obvious effect the Confederation decided to impose bans on overtime and piece-work from 18 January. A week before this threat was made, however, the Government gave the employers new cause for anxiety. The railwaymen had been engaged on a parallel wage claim and at this period railway settlements were regarded as setting a pattern for the nationalised industries and engineering for private industry. On 4 December the railwaymen

were awarded a 4s. a week increase by the industry's independent
tribunal – and promptly rejected it and threatened a national
strike a week before Christmas. Monckton and Lennox Boyd, the
Minister of Transport, joined in efforts to avert the strike. On 16
December the two Ministers went to see Churchill at No. 10
Downing Street, and on their return a settlement was reached
giving the men 4s. immediately, the promise of something more
within in two months and afterwards a complete re-examination
of the industry's wage structure.

If that was the Government's attitude to inflationary wage
increases, what hope was there that they would keep out of the
engineering dispute? Mills again took his office-bearers to see
Monckton on 30 December.

> They confirmed [Sir Percy reported afterwards] that the
> employers were unable to make use of the Minister's good
> offices to bring about further negotiations as it was impossible
> for them to make an offer. He [Monckton] was again urged to
> allow the Federation to face up to the situation and to meet the
> threat of a ban on piece-work and overtime by saying that,
> except in special cases, work would only be available under
> normal shop conditions.

Monckton was as usual sweetness itself – but the following afternoon he did exactly what Mills had tried to prevent. He
announced that he would set up a court of inquiry. The Confederation postponed their ban.

Since the ban was only postponed, the employers continued to
make ready for battle. A joint meeting of the General Council
and association executives in Church House on 6 January 1954,
passed the following resolution:

> This meeting, while reaffirming its co-operation with the Court
> of Inquiry set up by the Minister of Labour, records its oppo-
> sition to attempts to force up wage costs in the industry in the
> face of growing foreign competition, more particularly when
> in their view no justification exists for a claim for increased
> wages. It is resolved to resist any move intended to restrict out-
> put by a refusal to work to the conditions of employment
> established in the industry by general consent and consistent
> usage, and further, in the event of any such action, to take

measures to ensure that normal working conditions are restored.

These measures were spelt out in a letter sent to associations. Where an embargo was imposed, workers were to be given seven days' notice that they would be refused employment unless they returned to normal working. 'While it was appreciated that the issuing of such a notice would possibly involve a complete stoppage,' the Board recorded, 'it was felt that this new method of attack by the unions could only be defeated by immediate, positive and concerted action on the part of the employers, and members were strongly urged to take the action indicated.' The procedure had already been tried out by a firm at Treforest which gave notices to men operating a ban on piece-work in protest against continued employment of two workers who had refused to take part in the one-day strike. The ban there had been quickly lifted.

However the setting up of the court of inquiry, of which Lord Justice Morris was chairman, was for practical purposes the end of the matter. The court reported in February that there was justification for some increases, perhaps about a third of the original claim of 15 per cent. The Board thought that if they refused to accept the recommendation public opinion would be behind the unions and they would be fighting against the odds at great extra cost and loss of business. A new ballot of members resulted in a vote of 83,299 to 2740 for a settlement and in April agreement was reached on increases of 6s. 6d. for labourers, 7s. 6d. for semi-skilled and 8s. 6d. for craftsmen. The different increases for different levels of skill broke new ground. It was felt that the policy of uniform increases had restricted the skilled men's differential too much.

The recommendation for an increase was not the only part of the court's report which disturbed the employers. The court said that in comparing wages with the cost of living and other factors, rates rather than earnings were the best measuring rod, a view which the Federation described as 'entirely fallacious and unacceptable'. The court also recommended the establishment of a joint council for the industry to replace the system of *ad hoc* meetings when either side had anything to raise. The Board thought this would do nothing to obviate the cycle of wage claims, but would rather be an open invitation to the unions to bring them forward.

The court further pointed out that there was nothing about

the national interest in their terms of reference, and they had no evidence from the Government, but that they could not avoid the issue. They did not feel able to assess or quantify the dangers of wage increases to the national economy so they suggested the appointment of an 'authoritative and impartial body' which would consider the wider problems. The Federation, though not enthusiastic, were willing to co-operate through the British Employers' Confederation to see if there was any merit in the proposal. However the TUC said it was not feasible and so the idea was dropped.

1954 Wage Claim

Finally the court made another recommendation to simplify the wage structure. Renewed talks with the unions followed and later in the year the Board set up a sub-committee with J. J. Gracie, of English Electric, as chairman, but before any worthwhile progress had been made, the unions put in a new claim for 10s. for labourers and 15s. for craftsmen. Orders and profits were now increasing and there had been wage settlements in other industries, so there was no strong resistance this time and in March 1955, the Federation conceded increases of 11s. for skilled workers, 9s. 6d. for intermediate grades and 8s. for unskilled workers, leaving the structure for further examination. The South Wales, West of England and Wigan associations all wrote to the Federation regretting that the settlement had not been coupled with any simplification of the wage structure since some suggestions made by the Gracie committee had been approved by the associations, but it was pointed out that in the negotiations the unions had seemed interested only in a general wage increase.

1955 Wage Claim

The following year the same thing happened. Talks on the structure were interrupted by a new claim which was settled in February 1956, with increases of 12s. 6d. for skilled workers, 11s. for semi-skilled and 9s. 6d. for unskilled, the largest increases yet.

1956 Wage Claim

Within two months of this settlement the AEU national committee passed a resolution in favour of a new wage claim. The employers were incensed about this, so soon after the biggest increases they had ever conceded, and the following day agreed to tell the public and member firms that they regarded the action of the AEU as wholly irresponsible and contrary to national policy. An immediate press statement was issued declaring that a new claim would have to be resisted.

Though the statement was strongly worded, it was not enough for the Midlands and West of England associations, who determined that this time the Federation should say 'No' and mean it. The members in the motor industry, who were facing a recession, were particularly strongly opposed to any further general increase on top of the high wages they were already paying. Brigadier John (later Sir John) Barraclough, chairman of the Birmingham association, and Sir William Grant, chairman of the West of England association, agreed on a concerted move to stir the Federation into action. It was a formidable alliance. They were the only paid officials on the Federation Board by virtue of the fact that each was chairman of his regional committee. Barraclough was a professional soldier, much decorated in the First World War, who had been brought by Percy Mills from the Control Commission in Germany to take over the chairmanship of the Birmingham association in succession to General Baylay in 1951. Grant had been works manager of the Bristol Aeroplane Company and active in the affairs of the West of England association from 1920. He joined the association as the first full-time chairman in 1938. Both were outspoken and aggressive by nature and, while fundamentally loyal to the Federation, vigorous partisans of the policies of their own associations.

On 1 May Barraclough wrote to all the managing directors of his member firms: 'In my view we should not wait until the claim is tabled. Some positive action by employers should be taken now. We should make it clear to the unions, to the Government and to the country that the union demands are wholly irresponsible and *must be rejected*.' Barraclough added that his president and office-bearers concurred and invited the views of the industrial leaders without delay. The following day Grant sent a similar letter to his managing directors, asking for quick replies because he wanted to write to the Federation 'concurrently with other associations taking a similar line'. A few days later the Derby office-bearers did the same thing. The object was to get ammunition to put before the Board meeting at the end of the month.

Macarty told Barraclough that he was 'not exactly clear' as to the purpose of his letter. Barraclough replied that the Federation was 'at the crossroads'. There was a tendency to underestimate the discontent and general disgruntlement among members. There was a very real danger of a split in the Federation – particularly between the Midlands and those areas in which there were workers on or near the minimum. Employers were asking what the Federation was doing, what use they were making of the crucial period before the new claim was submitted. The object of his letter was to allay widespread discontent and restore confidence in the Federation. He suggested that resistance should be concerted with other organisations such as the British Employers' Confederation, the Chambers of Commerce and trade associations. A letter from Vincent Everard, now the second vice-president, reinforced the Midlands attitude. If there was another general increase, he said, a great number of Birmingham firms would withdraw from membership or attempt to negotiate a Midlands wage rate or form a breakaway organisation. The last, he said, was 'a very real possibility'. Soon hundreds of letters advocating a strong stand were being quoted to Broadway House.

The Federation leaders probably did not need much convincing, but they could not risk being let down again by the Government. Churchill and Monckton had been held responsible for previous surrenders. Monckton's strength, Lord Butler was to write later, 'lay in an ability to inject his own sweetness and light into the atmosphere. This strength was precisely what was wanted by Churchill who, with unhappy memories of the general strike to live down, was determined to pursue a policy of industrial appeasement, even at the cost of inflationary wage settlements'. But Churchill and Monckton had now been replaced by Sir Anthony Eden and Iain Macleod, and at the Exchequer was Percy Mills' friend, Harold Macmillan.

Mills was no longer president. He had stayed on a month over his three years to complete the previous negotiations and then been succeeded, in March, by Frederick C. Braby, generally known as 'Eric' Braby, a man of 59, the head of a comparatively small company, who had been active in the London association since 1929. His uncle had been prominent in the National Employers' Federation. He was also the Boy Scouts' County Commissioner for Kent. But Mills was still a force in the Federation and he insisted that the Government would back them this time. When the office-bearers expressed doubts, he took Braby along to No. 11 Downing Street, to see Macmillan. 'So long as I have anything to do with the Government we will stand behind you,' were his words as Braby remembers them.

The Government were in fact engaged in one of the periodic efforts to stop the inflationary spiral. A number of economic restrictions had been announced in February and in March Eden, accompanied by Macmillan and other Ministers, had a series of talks with leaders of the TUC, the British Employers' Confederation and the chairmen of the nationalised industries, whom private employers always accused of 'selling the pass' when efforts were made to restrain wage increases. There was general agreement on the need to keep down prices. The Government also published a White Paper on *The Economic Implications of Full Employment* on the same theme. Macmillan said in a speech at Newcastle in May that another round of wage increases could not be repeated without disaster. The TUC were not prepared to co-operate with the Conservative Government, particularly after the Budget cuts in subsidies, and policy had to be directed to keeping prices down and encouraging resistance to wage claims. 'For employers the course is clear,' said the *Employers' Confederation Bulletin*. 'It must be their duty to resist with the utmost firmness any wage increase which would cause an increase in the selling price of the product or service provided.'

At the May meeting of the Management Board it was decided, under pressure from Mills and the Midlands and West of England associations, to appeal to the unions not to bring forward a wage claim and to warn them that, if they did, the employers would have to reject it as it would be inimical to the interests of all concerned. During the following month the Government obtained undertakings from some nationalised industries to keep prices stable. And the Association of British Chambers of Commerce, the British Employers' Confederation, the Federation of British Industries and the National Union of Manufacturers made a joint recommendation to private industry to match their actions. Mills was present at a joint meeting with representatives of the Employers' Confederation and FBI and reported everyone had agreed that the time had come to face the unions. They decided to put this point of view to the Government when the next cycle of claims began and to ask the Government to keep out of it if the claims were rejected by employers.

The Federation found the opportunity to tell the unions that a new wage claim would be rejected on 28 June, when they had a meeting with them to reply to applications for a 40-hour week and improved holiday pay (which were turned down). They explained their action at a Press conference afterwards when Braby said they had appealed to the unions 'in a spirit of friendship and mutual respect' to think carefully before making another claim. There was some public criticism of the Federation for rejecting a claim even before they had received it. One suggestion was that so provocative an action would undermine the position of responsible union leaders.

The public image of engineering employers suffered a further severe blow the next day, when the British Motor Corporation sacked 6000 workers with one week's pay in lieu of notice. This abrupt action was taken in spite of remonstrances by the Birmingham association and the Federation. Joe Edwards, of BMC, had informed John Hope, the association secretary, on the Monday of the firm's intention to issue notices on the Friday, and Hope and Edwards went to London to see Macarty. Macarty warned Edwards that if they carried out their intention there would be an outcry from the Press and public, questions in Parliament and trouble with the men. But Edwards said that Leonard Lord, the head of the firm, was determined to go ahead. Lord's contention was that Sir John Black, at Standards, had been consulting the unions about necessary redundancies for months and that his velvet glove methods were getting him nowhere.

Lord's use of the mailed fist was immediately effective but resulted in the consequences that Macarty had forecast. Government, public and Press were shocked and the fifteen unions affected called a strike at all BMC factories. When it became clear that it would be difficult to settle the dispute without some special payments to the dismissed men, the Federation arranged a special meeting of the General Council on 8 August. They were anxious to avoid finding themselves committed to the principle of redundancy pay, but in view of the specal circumstances were willing to accept an *ex gratia* payment on an *ad hoc* basis to BMC men. The BMC eventually made an arrangement for compensation for employees with long service and promised that there would be consultation in future.

About the same time Braby met Macleod at a private lunch at the Royal Thames Yacht Club, and Macleod reaffirmed that the Ministry would not interfere if the Federation resisted a wage claim, but he expressed doubt whether all the Federation members would maintain the stand if there was trouble. He raised the possibility of the employers in their reply trying to divert the unions from wages to improvements in working conditions. This idea seems to have made some headway. The following month we find Braby writing to Macarty of 'loose talk about the possibility of our eventually granting something to the unions in lieu of general wage increases' and asking for estimates to be prepared of the costs of various possible fringe benefit concessions. But he felt, he said, that concessions of that nature would be very unpopular with most of their members and would do little or nothing to satiate the appetite of the unions. Macarty in reply referred to 'a slight outbreak of weakness in the knees in certain quarters'. Discreet steps were taken to dissuade Macleod from talking about fringe benefits at the Conservative party conference. The council of the Employers' Confederation announced that in their view no general wage increase nor any general change in terms of employment, which in either case would increase costs, would be justified.

By the time of the September Board meeting the Confederation had decided on a claim for a substantial increase and asked for a meeting. The Board approved a questionnaire to members, asking them whether they were in favour of outright rejection and 'In the event of actions against any or all employers to enforce this claim are you prepared to co-operate in any measures which may appear to the Management Board to be necessary even if they should involve your own establishment directly or indirectly, including a complete or partial stoppage of production?' Of those who voted, 91.9 per cent said they were in favour of outright rejection and 93.1 per cent that they were prepared to face a stoppage.

The President appointed an action committee consisting of the office-bearers and Greville Maginness. The publicity committee drew up a pamphlet for distribution. A survey was made of the proportion of workers on the admittedly low minimum rates which showed a decrease but there were still 14.82 per cent of labourers and 2.27 per cent of fitters. The President and other officers made informal approaches to the heads of some of the biggest companies, inside as well as outside the Federation, to make sure of their support. An analysis of membership showed that 41 groups, 22 combined engineering and shipbuilding establishments and 34 companies with more than 2000 manual workers, had among them nearly half the Federation vote.

The Confederation argued their claim in October, explaining that by 'substantial' they meant 10 per cent. The Federation rejected it on 29 November and the Shipbuilding Employers' Federation rejected a similar claim a fortnight later. Neither gave any hint of possible concessions, though arbitration tribunals were now beginning to award increases of three per cent in other industries – about the same as the increase in the cost of living since previous settlements. Macmillan in his speeches was still insisting that prices were being kept on a 'plateau of stability'. Observers suggested that some engineering firms would prefer a settlement of about three per cent to an all-out struggle. If so they were having no influence on Federation policy, though the recession in motors and some other sectors was not general throughout the industry.

A conference of Confederation union executives in January 1957, asked for another meeting and gave their executive authority to say that, failing a satisfactory conclusion, action would have to be taken to enforce the claim. The claim was presented again on 12 February and that to the shipbuilding employers the following day. So far the shipbuilding negotiations had, as was usual, followed closely those in engineering. But at their meeting on 13 February, the unions taunted the shipbuilding employers with always lagging behind, with the result that the next meeting was held before that with the engineers. The shipbuilders rejected the claim on 5 March and the engineering employers on 12 March. The change in order was of some importance because the shipbuilding industry was in a phase of relative prosperity. The unions called a national shipbuilding strike for 16 March.

While the long series of meetings had been pursuing its slow progress towards crisis, the country's economic position had suffered severe shocks. The collapse of the Suez adventure by Britain and France had resulted in loss of confidence and financial reserves. At the end of 1956 petrol rationing was introduced and an increase in the duty on petrol was followed by rises in bus fares and road transport charges. Macmillan's plateau of price stability was evidently in danger, though the Treasury Bulletin insisted that a temporary increase in petrol and oil duty was no justification for rises in wages and profits, which would permanently put up prices. In January Macmillan succeeded Eden as Prime Minister and Percy Mills became Lord Mills and Minister of Power.

It soon became evident the Government felt that after all they could not stand aside while the employers and the unions fought it out. Macmillan, working hard to restore Britain's international position, returned from a visit to Paris in March to find the country on the verge of becoming an industrial battlefield. Besides the threatened shipbuilding and engineering strikes, a railway strike was likely and trouble was brewing in the power stations and on the docks. With visions of a near-general strike, devaluation of the £, the collapse of the Government, Macmillan with the aid of Macleod set himself to restore peace.

On 12 March Macleod announced in the House of Commons that he had decided to refer the shipbuilding dispute to Lord Evershed, Master of the Rolls, as arbitrator. When Alfred Robens, shadow Minister, quoted Sir William Grant as saying, 'This time we do not want government interference. We want to fight it out ourselves. We have got to stand firm and prove to these fellows that things are not done so easily,' Macleod at once dissociated himself from these sentiments. The shipbuilding employers accepted the proposed arbitration the next day but the unions had already rejected it. On 18 March Macmillan made a major public speech at Leicester – the first since becoming Prime Minister – in which he appealed for peaceful settlement of the disputes by some form of arbitration rather than have recourse to 'self-destructive struggles'. With all the pressures on the economy, the industrial disputes were matters of national concern, he said.

'In the long run, and for the common good, the umpire is better than the duel.'

The following morning the unions decided to call out their engineering members in ten districts on 23 March. The districts were nearly all in marine areas where shipbuilding workers would already be out – Bristol, Merseyside, the Clyde, Manchester, Tyne and Blyth, the Wear, Tees and Hartlepool, Southampton, Belfast and Sheffield. The other districts were to be called out at two-weekly intervals until on 6 April the whole industry would be stopped. The same day that this decision was taken there was a meeting of historical importance to the Federation.

When Eric Braby arrived at Broadway House that morning he was greeted by Macarty with the news that Percy Mills wanted to see him. 'I think the Government are going to back down,' Macarty added. A much worried man, Braby went to see Mills at the Ministry of Power. The country could not afford strikes, Mills told him. Above all, it could not afford a railway strike. And if the Transport Commission gave way, he did not see how the engineering employers could hold the line. 'But you must hear this from the Prime Minister himself,' he added. Mills explained to Braby how to get into No. 10 by the secret entrance. When he got there he found Macmillan accompanied by Macleod and with them Sir John Hunter, president of the Shipbuilding Employers' Federation, Sir Brian Robertson, chairman of the British Transport Commission, and Sir Colin Anderson, president of the British Employers' Confederation. Accounts of the meeting differ in detail, but the substance is clear.

Macmillan, looking worried and unhappy, told them he was about to leave for the Caribbean for a meeting with Eisenhower to try to restore Anglo-American relations, but felt he could not leave the country in its present state of chaos. He conceded that the position was the responsibility of the Government. They had given the lead to stand firm but the employers had followed the lead with rather more enthusiasm than expected. The country had not prepared for something which would amount to a general strike as they had done in 1926. Macleod contributed 'great histrionics' about the danger of the country going bankrupt, the £ collapsing, and the Government falling. Macmillan asked Robertson if he could get a settlement, to which Robertson replied that he was sure he could if he was left alone to do it. 'I am afraid this means you too,' said Macmillan, turning to Braby.

Braby went back to Broadway House and told the Action Committee, now in almost continuous session. They seemed to him, as he put it afterwards, 'flabbergasted'. Their first reaction was that they must stand firm. They were under mandate to do so. Macmillan might be Prime Minister but he was not President of the Federation. Eventually they agreed that they must take into account the arguments about the interests of the country and the future of the Government. But they could not just give the unions what they wanted. They must get something in return. Braby felt himself in an impossible position and suggested he should resign, but the other office-bearers said that would do more harm than good.

Sir Brian Robertson's response to Macmillan's appeal was immediate. On 22 March, he over-ruled an arbitration award of 3 per cent and settled with the railwaymen for 5 per cent in return for a promise to continue to co-operate in efforts to increase efficiency. On the same day the shipbuilding employers agreed on a basis for negotiations. They offered an increase of 5 per cent in return for undertakings from the unions regarding restrictive practices, demarcation disputes and unofficial strikes. The Confederation, however, said they must have $7\frac{1}{2}$ per cent and the Minister at once set up a court of inquiry into the shipbuilding dispute.

Macleod's efforts to bring the Federation into line were redoubled. During the following week there were three consecutive days of discussion at the Ministry of Labour. The engineering strike had now started and the Ministry said that if the engineers would follow the example of the shipbuilders in making a cash offer, the unions would call it off. The Action Committee replied that in view of the attitude the unions had adopted to the shipbuilders' offer, they could not see their way to do likewise. But the Minister's pressure was unremitting. At times, it was said, he pleaded with tears in his eyes. And eventually the committee agreed to refer the question to the Management Board and General Council.

There followed on the morning of 28 March perhaps the most stormy Board meeting in the history of the Federation. Braby explained what had happened and said there was no time to ask the associations whether they would revise their mandate to reject the claim outright. The Action Committee had to give the Minister an answer that day. There were angry reactions from many members, particularly those from the Midlands and West of England. A proposal was put forward that the Action Committee be instructed 'to proceed into negotiations in the light of discussions at the meeting and make the best bargain they could in the circumstances'. An amendment that the matter be referred back to the associations for a further referendum was defeated by forty-two votes to eighteen. A second amendment that the Action Committee should not be authorised to go as far as the shipbuilding employers without referring back to the Board was defeated, with ten votes in favour. The original motion was then carried with only six against, but it was said afterwards that it had been 'touch and go'.

The Action Committee went straight on to see the Minister and said they were prepared to reopen talks on the same lines as in shipbuilding and gave him a copy of their *quid pro quo* proposals, which included undertakings regarding efficiency and a wage standstill for a year. But they warned him that they could not be expected to follow the shipbuilders' 5 per cent offer as conditions in the two industries were different. In fact they offered 3½ per cent, which was duly rejected. The Minister immediately set up a court of inquiry into the engineering dispute.

The engineering strike was extended to London on 30 March, but on 2 April the unions called off both strikes. The decision to call them off was largely determined by one man, William Carron (later Lord Carron) who had become president of the AEU less than a year earlier and was to be the most stalwart leader of moderate opinion in the AEU and the trade union movement generally for a decade. He had given a casting vote in favour of calling the strikes off at a meeting of his own executive, and the AEU attitude had proved decisive when the Confederation took their decision by 710,177 votes to 449,162. The Federation estimated that about 450,000 had taken part in the engineering strike. The number involved in shipbuilding was 160,000.

The two courts of inquiry reported on 2 May, recommending the alternatives of an increase of 8s. 6d. for skilled workers without conditions or 11s. with the proposed conditions on increased efficiency and a standstill. The unions chose the latter and finally, on 23 May, after the associations had voted to accept the court's recommendations, the Federation settled for 11s. for skilled workers, 10s. for intermediate grades and 9s. for unskilled – about 6½ per cent. Of the conditions, the year's standstill in wage claims was obviously important, but Macarty in his evidence to the court made no attempt to disguise the fact that the productivity clauses were little more than a face-saver. He referred to the document containing them as 'one of the forms of persuasion the Minister used when he suggested to us we ought to meet our friends to talk about present difficulties'. The clauses were largely speaking covered by existing agreements he said, but they were trying to find a form of words as 'a bridge over which we might resume negotiations'.

In addition to the recommendations on pay, the court suggested, like that of 1954, a national council for the industry, a provision in the Procedure for unresolved disputes to be referred to arbitration and, again like that of 1954, the creation of an authoritative and impartial body to examine the wider problems of wages policy.

Aftermath 1957–1964

The Tycoons Rouse Themselves – Midlands in Revolt
– Calls for a Motor Breakaway – Wage Structure
Tangle – Unofficial Strikes – Hints of New Thinking

The Federation's standing had never been so low as it was after
the 1957 back-down. The leaders were accused of adopting a
purely negative policy, of always saying 'No' to begin with and
then giving way in the end, of refusing to negotiate until they
were compelled to do so, of clinging to out-of-date attitudes, in
general of being 'bloody-minded' and at the same time weak.

Internally, there was a feeling among the members of having
been let down. Associations were angry and some of them near
revolt. With the Government, particularly Macleod, denying that
they had interfered in the Federation's decisions, they found difficulty in justifying themselves without making disclosures which
would be damaging to the national interest. It was known that
the Government had exerted some pressure, but the critics were
unaware of the part played by Macmillan. 'The Government
asured us that they had no intention of interfering with our decision in any way – so long as we did what they said,' was Kenneth
Hague's comment.

Would the employers have been justified in rejecting the
appeal by the Prime Minister? Perhaps they would have behaved
differently in Colonel Dyer's day, or even in that of Sir Allan
Smith. But the world had changed. Some, looking back at it
afterwards, thought they would have done better to stand out in
spite of everything, but probably most would say they had to
give way.

One result of the loss of employer morale was to remind the
industry's more individualistic tycoons of the Federation's existence. Few of them took much notice of it in the ordinary way.

They might have subordinates who attended its meetings, but they were too busy to bother. But now, feeling that the Federation had brought the industry's employers into disrepute, they decided they must do something about it.

One day early in May Viscount Knollys, the head of Vickers, rang up Hague, whom he had met during the war when Knollys was Governor of Bermuda and Hague was on a government mission which was held up there on the way to the United States, and invited him to a meeting at his flat. When Hague got there, he found Lord Chandos, head of Associated Electrical Industries, and others of the best-known industrialists in engineering. He was subjected to a barrage of criticisms of the Federation – its lack of constructive policy, its parochialism and so on. Could the Federation's leaders not get away from the attitude that all they had to discuss was whether an increase should be 5s. or 6s. a week – and then sit down and wait for the next claim? If the head of a comparatively small company like Braby was in the top position, the unions were bound to get the impression that the Federation did not speak for the real leaders. Hague said they would be only too pleased if the 'real leaders' took a more active part in the Federation. In reply they talked about the difficulty of finding time.

Hague was in an embarrasing position. As Deputy Chairman and Managing Director of Babcock and Wilcox, he was accepted by the tycoons as one of themselves. But he did not want to take part in such meetings behind the back of his president. He discussed the position with Maginness and told Macarty what was going on. Eventually it was arranged for Braby to face this formidable group of critics at an informal dinner, which took place at the Savoy on 21 May 1957. Those there included Knollys and Chandos, Sir Reginald Verdon Smith, chairman of the Bristol Aeroplane Company, Lord Tedder, chairman of Standard Motors, Sir George Nelson, managing director of the English Electric Company, Sir Frank Spriggs, managing director of Hawker Siddeley, Sir Reginald Rootes, deputy chairman of Rootes Motors, J. D. Pearson, chief executive and deputy chairman of Rolls-Royce, General Dunphie, managing director of Vickers, and Sir Harry Railing, chairman and director of the General Electric Company.

Chandos opened the attack. As Oliver Lyttelton, he had been

among the most successful of the business men brought into the War Cabinet. He was a member of the Conservative government from 1951 to 1954, when he returned to the chairmanship of his firm and was elected president of the Institute of Directors. He has been described as the natural spokesman of free enterprise in the fifties. A powerful man, who could be ruthless, he seldom minced his words and he did not now. Pay negotiations in the engineering industry, he said, had become a sort of 'ritual dance'. Like the boat race and the Derby, a pay claim would come up at a predictable time each year. Then there would be a great cluck-ing in the Federation. It was quite outrageous, they would say. They could not afford to pay higher wages, they would say – even in times when firms were spending many millions of pounds on expansion and development and giving money away in response to domestic claims. Then a few months would elapse and they would make an offer. It was not sensible to cry 'Wolf' every time. In some cases, a parade of negotiations went on even after the outcome had been settled behind the scenes.

Knollys said there was need for a much smaller body at the top than the Board. The scope of negotiations was too wide. More should be done at plant level. Verdon Smith criticised the Federa-tion's public relations. They should create better labour relations at all levels. Perhaps a joint industrial council, or some such body, by giving unions a sense of responsibility, would help. He went so far as to describe the holy 1922 procedure agreement as 'a menace'. Tedder suggested greater regional freedom in negotia-tions. Nelson supported the idea of a joint council. Dunphie won-dered whether it would be possible to have a policy committee made up of 'the people at this table'.

But Eric Braby at the head of the table, was not left alone to face the giants. Reginald Rootes defended all the Federation had done. They certainly represented a conglomeration of industries but by and large there was nothing wrong with the organisation, he said, though he agreed there were not enough young men on the Board. Spriggs said the employers had been right in rejecting the claim, and further resistance, which could bring down the Government, might be necessary. Even the fall of a government might be a worthwhile price to pay if it could achieve some stabi-lisation. Pearson turned the tables on the critics by declaring that if there were faults in the Federation, they could be laid at the

door of the guests. The member firms were the Federation and if
there was ground for criticism, the right course would be to support the local associations and so ensure the best possible representation on the Board. And Railing pointed out that quite a few top
executives so arranged their lives that they were able to give the
service without which the Federation could never have been
built up.

Braby himself made a spirited reply. They were trying to bring
younger men on to the Board, he said, and half a dozen had been
co-opted for that purpose the previous year. There would be no
difficulty in improving the representation if the right men were
available. As to its size, Braby explained the form and functions
of the smaller policy committee and of the President's Advisory
Committee of office-bearers and elder statesmen. As for the 'ritual
dance', he reminded his audience that on the two previous occasions, in 1955 and 1956, they had not refused increases, though
they had always reminded the unions of the continuing dangers
of inflation. There was need for the closest co-operation between
the Federation and the large organisations in it but – in reply to
Dunphie – he was most emphatically opposed to the creation of
any body outside the Federation which could be thought to
influence the policies and actions of the Federation.

It was obvious something had to be done to appease the
tycoons, but the talk at the dinner left it far from clear what it
could be. After much informal consultation, Hague eventually
found the answer. At their April meeting the following year, two
months after he had succeeded Braby as president, Hague told
the Board that after the 1957 crisis the office-bearers had received
'friendly and helpful criticism from influential persons, both
within and outside the industry'. There would be a wage claim
after the expiry of the standstill and it had been suggested that
some who had given advice, being federated employers, should
assist in deliberations on policy.

He therefore proposed – and the Board agreed – that the three
vice-presidents should in future be called deputy presidents
and that the General Council should be empowered to co-opt
up to ten vice-presidents consisting of 'persons whose personal
position and attributes render them in the opinion of the council
especially well qualified to further the objects and interests of the
Federation'. The first five were Chandos, Knollys, Maginness, K.

S. Peacock, chairman and managing director of Guest, Keen and Nettlefolds, and A. B. Waring, managing director of Joseph Lucas. They were followed by Sir Roy Dobson, who succeeded Spriggs as managing director of Hawker Siddeley, G. W. Harriman, deputy chairman and managing director of the British Motor Corporation, Sir Percy Lister, chairman of R. A. Lister & Co., and Reginald Rootes.

The arrangement has worked surprisingly well ever since. Few vice-presidents attend Board meetings very regularly but once or twice a year, when there is some major decision to be taken, the President calls them together to make sure of their support. It is helpful to the Federation to know where they stand and it gives the 'big boys' a sense of involvement in Federation policy-making. 'It was time we put football jerseys on them,' Hague said.

Meanwhile the rebellious associations had had to be assuaged, and this proved a longer process. Even before the court of inquiry had reported in 1957, the West of England association wrote to the Federation urging that immediate steps should be taken to review their constitutional machinery in respect of national wage negotiations and mandates from member firms. It was essential, they said, 'to devise some means of avoiding a repetition of the present situation.' Members at a meeting of the Coventry association said the Federation's offer had destroyed the whole basis of national negotiations and in Birmingham there were numerous questions and complaints. The final settlement intensified criticism. At a meeting of the Midland Regional Committee in September, representatives from Coventry said many member firms felt they had been completely let down and that there was no point in voting'. Birmingham representatives thought the trouble had arisen because of the way the original questionnaire was worded. No doubt the trade unions and the public, they said, gained the impression that the Board adopted a negative approach as a matter of routine. The committee decided to ask the President to receive a deputation.

On 15 October 1957, a deputation led by Ivan Yates, chairman of the regional committee and deputy president of the Birmingham association, and including leaders from Birmingham, Coventry, North Staffordshire and Shropshire, went to Broadway House to see Braby, who was accompanied by

Everard, Macarty and Happold. Yates told them that the Federation had been shaken to its foundations and something must be done quickly to restore the confidence of their members. There were, he conceded, many factors outside their control – the general economic situation, the ineffectiveness and vacillation of the Government, the growing aggressiveness of the unions, full employment and the international situation – but 'because these factors *do* exist and because they *are* outside our control, should we not make sure that our constitution and organisation are suitably adjusted to meet the circumstances which we cannot control?'

Yates' main theme was that 'it must not happen again'. Members must have an assurance that their votes mean something. 'We cannot expect our members repeatedly to go through all this formality of voting, and then accept with complacency results diametrically opposed to the purpose of their votes.' He attacked Macleod – whose behaviour during the crisis had alienated many of the employers – for a television interview in which he denied that the Government had brought any pressure on them *not* to give way.

> We had therefore the absurd situation in which for several months we were pursuing what we thought to be government policy (and what, in fact, had been declared to be government policy) only to be repudiated, openly and publicly, by the Minister of Labour himself. It may have been government policy (which obviously could not be declared) that events *should* take that course. It may have been that the Government wished us to do exactly what we did, with the intention of intervening when things got too 'hot'. Be that as it may, we, the engineering employers, in the eyes of the public, emerged from the proceedings as a body of reactionary and bloody-minded men who will yield only to *force majeure*.

Yates went on to ask whether, if substantial concessions were made by a nationalised industry such as the railways, they could ignore it; if great pressure were brought to bear by the Government, they could resist the pressure.

> I suspect that the office-bearers of the Federation think we can *not*. But many of our members think we can and should. . . . We must agree amongst ourselves whether or not government intervention is inevitable, and if so whether we

must yield to it. Our tactics must be adjusted accordingly. . . . Many of our members feel that the prestige of the Federation has never been so low as it is at the moment. We, in the Midlands, represent a large part of the Federation itself. We are in close touch with local conditions and local feeling. We think the Federation is at the crossroads. . . . There is widespread and deep-rooted dissatisfaction. . . . If this great Federation of ours is to maintain its position in the national economy of our country, we must do something different. If we carry on in the same old way, we shall become less and less effective if, indeed, we do not disintegrate altogether.

The delegation's positive proposal was that questionnaires should give the negotiating committee the widest powers of negotiation on the basis of the policy of the Board which would be verbally explained to associations by their presidents. Braby replied with a detailed account of the course of events and after some discussion it was decided to meet again on 18 December.

At the second meeting, Harold Heath, president of the Coventry association, led the deputation in the absence of Yates, and Braby's team was strengthened by the addition of Hague, Wallace, Maginness and G. R. Adamson.

It was Suez which changed everything [Braby explained to the rebels]. The Government were not prepared to face a stoppage on the railways, with the threat of a general strike to follow, for fear of the collapse of the £. What made it more difficult for us, as office-bearers, was that the Government naturally did not want their fears to receive any publicity, which would have been inevitable if the matter had been referred back to all our members by any means whatever.

Braby produced an analysis showing the varied way in which the Federation had treated the nine claims since the war. In one there had been three referenda, he pointed out, in another none. They had counsel's opinion that the constitution did not require a referendum unless a lock-out was recommended. The Board had complete authority to settle claims. 'We feel,' he added, 'that circumstances can vary so greatly that no useful purpose would be served by trying to decide now whether we should take a referendum or what form the questions should take in regard to future claims.'

The deputation were far from satisfied. Heath referred again to the deep-rooted dissatisfaction in the Midland area and said there was a danger of a breakaway by certain firms with the possible formation of an association of their own. The Midlands associations felt that the position should have been faced up to on 28 March in spite of the strong government pressure. Barraclough visualised 'ugly scenes' at forthcoming meetings of associations if members could not be assured that what had happened in the last wage negotiations would not happen again. A. W. Weekes, the Coventry director, took the same line.

Hague suggested that the best message which presidents of associations could convey to their members was that the Action Committee of the Federation had resisted the Government just as far as they could but eventually they were, in effect, forced to act as they did in view of the circumstances of the time. Their members would then ask, said the Midlanders, 'Who runs the engineering industry – the Government or the Federation?' Maginness replied that if the engineering employers had refused to do what was done, they would in fact have been 'at war' with the Government. But the meeting ended with the Midlands employers still restless and dissatisfied.

When the Board came to look back at the events leading to the 1957 settlement, they felt that they had been badly treated and misunderstood by everybody, inside and outside the Federation. They decided in August that they must do something to improve the Federation's image. They had paid for a full-page advertisement in most newspapers during the strike but that had had little impact. So they decided to publish a booklet to explain their conciliation procedures and their generally amicable relationship with the unions. The publicity committee ruled that it should be 'serious but not sombre'. Herman Roberts, industrial correspondent of the *Birmingham Post*, was commissioned to write it, but his text was subjected to much amendment by committees. The booklet was published at the end of 1958, a sober assessment of the Federation's development of negotiation and conciliation over the years. But the newspapers for the most part singled out one passage:

Twice in four years the Federation has been prepared to 'fight it out' with the unions. Clearly, the union's capacity to pay strike benefit was limited. Such a course, involving, as it would have done, the virtual closing down of the industry, might have been a worthwhile calculated risk. It was no occasion for the kind of compromise which would inevitably emerge from a court of inquiry. The Federation can hardly be blamed for heeding governmental warnings calling attention to the economic dangers of further wage increases. Like the Czechs in 1938, their complaint was that they were not allowed to resist in 1954 and 1957 after they had received every encouragement to have a firm purpose and to dare to make it known to the unions.

On the whole, the associations liked it, but there were more newspaper attacks and the public became more convinced than ever of the 'bloody-mindedness' of the Federation.

An old issue raised again by the court of inquiry was the establishment of a national joint council for the engineering industry. This was not to be just an arrangement for settling differences but 'a body which would concern itself positively with the productive efficiency of the industry'. The Federation had rejected the idea of a joint council at the time of the Whitley Committee recommendations in 1917 and again when it was proposed by the 1954 court of inquiry, arguing that, so far from doing anything to obviate the cycle of wage claims, it would be an open invitation to the unions to bring forward claims.

Several of the big industrialists had referred to the idea sympathetically at the Savoy Hotel dinner, however, and the Federation now went into it more carefully. Braby had informal talks with Carron, the AEU president, but found the unions had not developed their thinking on the subject any further since 1954. Following this, he was invited to discuss the question by Sir Harold Emerson, the Ministry of Labour Permanent Secretary, and, accompanied by Maginness and Macarty, went to see him and Sir Wilfred Neden, the Chief Industrial Commissioner. They told the Ministry officials that in their view some union leaders would use the regular meetings of such a council to air semi-political questions and to present more and more claims on behalf of their members. They did not think that formal discussions on such a body on such subjects as 'the productive efficiency of the industry' would be likely to achieve anything useful. The primary purpose of the Federation was to deal with wages and working conditions.

Sir Harold did not press the point hard but said people outside the industry did not appreciate the value of the disputes procedure and advised the Federation to pay more attention to 'window dressing'. He was pleased to hear about their proposed pamphlet. Shortly afterwards the Federation wrote formally to the Ministry opposing the proposal.

When Hague succeeded Braby as president in February 1958, he found himself faced with continued rumblings of revolt in the Midlands. The motor manufacturers in particular were exasperated, not only because wage rises had been conceded in spite of the mandate to give nothing but also because they took the form of general increases. They had for years been demanding that national increases should be confined to minimum rates, but had been constantly outvoted by other associations which were not prepared to face another experience like that which followed the minimum rates increase of 1950.

High wages in the motor industry had been a source of trouble to the Federation almost since motors began. In 1906 the minutes of the Birmingham and District Association recorded complaints that 'the cycle and motor industries' were responsible for much of the present unrest as employers in the motor trade were paying wages 'far in excess of the district engineering rates'. In 1914 the Austin Motor Company were elected to membership of the association 'subject to assurances that they would gradually bring their rates into conformity with district rates'. In 1927 earnings in motor manufacture were 28 per cent higher than in general engineering. One reason for their high wages was the seasonal character of their industry, which meant that they had to pay enough to attract workers from other sections of engineering when they were working flat out. Apart from that their rapid rate of growth during the preceding half century meant that they were constantly needing to attract new men.

The position became more difficult in the Second World War, when the industrial expansion in Coventry and other parts of the Midlands and West of England, described in Chapter 7, resulted in severe labour shortages in motor and aircraft firms and soaring piece-work prices. The Coventry toolroom agreement remained until 1971 'like a stomach ulcer', as one of their officials put it. In

1945, Sir John Black, the head of Standards, adopted a post-war wages policy of his own and entered into consultation with the unions without consulting the association. Interviewed by association office-bearers, Sir John said he had no intention of altering his proposals and that 'our lads are giving the production'. The association Board decided that the company had contravened the rules and when Sir John tendered the company's resignation it was agreed to waive the statutory six months' notice.

Ford and Vauxhalls were already outside the Federation so that only two of the big five of that time, the British Motor Corporation and Rootes, now remained within it. But inside or outside, Standards and the other motor companies in the Midlands continued to set the pace for wages. And with continued full employment the pace did not slacken. Frequent interruptions in the supplies of raw materials and components in the post-war years caused loss of working time which was compensated for by higher piece-work prices. When new models were introduced, the men expected to earn as much from the beginning as they had on the old ones, so that by the time the new model was run in they were earning substantially more. Rapid technological change made it the more difficult to adjust piece-work prices as it took place.

Motor manufacturers tended to be freebooters. Their attitude was that if anyone was to go short of labour, it would not be them. And they would often give way to a sudden unofficial demand from a group of workers rather than risk loss of production. They knew that when they had labour troubles their competitors were quick to take advantage of it. These attitudes were not confined to motor manufacturers, but they exhibited them to an exceptional degree.

Thus in the high wage areas the position got worse, not better. In 1956 the Coventry employers, basing their figures on returns under the toolroom agreement, found that from 1946 the average earnings of their skilled production workers had increased from 3s. 8½d. an hour to 7s. 4¾d., an increase of 3s. 8¼d. of which only 1s. 2½d. was due to national settlements. Comparing their figures with national figures obtained by the Federation at the time of wage applications, they found that in January 1948, the national average of skilled piece-workers was 3s. 4¼d. an hour, whereas the average in Coventry was 4s. 3¼d. By September 1955, the national average was 5s. 3½d. whereas the Coventry average was 7s. 3½d. Thus in seven and a half years the gap between Coventry and the country as a whole had widened from 10¾d. to 2s. During the previous year, they reckoned, Coventry employers had paid £11,500,000 more to their male manual workers than would have been paid if Coventry's wages had been no more than the national average.

As this process continued, the motor firms increasingly became impatient of the gratuitous and unnecessary additions to their labour costs, as it seemed to them, brought about by general wage increases. The Midlands, the West of England and some associations elsewhere had not experienced the troubles which followed the 1950 minimum wage settlement. Their piece-workers looked after themselves in their normal way. But firms in areas which had experienced the troubles were determined there should be no more national settlements limited to minimum rates or earnings, and they commanded a substantial Federation majority.

The result was a division in the Federation which lasted well into the sixties and made any agreed revision of the industry's wage structure impossible. The two things most obviously wrong with it were that the minimum rates were too low and that there was need for simplification by further consolidation. But to raise the minima to a respectable level would be excessively costly if all differentials were to be maintained and nobody could work out a method of consolidation which would not benefit the highest-paid piece-workers more than anybody. So though courts of inquiry recommended revision and simplification and newspapers criticised and unions made great capital of the low rates, the Federation could do nothing about it.

Throughout the fifties the problems of the motor industry and of the wage structure had become increasingly entangled. After the 1957 settlement, both the Birmingham association and the West of England region informed the Board that they were preparing reports on the wages structure and these reports were received in May the following year and referred to the Federation's Wages Stucture Committee.

The Birmingham proposals, forwarded in the name of the Midland Counties Regional Committee, included a recommendation that 'a new wage structure should improve present minimum levels of earnings rather than provide general increases for everyone'. The Board decided to wait until the new wage claim had been disposed of and then call together representatives of ten of the largest associations with opposing views on the subject. They met on 12 November 1958, and decided to call themselves the Ad Hoc Advisory Committee to the Management Board on Wages Structure and to meet again in January 1959, by which time a sub-committee of the London association was also expected to have produced a report. Meanwhile, however, something had to be done about the motor manufacturers, among whom there was much behind-the-scenes talk of a possible break-away from the Federation to form a Midlands or motor manu-facturing organisation.

It was not the first time there had been such talk. In 1953, after a big strike at Austin's, Leonard Lord, head of the British Motor Corporation, summoned Barraclough and John Hope, secretary of the Birmingham association, to see him at the 'Kremlin', as his Longbridge office was often called, and told them the motor manufacturers should form their own association. They pointed out that if the unions had two organisations to deal with, they would play up one against the other. 'In any case,' Barraclough said, 'you are too busy making motor cars to run an association.' He also suggested that if Lord was dissatisfied with the Federa-tion, he should put in writing his proposals for remedying its faults.

The present position was more serious. Standards, exasperated by constant unofficial strikes, overtime bans and go-slows, had ended their special wage agreements and rejoined the Federation. But they remained restive members and other motor companies were becoming ever more restive. On 26 November 1958, a fort-night after the meeting of the Ad Hoc Advisory Committee, Hague and Macarty went to Birmingham to meet the office-bearers and officials of the Birmingham and Coventry associa-tions and the heads of the chief federated motor firms. In the course of a wide-ranging discussion of the problems of low mini-mum rates and high earnings there was some pretty plain speaking.

Both Sir William Lyons, of Jaguars, and G. W. Harriman, of BMC, spoke of the 'great dissatisfaction' among Midland employers about the general increases of recent years. Hague in reply produced figures showing that between April 1954, and

May 1957, time-workers and piece-workers alike in the motor industry had enjoyed far greater increases than had been general throughout the country. The rest of the Federation, he reminded the motor manufacturers, considered that they had created their own troubles by allowing piece-work prices to get out of hand and were now trying to get national agreements of a kind which would cause difficulties for others, to escape from a situation of their own making.

Lyons retorted that his industry was rather tired of this criticism and pointed to the difficulties with which they had always been faced in the change-over from one model to another, and A. S. Dick, of Standards, said that in the light of the heavy capital investment in the motor industry and the greatly increased productivity, the fact that earnings had grown was to be expected. J. J. Gracie, now the president of the Birmingham association, said it was the low payers in the Federation who put the whole Federation into ill repute with the public.

Hague said it was an urgent necessity to avoid any split in the Federation, to which L. G. T. Farmer, of Rovers, replied that there was already a split on the question of wage structure, and Sir William Lyons said there was much support for the idea that engineers in the Midlands should consider whether it was possible for them to 'look after themselves' in matters of wages. Finally Hague suggested a first step might be to urge the individual employers to raise their rates, and then try to get an agreement with the unions on a minimum wage settlement.

At the meeting of the Ad Hoc Advisory Committee the following January it was suggested that a national technical committee of the Federation should be set up, composed of representatives of the motor firms, to discuss the possibility of excluding higher paid men from national wage increases. The Board had by now received new returns from associations showing that the number of workers still on minimum rates was declining but that the problem still existed. Less than two per cent of skilled men but nearly thirteen per cent of unskilled were on the minimum. The Board consulted associations on the possibility of asking firms to raise the pay of all these so that no one would remain on the minimum but this was opposed by associations with members employing 85.8 per cent of the fitters and 87.4 per cent of the labourers still on minimum rates.

Hague and Macarty met the motor industry leaders again on 14 May 1959, but by then the motor firms had become preoccupied with unofficial strikes. Barraclough had raised this subject at the December meeting of the Board, when he pointed out that the number of unofficial strikes was increasing and suggested that there should be some formal protest to the unions. Since 1 March the previous year, he said, there had been 132 strikes against members of his association, involving the direct loss of 500,000 man-hours. Among suggestions from his members had been new legislation, a meeting with union executives to ask them to discipline their members, a court of inquiry and an informal meeting with union leaders. The Board favoured the last suggestion.

The motor firms grew more and more exasperated, however, and this was reflected at the February Board meeting when Barraclough took a stronger line. The union leaders should be told, he urged, that employers would discharge shop stewards, where they were responsible, unless the unions took action to discipline them. He had no illusions as to what such action might mean but the situation was intolerable. There was a general feeling on the Board that if informal talks broke down action might have to be taken but the test case would have to be chosen very carefully.

So before meeting the motor manufacturers again, Hague had a talk with 'Bill' Carron, the AEU president. Carron, he reported, had confessed that he could not control the 'wild boys' but had also said that in many cases managements were to blame because they gave in easily and allowed the men to derive benefits from unofficial action. The result was weakening of the authority of union leaders. Sir William Lyons considered this was nothing but a red herring. A letter should be sent to the unions, he urged – and it should be given a lot of publicity – saying that the prerequisite of any future discussions on wages and working conditions was that the unions should give a definite undertaking that their members would in future observe agreements. The Federation should attack as hard as they could on the issue.

Hague said he believed communism was behind most unofficial strikes and the Federation should help those like Carron dedicated to oppose communism within the unions. He intended to ask for more informal talks but Carron had said he could not do anything until he (Carron) had been re-elected president. Lyons and several of the others pressed him persistently for stronger action, but he insisted that the first step was to have more informal talks, though stronger action might follow.

With regard to the complaints about general wage increases and the wage structure, Hague put the proposal that a national committee should be set up for the motor industry, with direct access to the Board to express their views. If the companies wished, the committee could negotiate separately on minimum rates only. The manufacturers were doubtful about this, but duly set up their committee with Sir Reginald Rootes as chairman. It does not appear to have done anything in particular.

None of the problems had been resolved. In May the following year the Midland Region once more wrote to the Federation saying that the minimum rates were unrealistic and ought to be raised. Demands for action about unofficial strikes – and informal talks with union leaders – went on, but the position continued to deteriorate. And by 1961 the motor manufacturers were once more talking about setting up their own organisation.

From this point we will try to follow the three threads of the tangle separately. The strike position got worse and worse. In 1960 for the first time more than half a million working days were lost in local strikes in the establishments where the strikes occurred and at least another 300,000 in plants indirectly affected. The year also saw an astonishing demonstration of the power of determined unofficial action to defeat the combined strength of the organised employers and unions.

In March the length of the working week was reduced from 44 to 42 hours. Some nightshift workers, mainly in Birmingham car factories, decided that the 42 hours should be worked on a four-night week of $10\frac{1}{2}$ hours a night. But the national agreement provided for five equal shifts. The unions were strongly opposed to anybody working a $10\frac{1}{2}$-hour shift, which they feared would undermine their case for shorter hours when they renewed their claim for a 40-hour week. The employers were equally opposed to it lest it be used as a stepping stone to a general four-day week. But 3,000 nightshift workers in the Midlands simply refused to work the Friday shift and men at one firm imposed an overtime ban. Eventually the union leaders and the Federation revised the agreement to allow for a short shift on Fridays, though still insisting that the other shifts should not be longer than $9\frac{1}{2}$ hours.

But when the 40-hour week was introduced a few years later, the nightshift workers repeated the operation and forced the employers and unions to agree to a four-shift week of 10 hours a night.

The unofficial strike situation had got so bad that it was causing national concern and at the end of 1960 John Hare (later Lord Blakenham), who had succeeded Edward Heath as Minister of Labour in July, decided to bring the two sides together to discuss the problem of labour relations in the industry. After a preliminary talk with Federation office-bearers, there was a series of meetings in 1961 with the chief motor manufacturers and union leaders.

Thus the motor firms got the meetings with the unions which they had been demanding. The result was a joint statement in April, sometimes referred to as a 'charter' for the industry, which declared that the parties attached paramount importance to the letter and spirit of the procedures. Both sides agreed to act in accordance with their respective constitutions to secure their observance. The employers promised to review their arrangements for the selection and training of supervisors and the unions the rules about the qualifications and training of shop stewards. There were general remarks about the importance of communications and about work study, wage systems, inter-union relations and training. It was agreed in December to review the results in about a year and in January 1963, the parties set up an eight-a-side study group to continue the work. The big non-federated firms, Ford and Vauxhall, took part in the meetings. But there were few signs of improvement in the situation.

It was while these talks were going on that some of the motor manufacturers revived the idea of having an organisation of their own. Just what form it should take they were not sure. Sir William Lyons seems to have thought at one time of a British Motor Manufacturers' Association which would negotiate on wages and other matters. Others envisaged an 'action committee' which would co-ordinate concerted action, if necessary at short notice. Or it might, some thought, be a motor section of the Federation. After contacts with Lyons, George Harriman, Geoffrey Rootes and George Farmer in 1961, J. R. Edwards, now at Pressed Steel, discussed the suggestions with Barraclough.

Barraclough insisted, as he had always done, that whatever

happened they must avoid the creation of a splinter group, which would result in their being 'weak everywhere and strong nowhere'. He also pointed out that motor companies should not take advantage of each other's labour troubles to further their own commercial ends. It was largely for this reason that the informal committee under Reginald Rootes had been set up, but it had achieved very little and to the best of his knowledge no longer functioned. But the 'charter' was a new development and something must be done to keep it alive. It would not be resented at Broadway House if a number of federated employers, with a special common problem, got together on a permanent basis to take co-ordinated action. But some sort of new look was required if Fords and Vauxhalls were to be attracted. If a committee was set up, it should be axiomatic that if one company was attacked, all were attacked. The committee should be a standing one and when a motor company was seriously embarrassed by a labour problem, the action committee should meet at immediate notice and agree on concerted action.

The manufacturers seem to have pondered over this for some time without making much progress and in March 1962, George Harriman approached Barraclough again with the suggestion that he should run a motor section for them. He agreed to do so if his association management board approved but he wished to continue as chairman of the board. Though part of the Federation, the section, as he saw it, would be autonomous, just as local associations were autonomous. It would have a small secretariat in London, but not at Broadway House. He concluded by warning the motor firms that it would be disastrous if the project were a 'flop' and that a lot of spadework would be necessary before it could be launched. Since nothing more was heard of the scheme it is to be presumed that the spadework was never done.

To return to the wage structure, when the Midlands wrote to the Federation again in May 1960, saying that minimum rates ought to be raised, the Board reconvened Gracie's wage structure sub-committee to consider four points – simplification, the raising of minimum rates only, if considered practicable, the establishment of reasonable differentials, and specimen figures to illustrate the effect of possible lines of action. Gracie tried hard to get agreement on some variation of the Birmingham proposals but met determined opposition led by Arthur Main, of Metropolitan-

Vickers, Manchester, chairman of the conference committee, and Gordon Baker, of Parsons, a future president. Both had suffered in the 1951 conflict. Main said his company had lost £1m. The go-slow at Parsons lasted eleven weeks. The sub-committee found their views irreconcilable and on October 1960, Gracie resigned from the chairmanship of the sub-committee after six years of trying to get an agreed policy. A report in *The Times* that he had resigned 'in disgust' caused indignation at Broadway House.

The wage structure discussions had now reached their lowest ebb. Looking for some way out of the impasse, the office-bearers decided to get outside advice and commissioned Cooper Brothers, a firm of chartered accountants, to examine the wages structure to see if simplification was a practical possibility. The accountants started by producing a series of questions which forced the Federation to do some hard thinking, and then presented a report which acted as a catalyst. The problem was debated throughout the Federation more intensively than ever. The Midlands went on putting their case. Leeds, Manchester and London associations all prepared memoranda. So did a number of individuals, including John Hope, the Birmingham secretary, and Arthur Main.

Cooper Brothers had laid more emphasis on establishing a minimum earnings level than on increasing the minimum rates and this was being actively debated. London's proposal was for increases in minimum earnings coupled with a small general increase. Barraclough arranged for trials to be made at a number of undertakings of BMC, Lucas and the Mint to find out the effects of a 'minimum rates or minimum earnings exercise'. In the autumn of 1962, two years after Gracie's resignation, the Federation felt confident enough to take the initiative in arranging a joint wage structure working party with the unions. The ghost of 1951 had not been laid. Members of the Board were still haunted by it a year later. But there had been the beginning of moves towards compromise and new thinking which were to culminate in the package deals of 1964 and 1968.

Another subject with which the Federation was much occupied during the decade beginning in 1954 was a redundancy policy, arising out of incidents in the motor industry. The unions proposed in April 1954, that there should be joint consultation at domestic level before workers were made redundant. As a result, the Board advised member firms to inform workers' representatives of coming redundancies at the earliest possible moment and explain how they intended to deal with it, but said that the final decision must rest with management. 'It is not desirable for any management to adopt any procedure which is designed to share the responsibility of decisions on redundancy.'

The unions complained that the Federation circular was provocative because it laid stress on 'the employer's sole right to dismiss workers at will, without any regard to social and moral responsibilities.' That might have been the end of the matter for the time being if the Federation had not been suddenly thrown on the defensive by BMC's dismissal in 1956 of 6000 workers without notice, referred to in the last chapter. The Board set up a sub-committee on the subject and when it reported sent a private letter of advice to associations. They wanted local agreements to avoid special redundancy payments becoming general, or overtime being put under joint control, or the one-week period of notice being altered or, if possible, any reference to short time. The subject kept cropping up and at the end of 1961, the Federation revised their guidance to stress that managements should give warning and explain the reasons for redundancies before the final decision was taken. Two years later, with the Government expressing sympathy for the idea of severance pay, the Federation drew up a code of good behaviour for members.

The code made no reference to compensation, but in other respects went a good deal further than their earlier guidance. It advocated that, having briefed supervision, firms should take an early opportunity of giving as full a report as possible to workers' representatives, who would be allowed to put forward suggestions for avoiding redundancy or dealing with it – suggestions which should be given proper consideration. If overtime could not be eliminated, it should be cut to a minimum, and recruitment of classes of labour affected should be suspended. Careful consideration should be given to wastage, the possibility of transfers and retirements, the amount of sub-contract work and, though it was normally uneconomic, the practicability of short-time working. The code represented the Federation's policy when, at the end of 1964, the Labour Government opened discussions on their proposed Redundancy Payments Bill.

The period from February 1960, to February 1964, was one of transition. Sir Kenneth Hague, president from 1958 to 1960, had led the Federation through the storm after the 1957 crisis. The presidencies of Vincent Everard and Sir Kenneth Allen, which followed, saw the stirrings of new thinking which was increasingly to manifest itself from 1964 onwards. The successive presidents from Hague onwards had maintained a close relationship with William Carron, the AEU president, with whom they had frequent meetings over lunches, after negotiations, or in deck chairs on the beach at whatever seaside resort the trade union confederation chose for its annual conference. Carron was a tough, round-faced little man, a Roman Catholic who opposed the communists in the engineering unions with a fierce determination, and by and large maintained an astonishing dominance over the irresponsible 'militants'. The informal contacts with him, and with some other union leaders, helped both sides to understand each other's position without committing their organisations.

On the surface not much changed. The annual wage claims came and went as before. The 1957 settlement provided for a year's standstill but a month after it was concluded the unions put in a claim for a 40-hour week without loss of pay and improved holiday payments. The Federation considered this a violation of the terms of the settlement and rejected it. Negotiations dragged on until the end of 1958, when the claim was referred to the Industrial Disputes Tribunal. The tribunal (about to go out of existence) did not think it appropriate to make an award which would have such far-reaching consequences but suggested the parties should renew negotiations when circumstances changed.

Meanwhile, a year after the settlement a new wage claim duly arrived for an increase of not less than 6 per cent on wage rates and, in view of the fact that a pattern had been set in other industries, resulted six months later in increases of 7s. 4d. a week for skilled workers, 6s. for intermediate grades and 6s. for labourers – about 4 per cent. The following year the claim was for £1 and a 40-hour week and in January 1960 the unions renewed their £1-a-week claim and obtained increases ranging from 7s. for women to 8s. 6d. for skilled workers.

In the 1961–2 negotiations, the Federation once more decided to stand firm, but this time without the ignominious results of their previous attempts. It was the period of the 'pay pause' initiated by Selwyn Lloyd as Chancellor of the Exchequer. There was no Government interference and the unions played into the employers' hand by misjudging the temper of their members, as they did in 1950. Concessions were made in the end, but they were the result of changed circumstances, not outside pressures.

The claim submitted in September 1961, was for an unspecified increase for men, for the women's minimum to be brought up to that of labourers, and again for a 40-hour week. The Board, backed by an almost unanimous referendum, rejected it altogether. In addition to their usual arguments, they contended that the proximity of Britain's possible entry into the Common Market made it a first responsibility of managements to reduce costs. The Confederation called a one-day token strike on 5 February 1962, which was fairly well observed but did not have any apparent effect on the employers, so they called another on 5 March. Then the unions balloted their members on a full stoppage but failed to get the necessary two-thirds majority. Less than half the eligible membership voted and 60 per cent of those voting were against a strike.

With their sting drawn, the unions asked for another meeting with the Federation, at which they pointed out that the cost of living was nearly 7 per cent higher than at the last settlement and that $5\frac{1}{2}$ million workers had received increases above the maximum of $2\frac{1}{2}$ per cent recommended by the Chancellor. The employers felt they could not stand aside from the general pattern and conceded 6s. for skilled workers, 5s. 6d. for semi-skilled and 5s. for unskilled and women. It was from this stronger position that the Federation put forward their proposal for a joint committee on the wages structure.

In 1963 the unions claimed substantial increases in the minimum rates and progressive wage increases on the basis of a long-term agreement. This raised the issues on which Federation members had been arguing for so long but they were still not ready for them. Questionnaires to members had inconclusive results and it was decided once again to offer general increases on the normal pattern. They first suggested increases from 5s. to 6s. but it soon became clear that the unions would not accept anything like that unless they were also given the 40-hour week. They decided on an overtime ban from 25 November and a piece-work ban from the following 6 January. Without a mandate to concede a 40-hour week, the Federation settled in December for 10s. 6d. for skilled men, 10s. for semi-skilled, 9s. 6d. for labourers and 10s. for women. But a fortnight later the shipbuilding employers settled for smaller increases and the 40-hour week to be conceded in two stages. Both settlements were referred by the Government to the newly-formed National Incomes Commission (Nicky) for examination. The Board decided to examine the question of a long-term contract.

A number of issues raised during these negotiations – increases in minimum rates, a long-term agreement, the higher increase for women than labourers, the different settlement for shipbuilding workers, the reference of the agreement to an independent body – were to have their influence on the new developments in Federation policy which will be the subject of the next chapter.

CHAPTER 10

Wider Horizons 1964-1971

President with a Plan – Package Deals – Jukes Moves
In – Fewer and Bigger Associations – New Services –
Death of the Procedure – National Negotiations Break
Down

When Stephen (later Sir Stephen) Brown became president of the
Federation in February 1964, he had a five-point programme of
fundamental change worked out in his mind. It was based partly
on trends already discernible, partly on discussions with other
office-bearers during the preceding years, partly on his own vision
of a future Federation with a new purpose and a new image. He
wanted to see it try to anticipate and mould events instead of
merely reacting to them. He wanted to see it contribute by the
form of its agreements and by the development of its services
to an improvement in the efficiency and productivity of the
industry. He wanted it to be less a combative organisation, more
a constructive one.

Firstly, Brown wanted to persuade the employers and the
unions to accept the concept of a comprehensive long-term agreement, carefully planned in advance, which would relieve both
sides from their constant preoccupation with annual claims.
Like Lord Chandos earlier, he was disillusioned with the annual
round of negotiations which seemed to him little better than a
charade, in which both sides presented long statements and
masses of statistics and then said to each other, in effect, 'Now,
let's get down to horse-trading'. (There is a room at Broadway
House sometimes called 'the horse-box'. It was there that two or
three leaders from each side used to get together informally after
the set pieces had been staged.)

Secondly, he wanted to see the numerous small associations
welded together into units large enough to provide the new ser-

vices needed in a period when local bargaining was growing in importance and changing in character. Thirdly, he wanted the scope of the Federation itself to be enlarged so that it could play a more significant part in the improvement of industrial relations and in the industrial and economic growth of the nation. Fourthly, he wanted an amalgamation with the Shipbuilding Employers' Federation, which regularly negotiated with the same unions on similar claims but sometimes reached divergent results as in their recent embarrassing agreement to concede the 40-hour week.

His fifth objective, which Brown regarded as a pre-condition of much of the rest, was to put in charge at Broadway House some-one from outside with the vision and persuasiveness and tact to build and spread through the Federation new attitudes and a new approach to old problems. Brown felt that the choice of a director with Macarty's uncompromising attitude to the trade unions might have been appropriate at the time of his appointment, and that he had served the Federation well, but that he would be unsympathetic to – and not the man to bring about – the changes which Brown wished to see. Macarty was in any case due to retire in three years' time. Perhaps he could be persuaded to make way a little earlier for someone with different qualities.

Brown was 58 when he became president, a leader in a con-ventional mould – Conservative, Church of England, fond of golf and shooting and fishing, with a strong sense of public service. His firm, Stone-Platt Industries, is a group of medium size with plants spread over five association areas. He became a member of a Federation district committee as far back as 1936 and was president of the London association from 1958-9. He was a thoughtful man, a firm and persuasive negotiator, who showed an ability to enlist the co-operation of others in the pro-jects he had in mind.

Preparations for the attempt to negotiate a long-term package agreement were already in train when Brown assumed office. The joint working party on the wage structure had suspended its work during the 1963 negotiations but the employers' side continued to meet and drew up a plan for a package deal which was accepted by the Board and presented to the unions in June 1964. The posi-tion was complicated by the fact that the unions had renewed their claim for a 40-hour week almost immediately after it had been promised by the shipbuilding employers. They now insisted that this claim must be dealt with first. This caused some delay but in August it was agreed that the working week should be reduced to 41 hours in December, as in the shipbuilding arrangement, and that the 40-hour week would be considered in relation to the package deal.

There followed a series of meetings by a joint working party, similar in composition to that on the wages structure, and the three-year agreement was finally accepted by both sides on 22 December. The success gratified and probably somewhat surprised the negotiators on both sides. Many employers had had doubts about the wisdom of committing themselves so far in advance but Brown had taken the precaution of discussing it with the vice-presidents to get the support of the big groups before the associations were asked to make their decision.

Many of the unions had also initially been extremely suspicious. The first reaction to the proposals by Ted Hill, the boilermakers' leader, was that they were 'a load of tripe'. But Carron supported the plan and worked hard to surmount the difficulties. The Federation hailed the agreement as one of the most outstanding events in nearly seventy years of engineering negotiations.

> I would personally like to give full credit to you and your colleagues for the very constructive way in which these negotiations have been carried out [said Stephen Brown to Carron at the final meeting]. I hope you would agree with me, Sir William, that if we can bring to bear the same degree of constructive thought, tolerance and understanding to our other major issues, then there is quite a rosy outlook for industrial relations in our industry.

The agreement was much the most comprehensive the Federation had negotiated, at least since 1922. There were to be two small general increases (5s. for skilled workers) in 1966 and 1967. There were also to be minimum earnings levels above the existing minimum rates which would go up (by 6s. for skilled workers) every six months for three years, with adjustments where the district rates were higher than the national minimum. At the end of the three years the minimum earnings levels would be converted into new minimum time rates. Women's minimum earnings were raised by 7s. every six months and the pay of apprentices was raised to higher percentages of the fitter's time rate. There were to be two additional days of paid holidays, one in 1965 and one in 1966. The 40-hour week was to be introduced at the same time as in shipbuilding in July 1965.

In return for these concessions, the unions agreed that there should be no national or local claims on wages or working conditions, except to remedy anomalies or inequities within an establishment. But a new general claim would be permissible if the index of retail prices rose by five points and maintained the increase for three months in any year of the agreement. The unions also conceded that the guaranteed week should be automatically suspended if work was dislocated by a dispute in another federated factory – a change of great benefit to some employers, particularly in the motor industry, in the strike-happy years to come.

The agreement ingeniously resolved for the time being the long dispute among employers about general or minimum increases. Its most important feature was the attempt to stop the continual increase in earnings at two levels by ruling out local claims – but many employers had doubts about whether this provision would be fully observed.

The difficulties caused by the shipbuilders' 40-hour agreement reinforced the president's determination to bring about a merger if he could. Early in 1965 he met G. H. Holden, president of the Shipbuilding Employers' Federation, and others over dinner and afterwards wrote to him summarising the gains which would come from amalgamation as he saw it. Because they negotiated with the same unions and employed the same kinds of worker, he said, they would be in a stronger position. There was not that much difference between custom and practice in shipbuilding and in heavy engineering. There were in the SEF two or three 'composite' firms – firms with both shipbuilding and engineering interests – who had to apply any concessions contained in a shipbuilding settlement to their engineering activities as well, which was often an embarrassment in engineering negotiations. Moreover the talks were going on which led to the merging of the Federation of British Industries, the British Employers' Confederation and the National Association of British Manufacturers into the Confederation of British Industry and he and some other engineering leaders feared that labour and industrial considerations would be swamped by commercial considerations in the new body. So it would help if the engineers and shipbuilders could speak with a united voice.

After this discussions went on for some time and at first the shipbuilders seemed to respond favourably but in the end they decided they would rather remain independent than become a small cog in the big engineering machine. Partly to protect themselves against any future take-over bid, they negotiated an amalgamation with the industry's two trade associations to form the Shipbuilders' and Repairers' National Association. This was Brown's one major disappointment.

The merger of the Employers' Confederation and the FBI, incidentally, caused the Federation quite a lot of worry. The proposed constitution, based on a report by an independent commission, seemed to them a threat to themselves and other employers' organisations mainly because it would allow direct membership and representation on the labour committee to individual firms. If companies paid subscriptions to the new body, the Federation argued, they might not also wish to pay to their employers' organisation, particularly if they could exercise influence through the labour committee. They also considered it unsatisfactory that the largest federation should have only one vote on the 'unwieldy' 400-member council. On the other hand many members of the Board were strongly in favour of a single employers' organisation, as a counterweight to the TUC, because they believed it would increase their power to influence the ever more extensive intervention by the Government in industrial affairs. They told the confederation that the proposed constitution was 'not acceptable in certain fundamental aspects' and insisted that a decision be deferred for up to a year.

As a result the BEC set up a working party, on which the Federation was represented, to review the arrangements for handling labour and social affairs, and eventually terms were negotiated which the Federation considered acceptable. In 1965 the CBI was established with Maurice Laing, president of the Employers' Confederation, as the first president, and Kenneth Allen as chairman of a Labour and Social Affairs Committee.

Meanwhile Stephen Brown, with the help of Kenneth Allen and others, was looking for a new director-general. Macarty was given this title instead of that of director in October 1964, on the grounds that the work of the Federation was growing in importance. Alan Swinden, the deputy director, was made director. When the new man took over from Macarty he would thus be freed from administrative responsibilities to devote himself to the broad guidance of the organisation. Brown and Allen talked to possible candidates over a wide field – industry, the services, the civil service, the law – and eventually came down to a short-list of three, all of them lawyers, not because they wanted a lawyer, but because it happened that way.

Of these the one they chose was Martin Jukes, QC, a man of 55 who had been at the Bar for thirty-two years. In December 1964, Jukes was appointed director-general designate and it was understood that he would take over from Macarty at the annual meeting in February 1966. Macarty, somewhat reluctantly, would become a consultant for his last year, during which he would travel widely.

Jukes, a native of Purley, in Surrey, had specialised at the Bar in insurance work of one kind and another and had handled a large number of industrial injury cases, so that he knew something of the way work was organised in factories. He was not unknown at Broadway House as on occasion he had been called in to advise the Federation on legal problems. In the ordinary course of events he might well have become a High Court judge before many years had passed. Stephen Brown persuaded him to abandon his legal career by laying stress on the challenging nature of the job which had to be done at Broadway House. The Federation, Brown told him, had not moved with the times and they were deliberately looking for someone who could take a broad, unbiased view of it and had the tact and diplomacy to carry through the essential changes.

Jukes was well suited to the task. He had not the detailed knowledge of the industry or the Federation with which Macarty started but he had a receptive mind and a persuasive tongue. With an unassuming manner and a quiet sense of humour, it was as natural to him to establish friendly relations with those outside – trade union leaders, civil servants, journalists – as it was for Macarty to irritate them. The methods he adopted within the Federation were diametrically opposed to those adopted by Allan Smith or Alexander Ramsay in his later years. Instead of trying to impose his will on the Federation, he tried to induce all those with influence in it to reach the conclusions he wished them to reach.

Jukes spent his thirteen months as director-general designate learning about the Federation, its nature and traditions, the way it worked, the people with whom he would have to deal. He spent a lot of time visiting the associations, getting to understand their different attitudes. He was chairman of a committee set up to prepare the Federation's evidence to the Donovan Commission, most of which he drafted. He visited five European countries to study their industrial relations set-up. He was also chairman of a committee on the organisation of the Federation. He did a lot of reading, studied the latest developments in management practice and the work of the behavioural scientists and interpreted the history of the Federation in the light of their theories. By the time he took over, he had the outlines of a programme in mind.

Apart from the Board itself, there were two very different sets of men he had to carry with him to bring about the kind of radical changes which Brown had envisaged and which Jukes had assured himself were desirable. Neither of the two groups had hitherto played a direct part in Federation policy-making.

On the one hand were the vice-presidents, the heads of the great industrial groups. Perhaps prima donnas does not exactly sum them up, but they were men accustomed to go their own way, to give orders and see them obeyed – men not easily harnessed to a collective viewpoint. Many of them would not be familiar with the intricacies of industrial relations, but for the most part they were men of alert mind, receptive to new ideas, hard to convince but, once convinced, decisive in their reactions. These men had the power to order or recommend their companies in associations all over the country to vote for or against any proposal, and some, though not all, were accustomed to do so. The two giants of the Federation, the General Electric Company and British Leyland, have between them 18 per cent of the votes. The twelve biggest engineering groups have 43 per cent of the votes. On some of the most important issues, each of the very biggest groups could, for practical purposes, exercise a power of veto.

On the other hand there were the chief officials of the associations, deeply versed in the lore of negotiation and procedure, inheritors of generations-old traditions, some imprisoned within those traditions but some already breaking away from them. The group had been by deliberate intent excluded from the Federation's policy-making bodies. It has been mentioned that Barraclough and Grant were members of the Board in the 1950s by virtue of the fact that they were chairmen of their regional committees. But when they went, the rules were changed to prevent that happening again. Their successors may attend the meetings but neither speak or vote. The Federation was still anxious, as Dr Campbell put it in 1933, to avoid the fate of Carthage by relying on a professional army. Nevertheless these directors (or chairmen or secretaries) had great influence in their associations and new policies could not be operated effectively without their co-operation.

Jukes' plan was to bring these two groups – and other important groups – into the formation of policy before it reached the Board, not after the Board had arrived at its recommendations. In doing so he achieved a highly-developed system of sectional participation.

The Federation, the basic structure of which had changed little since Allan Smith established it in 1924, was already a highly democratic organisation in which the associations had a great deal of autonomy and the membership was normally consulted by means of a referendum on any important decision. The association meetings at which votes were cast were commonly attended by 80 or 90 per cent of the member companies, who were helped to make up their minds by an explanation from their various presidents of the way the Board was thinking.

Nevertheless the need to give a simple 'yes' or 'no' to a few questions tended to polarise opinion and frequently made it hard to get a clear mandate. The Board did not usually proceed with a proposal if there was a substantial minority against it. It would be particularly difficult by a referendum to get a useful indication of the attitude of members on the complex plans now beginning to emerge from Broadway House, such as proposals for a package deal or for a staff charter or for the reform of the Federation or for basic changes in the Procedure. But if every significant section of the organisation had already thrashed a question out, the Federation could be well on the way to a consensus before the members voted.

There had been some progress in this direction before Jukes took over. The policy committee set up during the war, to enable more thorough discussion of important issues than is possible on the much larger Board, had been retained and met regularly every month eight days before the Board, taking no decisions but usefully clarifying issues. From Kenneth Allen's time it had been the custom for the office-bearers to meet over dinner on the evening before the policy committee meeting. There was also the President's Advisory Committee, consisting of ex-presidents and one or two others, who were called together as required to bring their experience to bear on particularly knotty problems. Occasionally the vice-presidents were consulted and there were infrequent meetings of association directors for specific purposes.

Jukes, with the able backing of Gordon Baker, who became president on the same day that Jukes was confirmed in office, built on these beginnings. The maximum number of vice-presidents was increased from ten to twenty to make sure that all the major groups could be included. They were consulted at an earlier stage in policy-making and more frequently.

The association directors were dealt with more formally. A month after he assumed office, Jukes had a week-end conference with them to consider the future of the Federation. What were they there for? Where were they going? He had prepared a discussion paper outlining possible developments, most of which were afterwards accepted and brought into operation. After this the directors of the large associations, who had hitherto come together irregularly, became the Director-General's Advisory Committee, meeting monthly on the day before the policy committee meeting, so that Jukes would have first-hand information about their views to put before the policy committee and Board. Jukes also set up a Chief Personnel Executives' Consultative Group, consisting of the chief labour relations men from about thirty of the biggest companies. This meets every two months and provides a technically better informed if less decisive indication of the attitudes of the big groups than can be obtained from the vice-presidents. Then he established a long-range planning committee, composed of the senior members of his own staff. This brings yet another group, the leading men at Broadway House into the collective framing of policy. They found before long that the things they were discussing were not all so very long-range so they now call themselves simply the Planning Committee.

With this network established, proposals for important new policy developments are likely to be discussed by top industrialists, by leading association directors, by personnel officers of the biggest companies, by influential regional representatives (on the Board) and by senior staff at Broadway House before they go to the members for decision.

But an extension of the Federation's services depended not only on ability to secure understanding and acceptance of the proposed changes but also on ability to put them into effect. That meant a restructuring of the associations and of Broadway House staff, and the promotion and recruitment of men with forward-looking minds.

There were thirty-nine associations when Jukes took over, nine fewer than in 1945, mainly because six in Yorkshire had merged in the West Riding association in 1960. But many of those left were far too small to provide the extended services envisaged. Often they had part-time secretaries – local solicitors or chartered accountants or the secretary of some neighbouring larger association. Jukes drew up a plan to reduce the number of associations to about twelve, a plan for which he secured the support of all sections of the Federation. But theoretical support for amalgamations is a very different matter from carrying them through in spite of vested interests and local and personal rivalries and pride. There were some small early successes but it was several years before continual effort and persuasion really bore fruit.

Events in Lancashire and Cheshire illustrate the difficulties. This was the area with greatest scope for rationalisation. There were thirteen associations there, six with part-time secretaries. As a consequence they had probably the most active regional organisation in the country – some regional committees do practically nothing but elect their officials and appoint reresentatives to the Federation Board. In 1966 the Chester part-time secretary retired and the association joined up with Manchester. Then Cammell Laird at Birkenhead decided to go over entirely to shipbuilding conditions and what was left of the Birkenhead association merged with Liverpool. The remaining eleven set up a working party which had meetings lasting over two years, trying out various possibilities and finding none of them easy.

In the end Liverpool and St Helens, followed by Oldham, decided to go in with Manchester, to form the South Lancashire,

Cheshire and North Wales Association, later joined by Blackburn and Burnley, who had shared a solicitor secretary. Barrow might have come in but were told they could more conveniently merge with the North-east coast, which they did not do. Preston, Wigan and Rochdale remained independent. The sum result was that thirteen associations were reduced to five, but there emerged a sort of Pakistan situation, with Wigan and Rochdale separating Blackburn and Burnley from the rest of the South Lancashire association.

Other main developments were the merging of Leicester, Lincoln and Nottingham, later joined by Derby, to form the East Midlands Association and of Bedfordshire, Cambridge and Peterborough to form the Mid-Anglian Association. Hull joined the West Riding in 1966 and Halifax joined it in 1971, when North Staffs joined the West Midlands. In five years the thirty-nine had been reduced to twenty-two. The big new associations have to pay a lot of attention to their internal organisation to maintain contacts with widely dispersed members. Some have set up district committees, as the widespreading London association had done many years before.

At Broadway House, consultants were called in to advise on the staff structure. After they reported in 1968, the structure was reshaped to clarify the obscure division of responsibilities. The changes included the creation of a separate industrial relations department under a director who was freed from the administrative duties with which he had previously been encumbered to concentrate on national negotiations and procedural conferences, the handling of industrial disputes at Federation level and the tendering of any advice and assistance required on industrial relations problems. The report also reinforced Jukes' intention to develop the planning, research and advisory functions of the Federation.

To implement the new policies and methods, new men were needed. The low level of salaries and restricted outlook in Macarty's time had not encouraged the emergence of able men with forward-looking attitudes, but one or two had begun to appear. There was Alan Swinden, a young man from Rolls-Royce who joined the Federation in 1955 and had been deputy director since 1956. It was commonly assumed that he was being groomed for the succession. He resigned in June 1965, to become director of the Engineering Industry Training Board but during his ten years with the Federation he had influenced it towards less restrictive and inward-looking attitudes.

Another and major figure was Pat Lowry, a grammar school boy from Leicester who had joined the Federation staff in 1938 at the age of 18. After seven years war absence, he returned to the statistical department and took a degree at the London School of Economics in his spare time. He became secretary in 1964, in succession to Ernest Happold, and director in December 1965, with overall responsibility for industrial relations. In that capacity he established a national reputation but he left in 1970 to become first director of industrial relations in the British Leyland Motor Corporation.

By then new men were beginning to make their mark. One was a keen-witted, resourceful and self-confident young man named Michael Bett. Bett was the first of a new breed of Federation officials, coming to the staff direct from the university in 1958 and after three years under Lowry going to Manchester for five years, familiarising himself with works conference and local conference work as assistant and then deputy director. He returned to Broadway House in 1966. When Lowry left, Bett became his successor but in 1972 he accepted the position as Director of Personnel for the General Electric Company. Thus the two giants of the Federation both have chief labour relations men drawn from Broadway House.

Several other young university men have since started a similar career pattern but have often been snapped up by private firms on their way up the ladder. While there is no systematic training scheme, a good deal is done in an *ad hoc* way. They are all given several weeks with associations to get to know the job at local level. Some are given time off to attend courses at association training centres or elsewhere or to sit the exams of the Institute of Personnel Management. One was released to take a higher degree at London University. Members of the staff often go to one-day or two-day management conferences and since the Federation got a computer many have attended computer courses of one kind or another. After two or three years the young men are encouraged to get a job with an association, where they can be toughened by direct contact with member firms and union officials and are more likely to be given responsibility early.

Whether they do so or not depends on their own initiative and the chance of a vacancy occurring at the right time.

There is a good deal of staff movement between the Federation and some of the associations. Baker, when he was president, wanted to have a more formal career structure but not all associations are enthusiastic. London, for instance, differs from the Federation in believing that industrial relations staff should all have industrial experience, and brings in men of from 35 to 45 from the line management of member firms.

A step taken during Fielding's presidency was to make it easier for big men in the industry, preoccupied with their far-flung empires, to accept at the same time the burdens of Federation office. The period of office was reduced from three years to two in Percy Mills' time, but that still meant a stint of six years – two as second deputy president, two as first deputy president and two as president. In 1969 it was decided that there should be only one deputy president (in addition to the chairman of the finance committee) so that the office-bearing period was reduced to four years, with the immediate past president available for consultation.

Having sketched the reshaping of the Federation, it is time to come to the new policies and services for which it was designed. To outsiders the most obvious development was a change in the Federation's attitude to publicity. It had shut itself away in Ramsay's time. Allan Smith joined in public controversies through Federation pamphlets and speeches, but Ramsay gave up even an annual report to members. The feeling seems to have been that the public regarded employers as hard-faced men who kept the workers in subjection, so that the less attention they drew to themselves the better. They were slow to realise, in the post-war era of inflationary wage claims and unofficial strikes, that the public attitude was changing.

In 1950 there appeared the first annual report since 1933 but it was treated as a highly confidential document. Members kept pressing for more to be done to counter trade union propaganda, but for some years with little result. Even the rare press hand-outs were delivered in envelopes marked 'private and confidential'.

At last, in 1953, a publicity officer was appointed. Increased unobtrusive use was also made of Aims of Industry and the Economic League. It was not until Jukes took over, however, that publicity was allowed to develop freely. A publications editor was appointed in 1969. The annual report acquired a glossy look and ceased to be private and confidential. Since September that year there has been a monthly bulletin, *EEF News*. And in 1970 a history of the Federation was commissioned.

Health and safety was another field in which the Federation expanded its services. A safety committee had been set up in 1962, and published one or two booklets, but had not been very active. In 1966, with the toll of industrial accidents getting worse, a full-time Federation safety adviser was appointed and the following year a new health and safety committee with Kenneth Allen as chairman. Associations began to set up safety committees of managers. It was agreed to build up an advisory service for member firms and associations were urged to appoint safety advisers but by 1971 only three had made full-time appointments. In October 1971, the Federation launched a major campaign aimed at reducing injuries in member companies by 25 per cent in two years. Targets were set for individual companies based on accident statistics.

The research department, which Macarty had resisted so long, was established in June 1967, 'to provide the office-bearers and directorate with more and better information on which to make decisions on matters on which they are immediately involved, but also to make a contribution to the extension of knowledge in the industrial relations field.' Macarty must have shuddered if he saw the last phrase. The man brought in to run it, Edward J. Robertson, built up a team of research workers which in 1971 numbered seven, including three economists. He also took over responsibility for the statistical department and for the computer, when the Federation bought one in 1969 to widen the factual base of its work.

The first of a series of research papers, by Robertson himself, was on 'Productivity Bargaining and the Engineering Industry', and marked a turning point in the Federation's attitude towards this form of bargaining. The vogue for productivity bargaining, which began with the Esso agreements at their Fawley oil refinery in 1960, had at first spread slowly but the pace quickened as a result of the significance given to it in the Labour Government's prices and incomes policy from 1965 onwards.

The Federation were suspicious of the concept but, after a

Prices and Incomes Board report in 1967, asked Robertson to prepare a document dealing with its possible dangers and problems as well as its benefits. In the same period they were extremely critical of the CBI/ TUC 'productivity initiative' which they complained had been concluded without any detailed consultation with the Federation – something they always advocated when the CBI entered the industrial relations field. They warned members that the document did not give a general licence to workers to claim increased wages in respect of every concession they made towards an improved use of productive resources.

However, when Robertson's report came down firmly in favour of genuine productivity bargaining, not so much because of its contribution to incomes policy as because it represented a movement towards joint responsibility for the effort-wage bargain, the Board strongly approved it and, as will be seen, productivity bargaining had an important place in the second package deal.

Robertson was also active in the development of WEM (Western European Metal Trades Employers' Organisation), which started in Kenneth Allen's time when he invited representatives of the engineering employers' organisations from thirteen countries to a meeting in London. At first a liaison committee arranged occasional meetings of presidents and directors, but in recent years it has become a working organisation with a technical committee meeting three or four times a year. This committee has prepared reports on progress in the various countries towards staff status for manual workers, on manual worker representation at plant level negotiations and on workers' representation on the boards of companies. It runs a statistical exchange covering rates, earnings, conditions and employer benefits in the WEM countries. Relations have been established with ORGALIME, representing European trade associations, and Martin Jukes is chairman of a committee preparing for a link-up of the two bodies. The contacts made at these meetings were expected to be useful when Britain joins the Common Market.

Far the most significant and courageous of Jukes' innovations was the creation in 1969 of the Federation Advisory Services – courageous because it ran counter to many members' conception of what the Federation was for. It was something quite different from the traditional fire-fighting and horse-trading roles. The research department was regarded as a bit of nonsense by some of the hard-headed men in the associations who prided themselves on their practical common sense, but it did not impinge on them except when it sent them new forms to fill in. So they looked upon it tolerantly. If Martin Jukes wanted something to play with in his ivory tower in Tothill Street, let him have it. Perhaps it would impress the Government.

The advisory service was something different. As they understood it, the Federation was going to enter their territory and tell their members how to manage their businesses. That, they considered, was definitely not the Federation's job. If companies needed advice, going beyond what the associations had always been ready to give them, they could call in consultants..

Jukes conceded nothing to this point of view. With the rather hesitant backing of his office-bearers, he not only established his new department but emphasised its importance by bringing a man from outside to take charge and making him one of the Federation's two directors, responsible only to him. The man appointed was an industrial consultant, E. de B. Marsh, with all the fluency and tact which a good consultant needs to overcome inbred habits and prejudices. He found in his first six months, during which he spent a lot of time with the associations explaining what he hoped to do, that those qualities were much needed. When he had got his team together, he took great care to do nothing except through or with an association. Some of them welcomed the service from the beginning and he gradually wore down the suspicions of some others.

The purpose of the service is 'to offer guidance, help and assistance in the general field of manpower utilization to enable managements to bring about improvements in company effectiveness, provide potential for higher earnings and improve industrial relations'. For the first time in its history the Federation was prepared to devote a substantial part of its resources to prevention rather than cure. Marsh was helped to get a good start by the fact that he began his work for the Federation just after the 1968 package deal. The package was designed to stimulate productivity bargaining, of which many managements had little knowledge.

The demand for the service steadily increased and by the

end of three years over 150 small and middle-sized firms had been helped to embark on action programmes, apart from many others who had been assisted in a minor way. Some of the larger associations have appointed their own advisers to co-operate with those of the Federation and it is hoped that eventually all will do so.

The establishment of the advisory service was complementary to the extension of association management training centres which the Federation encouraged by the promise of initial financial support. The West of England association were pioneers in this, far back in the beginning of 1953, when they started their own training department. They concentrated first on courses for work study engineers and senior management, but before long added others for foremen and shop stewards and extended their field to cover production planning and control, interviewing and selection methods, job evaluation, organisation and methods, and ergonomics. West country firms were given priority but before long students were going in from engineering firms in other parts of the country and from developed and developing countries abroad. Using the centre as the base, an advisory service was built up to give help to member firms.

In 1967 the West of England organised an appreciation course for officials and chairmen of federated associations and after that new training centres were established by Coventry at Leamington Spa, by the North-west region at Buxton, by the West Midlands at Malvern and, in 1971, by the West Riding, Sheffield and North-east Coast associations jointly at Leeds. Training courses were also sponsored by other associations, for instance by the East Midlands, by South Wales and by the Scottish association at Strathclyde University.

The expansion of Federation services meant a growth in the staff at Broadway House from 60 to 100 in five years, with most of the addition in the advisory and research departments, where high-salaried men were required. The headquarters began to strain at the seams and spread into an annex round the corner. With members of committees constantly coming and going, and a multiplication of documents, Broadway House fermented with activity as never before. The salary bill went up from £142,000 to £235,000 a year and the expenses of members coming in on Federation business reached between £60,000 and £70,000.

While the Federation was being gradually reshaped, the first package deal came to an end. Prolonged negotiations for a second such deal concluded, in October 1968, in one of the most dramatic weeks in the Federation's history, when a national strike was avoided by what seemed at the time almost a miracle.

Circumstances had changed a lot since the first package agreement. The Labour government which came into power in the autumn of 1964 had responded to the challenge of inflation and balance of payment difficulties by a greater degree of intervention in the industrial negotiating process than the country had known in peace-time. A voluntary prices and incomes policy was accepted unenthusiastically by all parties and in 1965 a National Board for Prices and Incomes was set up to investigate claims or settlements referred to it by the Government. These measures proved inadequate and in July 1966, the Government imposed a six-months' standstill on all income and price increases to be followed by a further six months of severe restraint. After July 1967, government policy provided for a nil norm for wage increases with certain exceptions which included workers making a direct contribution to increased productivity and those whose pay was too low to maintain a reasonable standard of living. As it happened, the only impact of the incomes policy on the implementation of the 1964 package was that general increases planned for March 1967, had to be deferred for four months. But in the summer of that year the Government referred the package to the Prices and Incomes Board and made it clear that they expected the parties to wait for the PIB report before coming to any conclusions about their next agreement. In November 1967, the £ was devalued.

This was the national background when the 1964 package reached its final stage on 1 January 1968. But there had been another change of perhaps more long-term importance for the Federation. Lord Carron retired from the presidency of the AEU in November 1967, and a militant left-winger, Hugh Scanlon, defeated the more right-wing John Boyd in the ballot for his successor. Scanlon had developed his talent for leadership in the hard school of Trafford Park. A smallish, wiry man, he was a brilliant negotiator with an exceptionally agile mind. He was also an ex-communist, a fervent opponent of any form of incomes policy, an apostle of workers' control in industry and, though he could be companionable in his personal relationships, he showed a hard hostility to employers as employers which created an atmosphere very different from that of Carron's day.

On the Federation side, James Fielding, from a Gloucester firm making hydraulic presses, succeeded Gordon Baker as president in February 1968, before the main negotiations began. A big, tough, determined man, who had for many years been active in the West of England association, he was well able to stand up to Scanlon whom he described to reporters in a moment of irritation as 'a provocative chap to deal with'.

Both sides were moderately pleased with the results of the 1964 package and by the summer of 1967 were preparing for a new one. On 31 October, the unions formally submitted their claim, an extremely comprehensive one which was later narrowed down to four basic demands – a general increase, an initial skilled time rate of £15 a week rising to £20, a third week's holiday and equal pay for women. Before replying, the Federation awaited the report of the PIB which when it came was critical of the results of the 1964 package and recommended a one-year agreement with no general increase but substantial increases in the minimum time rates and specific guide lines on productivity.

The point about guide lines on productivity was reinforced by the Donovan Commission's report in May. The Federation accepted both that and the proposal that there should be no more general increases, but they rejected the idea of a one-year agreement. 'We had broken away from the annual round of wage bargaining in which all long-term considerations were sacrificed to the necessity of arriving at an agreement for the short term and we were not prepared to encourage a return to that situation,' said Fielding afterwards.

A series of conferences in March and April left the two sides wide apart and the unions called a one-day strike on 15 May, a warning shot across the bows which, as on previous occasions, had no apparent effect on the situation. There followed informal talks, during which the Federation offered small general increases, while the unions were making demands which would substantially increases costs but said nothing about productivity clauses. Agreement seemed little nearer and the CSEU called a national strike for 21 October. The associations were consulted and gave solid support for the stand taken by the Federation negotiators.

On Monday 14 October, the Minister, Mrs Barbara Castle, called the two sides to the Department of Employment and Productivity and there followed a solid week of negotiations, often lasting late into the night, which occupied altogether 88 hours. The Federation were determined not to improve their offer any further unless they got specific concessions on productivity, a determination endorsed at a meeting of the vice-presidents on the Tuesday night and of the Board the following day. In an attempt to break the deadlock, the Federation then offered a £19 skilled minimum at the end of three years if their conditions were accepted.

Agreement seemed close when there was a sudden flare-up over women's pay. They were to receive slightly smaller general increases than labourers and their minimum rates, in the end, were to be £13 a week – £2 a week below those of labourers. Marion Veitch, of the General and Municipal Workers, accused the union leaders of selling the women down the river. Somewhat shamefacedly, the unions decided to stand out for £14 for the women. The Federation negotiators were firm against this because it would not have been acceptable to those members, particularly in electrical engineering, who employed a large proportion of women. The women in any case stood to gain most from the proposed settlement because far more women than men were employed at or near the existing minimum rates.

Barbara Castle called in the two sides and upbraided them for leaving women's pay until the very end, suggesting that the offer to women should be increased at the expense of those to the men. The suggestion was not well received and negotiations again broke down. A strike now seemed inevitable, but to everybody's surprise the AEU national committee overruled Scanlon and their executive and voted against this. So the strike was called off at the last minute but there was still no agreement and it was not until 10 December that the unions accepted the terms on condition that a joint working party would consider national job grading with special reference to women.

The agreement provided for two small general increases – 6s. each for skilled workers, for raising the skilled men's minimum time rate by stages to £19 and for three additional holidays, so

that by 1970 manual workers would have three weeks' holiday in
addition to the six statutory days. In return the unions promised
to accept such techniques as method study, work measurement
and job evaluation and to co-operate in eliminating such impedi-
ments to labour efficiency as the uneconomic manning of
machines, lack of flexibility in the use of labour and resistance to
shift working.

Improvements in pay and conditions at domestic level were
allowable 'provided that there is a measured increase in labour
productivity or efficiency to which the efforts of the workers
concerned have contributed'. The only exceptions to these
requirements were where a comprehensive new wage structure
was introduced or where wages of an individual or group of individuals were found to be out of line with prevailing wage patterns
in the establishment concerned.

The package was a marked advance on that of 1964 because
the productivity clauses were specific. If it had been fully
observed it would have proved the most valuable agreement in
the Federation's history. But it was not fully observed.

During 1969 it went reasonably well, but in 1970 there was a
national wages explosion, accompanied by a national strikes
explosion. The Labour government, preparing for the run-up to
the general election, abandoned any attempt to restrain it. The
unions seized the opportunity to try to make up for the years of
incomes policy restriction and the drop in real wages which
inevitably resulted from devaluation. Engineering workers, tied
to the package deal but seeing prices soaring and big increases
being negotiated all around them, broke loose at local level.
Some wanted to reopen the agreement but Scanlon insisted
that they keep their national bargain. The second package,
unlike the first, contained no safeguard against a steep rise in
prices.

Local claims multiplied, many ignoring the agreement's productivity clauses, and were often accompanied by immediate
threat of industrial action. The number of strikes reached record
levels, although in many cases employers offered little resistance.
The February board meeting considered a letter from the West
Midlands Association complaining that the agreement was being
flouted and urging that they should take the matter up with
CSEU and the Department of Employment and Productivity.

Not all associations were equally affected but South Lancashire said they were experiencing the same thing and a West of England spokesman said the situation was deteriorating at an alarming rate. Unions in some firms were said to be refusing to consider productivity bargains because in others increases had been conceded without conditions.

The Federation asked the CSEU for a meeting but Scanlon declined on the grounds that the Federation had refused to discuss claims for changes in the guaranteed week and qualifying conditions for statutory holidays, arguing that they were ruled out by the agreement. The March board meeting was indignant. There was talk of united action. Denby Bamford, the new president, said he would consult the chief executives of the major companies who would have to implement a policy of firmness. The major institutional investors would also be told the facts of the situation in the hope that they would support managements in any confrontation with the unions. It was decided to introduce an 'early warning' system under which firms would inform their associations as soon as they received an unconstitutional claim. They could then be helped to work out a counter-offer with productivity clauses, or local union officials could be asked to stop it.

However, Bamford and Jukes had an informal meeting with Scanlon, after which it was agreed that associations should arrange meetings on the subject with confederation district committees. Scanlon, it was reported, took the view that unions were entitled to bend the agreement as far as possible short of unconstitutional action. If firms conceded the claims, it was their own fault. Several associations reported that they had found local meetings useful and that the unions assured them they continued to recognise the sanctity of agreements. Whether or not the meetings had anything to do with it, the flood of strikes began to subside in June.

The Federation also tried to impress upon the Government the dangers of the situation and this led to a research document, 'Current Economic Problems in the Engineering Industry', for which a new Advisory Group, with economic advisers from a number of big companies as members, was responsible. Initially they intended to present it to Roy Jenkins, Labour Chancellor of the Exchequer, to emphasise the disastrous effect of his policy, but when the time came Anthony Barber was in his place and they found themselves talking to the converted.

The document was based on a survey of the industry which showed that earnings were going up at an annual rate of between 11 and 14 per cent, that productivity was going up at a little over $3\frac{1}{2}$ per cent, that unit costs were rising at a rate of $8\frac{1}{2}$ per cent, that profit margins were being squeezed and that most firms were not planning to increase their capital expenditure. Bamford and a strong delegation, including several vice-presidents, asked that the Government should press ahead with their industrial relations legislation, take a firm stand on wages in the sectors they controlled, leave firms free to raise prices in order not to further reduce cash flows and investment, ease credit pressures on the banks as applied to manufacturing industry, and recognise in their fiscal policies that adequate profitability was the prerequisite of investment for the future – much of this well outside the Federation's habitual industrial relations field.

This was the first occasion, at least in recent times, on which the Federation had tackled the Chancellor, and after this an economic statement became an annual affair. The Federation felt there was a need to discuss directly with the Government the problems of Britain's biggest industry, rather than leave the representation of the employers' point of view entirely to the CBI, which because of its comprehensiveness had to compromise between the various shades of opinion among employers in many different industries. With the establishment of the research department and the economic advisory group, the Federation was well equipped to present effectively its own clear-cut case. It afterwards made direct representations to other government ministries, in addition to the Department of Employment, such as that of Health and Social Security.

The Federation's economic initiatives inevitably cut across the field of the trade associations to some extent. In doing so they were filling a vacuum. There are some seventy trade associations in the engineering industry, but none able to speak for the industry as a whole. Generally the Federation and the associations kept meticulously to their own fields. They had an overlapping interest in training and in 1970 the Federation initiated a series of meetings with representatives of some twenty or thirty of the associations, at which it was agreed that there should be exchanges of statistics and information. The CBI has endeavoured to bring about mergers between industrial trade associations and employers' organisations, but this has not been regarded as practical in engineering in which so many associations represent so many different interests.

The reminder to the Chancellor about industrial relations legislation followed consistent Federation pressure for a new legal framework from the time the Donovan commission was set up in 1965. In their evidence to the commission, the Federation advocated that procedural agreements – but not substantive agreements – should be made enforceable. This went further than the initial proposals of the CBI, who found a lot of difficulties in the way of legal enforceability, but the CBI later came into line. The Federation also wanted an independent tribunal to deal with restrictive labour practices, but the commission rejected their suggestions. The Federation thought the Labour Party's first proposals in the White Paper, *In Place of Strife*, took a small step towards bringing the rule of law into industrial affairs and strongly criticised the Government for dropping what became known as the 'penal clauses' under TUC pressure.

They generally welcomed the Conservative Government's Industrial Relations Bill but were disturbed because it did not make any provision for an industry-wide disputes procedure to be imposed and made enforceable against the will of either party, though this could be done with company procedures in some circumstances. When they first saw Robert Carr's discussion paper they thought it must be a mistake, and when they found it was deliberate they exerted pressure by every means open to them to get Carr to change his mind, but without success. This soon proved to be important.

The engineering Procedure was coming under outside criticism at this time, among others by the Donovan Commission and the Prices and Incomes Board, and newspapers kept referring to it as 'long-winded' or 'outmoded' or 'discredited'. The unions always complained that it was unfair and antiquated and had been imposed on them by force after the 1922 lock-out and ought to lay down that the *status quo* must be observed while any disputed employer's decision was going through the Procedure. But persistent efforts to get it changed from the 1930s onwards resulted only in minor modifications in 1955 after three years of negotiation. The Board had regularly insisted that they could not entertain any proposal which 'derogated from the right of managements to manage their establishments'.

Towards the end of 1965, the CSEU were again proposing amendments and as Donovan was expected to say something on the subject, the Board set up a committee with Gordon Baker as chairman and there was a joint working party. The unions argued that unconstitutional strikes were due to the workers having lost faith in the Procedure but while strikes in breach of it were growing in number the use of the Procedure was also increasing. Between 1955 and 1965 the annual number of manual works conferences had risen from about 1,500 to more than 4000 and the number of central conference cases from 113 to 435. In fact the numbers were still increasing and went on doing so until in the peak year of 1970 there were more than 5000 works conferences and 647 central conference cases.

Long gone were the leisurely pre-war days when in most months there were only six or a dozen cases and only one court was needed. The employers then would finish their eve-of-confererence meeting in the Royal Station Hotel at York before 10 o'clock on the Thursday and settle down to a game of bridge or join the trade unionists for a session in the lounge which might go on into the early hours. The court would sit at 10 a.m. on the Friday and adjourn for a couple of hours for lunch to help the unionists spin out the time (their expenses were on a half-day basis).

Now the employers' committee meeting seldom finished before midnight and the following day several courts would sit simultaneously to get through the crowded case-list. At the last central conference of all, in December 1971, the record of nine courts on one day was equalled. Nevertheless the old amicable atmosphere remained – an atmosphere which has never existed in the white collar central conferences at Broadway House. It was partly due to the personalities of some of the post-war chairmen of the employers' conference committee.

There was John Green, from a Sheffield special steel firm, a huge Falstaff of a man, over six feet high and weighing 23 stone, a lover of good food and good drink, who used to progress through the hotel lounge like a battleship and got on splendidly with the union leaders. But he joined the Labour Government's nationalised steel corporation in 1950 and was never again mentioned in Federation circles.

A few years later there was C. S. Oliver, from a small Coventry firm, a deliberately unassertive but skilful operator who got the reputation of having started a new policy of conciliation and compromise, though it was Green who began it. Some members thought Chris Oliver compromised too much. But Arthur Main, who followed him, was perhaps the most respected chairman of them all, known to be firm but fair with unions and employers alike.

Many of the union leaders believed at heart in York and the Procedure as a means of settling disputes, though they seldom said so in public. Occasionally they did. 'If only workers will have faith in the Procedure and let it work properly, justice nearly always can be obtained without the sacrifice and loss of earnings and output involved in strikes,' said an article in the AEU journal in 1965. Even though it worked in practice, the form of the Procedure, which has been described as 'employer conciliation', with union representatives appearing before an employers' court, was open to criticism.

Baker's committee produced some not very radical proposals to speed up the Procedure and improve the shop steward arrangements. These were formally submitted to the unions in 1967 but the unions ignored them. Jukes and Lowry were not satisfied. They believed the time had come when basic improvements were possible and were conscious that criticisms of the Procedure, however unjustified, were damaging to the Federation's new image. in February 1969, Lowry put to the Board proposals which would have meant completely recasting the Procedure.

It was the first time proposals by the staff for major changes had been presented to the Board without any committee of employers being set up first and without reference to the associations. But the now accepted practice of consulting the vice-presidents, the director-general's advisory committee and so on was carried out, so that while the proposals may have surprised some members of the Board, most were aware of what was coming. The proposals went far beyond anything that had been offered to the unions before. The Procedure was to end at local conference stage, except for questions arising over the interpretation or application of national agreements, a national industrial relations council was to be set up for the industry, and the final stage of the domestic procedure was to be a joint works committee, through which all individual, sectional or factory claims would have to pass before reference to the external stage. Thus the national joint council, which the Federation had so often rejected, was conceded and the channelling of domestic claims through works committees would go some way to meet the criticism, by Donovan and others, that the Procedure encouraged the fragmentation of bargaining. Ending the Procedure at local conference would in many cases mean speedier decisions.

Negotiations went on for two-and-a-half years, partly because of delay in 1970 while the unions waited to see what the Industrial Relations Bill was going to be like. Now that it was offered to them, the unions were divided among themselves as to whether they wanted a national council, or works committees through which all disputed domestic claims would have to be passed, mainly because both would give the amalgamated engineers a dominant position. But the main issue was once again the *Status Quo*.

At one point in June 1970, a revised Federation formula was believed to have resolved it. Both sides accepted that a management decision within the framework of an existing agreement or established practice could be implemented without going through the Procedure, and that where a decision meant departing from an agreement or practice the employer must get agreement or go through the Procedure before implementation. But after the Conservative victory in the general election the same month, and during the run-up to the Industrial Relations Act, Scanlon's line hardened. First he reopened the argument by suggesting that an employer should also have to get agreement or go through the Procedure where a proposed new condition was not covered by any agreement or practice – a 'green fields' situation, as it came to be called The Federation declined to accept this, though they conceded there should be prior consultation where possible.

After an interval of some months, during which there was much discussion about a union demand that any agreement should not be legally enforceable, the unions went back to their original proposed wording of October 1969.

It is accepted by the trade unions that management have the

right to manage and to expect all normal management decisions concerning the efficient operation of the establishment to be implemented by workers immediately, except that any decisions which alter the established wages, working conditions, practices, manning, dismissals (except for gross industrial misconduct) or redundancy to which the workpeople concerned object, shall not be implemented until the local conference procedure has been exhausted.

The employers said that such an all-inclusive list of exceptions would give a single workman – a single trouble-maker anywhere – the right to halt management decisions (even when they were acting in accordance with agreements) and impair their ability to run a factory efficiently. To keep the wheels turning, certain management decisions at shop floor level had to be implemented almost immediately. This view was endorsed by an almost 100 per cent vote of the membership. In September 1971, the unions gave three months' notice to end the Procedure agreement for manual workers.

Just before this, with the 1968 package running out, the unions had submitted an enormous claim for improvements in pay and conditions. It included a substantial general wage increase, £6 extra on the minimum rate for skilled workers, four weeks annual holiday and ten statutory holidays, a 35-hour working week, equal pay for women, and numerous other demands, all to operate from January 1972, the month after the last improvements under the 1968 package. Bamford told the union leaders that to concede it would add at least 40 per cent to labour costs, without allowing for the equal pay item, and would wipe out all profits for the majority of companies. He also pointed out that average earnings of manual workers had risen by 13 per cent between June 1970 and June 1971, almost entirely through plant bargaining. The Federation offered no general increase and only £1.50 on the craftsmen's minimum.

The union claim was so big as to give the impression that a breakdown was intended from the beginning. Certainly the Federation offer provided no basis for negotiation. Scanlon hinted informally in December that other claims were negotiable if a £25 minimum was accepted, but the Federation had no mandate to offer that amount. When told this, Scanlon abruptly broke off the talks. He was so angry that he cancelled a meeting at the Department of Employment where a last attempt was to have been made to save the Procedure. The CSEU decided to terminate all relations with the Federation at national and local level and to press their demands at the undertakings. They would not even meet the Federation to talk about safety or training.

'The prospect that confronts us is a round of costly claims backed by the threat of disruptive action,' said Bamford in his presidential address in February 1972. 'The unions will not find us unprepared to meet these pressures. If the unions are out to test the fibre of our unity, we should leave them in no doubt as to its durability.'

Thus at one blow, temporarily or permanently, national negotiations and the manual workers' Procedure were brought to an end. The unions set out to press their claims domestically and to negotiate company procedures. Many pages of history were turned back.*

The main principles of the Procedure had been in operation for nearly 74 years. During the whole period the grand total of central conference cases was 11,150. How many cases went to the earlier stages in former times is not known but in the 15 years from 1957 to 1971 there were 50,486 cases in works conferences, 12,268 in local conferences and 5490 in central conference. In the final decade the proportion of failures to agree at central conference varied from 37 to 51 per cent of central conference cases but only from 4 to 6 per cent of the cases that entered works conferences. Over the years, tens of thousands of stoppages must have been averted by the now discarded Procedure.

---

* National negotiations were revived, and an agreement reached, in August 1972, when it was also agreed that discussions about a new Procedure should be resumed.

CHAPTER II

White Collars and Others 1947–1971

Apprentice Revolts – Women and Equal Pay – Spider-
men – The Militant Draughtsmen – Guerrilla Counter-
attack – Recognition Rivals

In the first years after the Second World War, the Federation's
collective bargaining followed a rather simple pattern. Main
negotiations were concerned with the pay and conditions of adult
male manual workers. Settlements were accompanied by proportionate increases for juveniles. Then related settlements would be
made for other groups of workers – those with special skills like
patternmakers, women, special sections of manual workers like
those employed on outside construction sites, and staff workers.
At first, though they had gained ground during the war, they
were all comparatively weak and by and large had to take what
they were offered. But as the years passed these groups grew in
numbers and bargaining power until some of them, notably the
draughtsmen, could challenge the power of the employers. And
the Federation increasingly adjusted its policies to the special
needs of particular groups.

The apprentices rebelled twice. In the post-war years they
were paid on a scale rising from $22\frac{1}{2}$ per cent of the skilled fitter's
rate at 15 years of age to $62\frac{1}{2}$ per cent at 20, and repeated efforts
to get an increase in the percentages were rejected. Then in
both 1952 and 1960 unofficial strikes spread from Glasgow to
other parts of Britain in support of new claims. Both strikes were
followed by flat rate increases.

In 1961 the CSEU demanded negotiating rights for inden-
tured apprentices, who were excluded when such rights were
granted for other youths in 1937. There was determined opposition from the Midlands block of associations, including Birmingham and Coventry, which had been little affected by the 1960

strike. The Board thought it illogical to reject the claim and set themselves to persuade the opposition associations to change their minds. It took three years but in the end all the bigger associations except Coventry gave way and the claim was conceded. The unions promised never to call apprentices out on strike and the Federation said they would neither lock them out nor ask them to do the work of adult strikers.

The Federation and some of the associations had always paid a good deal of attention to apprentice training and this increased when the Engineering Industry Training Board got to work from 1965 onwards. The Federation itself and eight associations have training officers. The 1968 package deal provided for training to end at 20, with payment of the adult rate at that age, instead of 21.

The pay of women workers did not present any serious problem to the Federation until the late sixties. Negotiations were at first conducted by a group of five unions – the AEU, the two general workers' unions, the electricians and the foundry workers, but from 1959 the CSEU included women in their manual workers' claim. Applications were made for a grading scheme in the first post-war years and for a number of years after that the unions regularly asked for the male labourer's rate for women or at least that they should get increases equal to those of labourers. The claims were regularly rejected without untoward results and the women usually got 6d. or 1s. a week less than labourers.

In 1962, with equal pay becoming a more live issue, they got for the first time the same increases as labourers, in 1963 they got 6d. a week more and the 1964 package deal provided for the gap with the labourer's rate to be steadily reduced over the following three years. Negotiations for the second package deal, as was mentioned in the last chapter, almost broke down over women's pay.

Though the relative position of women had improved, the Equal Pay Act meant there would be a huge addition to the industry's wage and salary bills from the end of 1975. In 1971 about 215,000 females were employed by federated firms on manual work and 180,000 on clerical and other staff work (counting a part-time employee as half in each case). Firms employing a large proportion of women were faced with an increase in labour costs of anything up to 30 per cent. The Federation devised a pay structure for staff workers which would introduce a new national minimum rate without sex discrimination at a lower level than the existing men's minimum rate for those who performed a 'routine clerical function'. But by the end of 1971 they had not persuaded any union to accept the idea.

The special sections in which the Federation negotiated separate agreements from those of factory workers through national technical committees representative of interested firms, covered such employments as site construction and erection work, lift erection, patent glazing, installation of telephone exchange equipment, typewriter service and scale and weighing machine installation, a number of different unions being involved. While wage rates normally followed general engineering, there were often difficult negotiations on such matters as allowances for working at a height, radius (or travelling) allowances, lodging allowances, meal allowances and 'wet time' allowances for those prevented from working by bad weather. At first after the war there were numerous references to the National Arbitration Tribunal and later the Industrial Disputes Tribunal arising out of these negotiations but in time most claims came to be settled by negotiation. Occasionally the unions resorted to strikes. Lift erectors did so in London in 1951 and in Glasgow in 1968. But the most important dispute was the snowball strike by 'spidermen' in 1954–5.

This arose out of a claim by the Constructional Engineering Union for increases for men on outside erection work 'to bridge the gap between the qualified steelwork erector's rate and that of other craftsmen in the building industry'. The claim was rejected and on 25 October the union called a strike at eleven steelwork erection sites in the City of London and extended it to other sites in different parts of the country the following month. The Minister of Labour referred the dispute to the Industrial Disputes Tribunal, but the union refused to give evidence to the tribunal or to call off the strikes, even after the tribunal on 3 January 1955, had awarded in favour of the employers 'on the evidence before them'. The employers then replied with a ban on overtime and week-end work from 21 January to reduce maximum hours to 44 a week on outside sites. On this the union called out men on nine more sites, and continued to extend the strike in February. The men finally returned to work and the employers called off their

overtime ban on 21 March. The men were conceded an increase
of 1¾d. an hour.

The Board were disturbed because unofficial talks had taken
place while the Federation ban was in operation and set up a
committee of investigation which recommended that in future
informal negotiations should only be conducted by the Federation or with their full approval and that any committee handling
a dispute should include at least two representatives of the Board.
The strike was important because the way the union ignored the
tribunal added force to the employers' contention that the Industrial Disputes Order operated in a one-sided way. The tribunal
was abolished in 1959.

From the middle sixties onwards the special sections increasingly presented their own particular problems which could not be
resolved simply by following the pattern set in the factory
workers' negotiations. The Federation developed a new flexibility in order to deal with them. A special procedure agreement
was made for workers on outside erection in 1961 but unofficial
strikes on big sites, particularly power stations, were causing
concern. In 1967, the Federation decided to set up a Site Contractors' Policy Committee to co-ordinate the work of five
national technical committees dealing with various kinds of outside erection, but complications were caused by the formation of
a non-federated Oil and Chemical Plant Constructors' Association, representing a few large employers. Efforts were made to
integrate the two bodies but were hindered by the level of concessions made by the association. In 1969 the Federation began
to vary its policy on site negotiations from that adopted for factory workers and in 1972 succeeded in reaching a national agreement after the CSEU had broken off the general manual
workers' wage negotiations. In several of the special sections negotiations, which covered some 25,000 workers, now took place on
a basis peculiar to the workers involved.

Far and away the most serious problems for the Federation,
however, were created by the white collar unions. When the war
ended five staff unions had procedural agreements with the
Federation – the Association of Engineering and Shipbuilding
Draughtsmen (AESD) which in 1961 became the Draughtsmen's and Allied Technicians' Association (DATA) and in 1971
the Amalgamated Union of Engineering Workers – Technical

and Supervisory Section (AUEW–TASS); the Association of Supervisory Staffs, Executives and Technicians (ASSET) and the Association of Scientific Workers, which in 1968 merged to form the Association of Scientific, Technical and Managerial Staffs (ASTMS); and the two mainly clerical organisations, the Clerical and Administrative Workers' Union (CAWU), later the Association of Professional, Executive, Clerical and Computer Staff (APEX), and the National Association of Clerical and Supervisory Staffs, later the Association of Clerical, Technical and Supervisory Staffs, the clerical section of the Transport and General Workers' Union, afterwards joined by a third, the clerical section of the General and Municipal Workers' Union. (The numerous changes of name reflect the expanding and conflicting ambitions of the unions.)

The Federation engaged in national negotiations with all of them except ASSET, but instead of concluding formal agreements recommended their members to make the agreed concessions. Some member firms remained uncomfortable about having any national negotiations on staff pay, even though the Federation had been given authority to conduct such negotiations in 1945, and for a decade there were occasional grumbles about it.

This became associated to some extent with the opposition in the Midlands to general increases for anybody. In 1952, for instance, Coventry and some others complained about a general increase, urging that firms which had given merit or cost-of-living increases should be safeguarded. Basic staff salaries and conditions, they said, must always be the prerogative of individual managements.

The Federation were at pains to prevent any link between the staff and manual workers. For several years they resisted claims from staff unions to sit with manual union officials as representatives of the CSEU, which they were debarred by the procedure agreements from doing. 'Staff workers have always been treated on a different basis from manual unions,' the Board informed the CSEU in 1949. 'Joint discussions would disregard the entirely different basis on which the two sections are employed.' They also opposed staff representation on joint production committees though in 1949 they accepted that technical staff directly concerned with production might be permitted to elect a member –

so long as manual workers had no part in the voting – but continued to exclude clerical workers.

In 1954, after the draughtsmen had got an increase, the Board decided to offer it to the clerical workers too. The clerical workers had not been militant, Board members remarked, and only a small proportion were organised, and to treat them worse than the draughtsmen might encourage union membership.

ASSET made repeated attempts to get their procedure agreement revised to allow for national bargaining and were each time refused, though in 1957 they were allowed as 'an act of courtesy' to attend a conference with other staff unions on hours of work. ASSET were making some progress at that time and in 1958 contended that the Federation's position was no longer tenable, about 18,000 of their 21,000 members being employed in engineering. The Board arranged a survey which showed that, except in Birmingham, Coventry, Scotland and the West of England, ASSET membership was 'nil or insignificant'. They then replied that the union's membership was very low compared with the total and that it was unnecessary to accord negotiating rights to a union with only 20,000 members.

ASSET also kept pressing for the non-union rule of the Foremen and Staff Mutual Benefit Society (FSMBS) to be removed. The Federation always replied, as they were still doing when approached by the CSEU in 1960, that the FSMBS had its own constitution and it was in no way controlled by the Federation, though many engineering firms were members.

The Federation's problem was to devise a policy which would induce foremen to consider themselves members of the management team and to persuade federated firms to concede them working conditions which would not give rise to a sense of grievance so that, while at liberty to join a union, foremen would not be disposed to do so. After ASSET was recognised in 1944, the FSMBS several times asked for the right to raise issues collectively with associations or the Federation. The Board pointed out that their constitution did not empower them to deal with wages or working conditions, but revised their memorandum on the status of foremen and encouraged the formation of foremen's representative committees in works and periodic meetings with managements for general discussions. From time to time the Federation sent out circulars encouraging member firms to join

he society, and in 1958 warned members of 'encroachment' by
ASSET.

The draughtsmen in the fifties and other staff unions in the
sixties became a source of increasing trouble to the Federation.
Accurate figures cannot be come by, but the total membership
of staff unions in engineering must at least have quadrupled
between 1945 and 1970. Their expansion is partly a reflection of
growth in the number of white collar workers in the industry.
Figures for staff employed by member firms are not available
before 1954, but between then and 1971 the number of full-
timers rose from 413,500 to 705,700, an increase of 70 per cent,
while the number of manual workers showed comparatively little
change. At the time of writing there are more than half as many
staff as manual workers, whereas in 1954 there were less than
one third as many. The growing strength of the unions depended
not only on their rise in membership but also on the increased
concentration of white collar workers in large groups in big companies, on a changed attitude among such workers towards
union membership and, most of all, on full employment.
Draughtsmen were specially scarce from the end of the war until
about 1970.

The draughtsmen's union was a well-run, well-disciplined
organisation, based on office groups and thorough in its collection of information about pay and conditions in the offices where
its members worked. Its contributions were large enough to
enable it to give four-fifths of their pay to men called out on
strike. Because draughtsmen come mainly from shop-floor
apprentices, they inherit craft traditions more than most white
collar associations. George Doughty, an able and intelligent official, has been their general secretary since 1952. Under his leadership, the union so plagued the employers by the skilful
manipulation of national and domestic bargaining as for a time
to undermine their confidence in the Federation's ability to
handle the problem, but as it entered the seventies, with left-wing
extremists strongly entrenched on its executive, it seemed to
over-reach itself.

The draughtsmen's union maintained a nucleus of membership between the wars more successfully than the other white
collar unions and after the Second World War its rapid
expansion came earlier. Within five years its activities were

already causing anxiety. It had long been its aim, as it was of the scientific and clerical unions, to get agreement on 'wage-for-age' scales of pay providing for annual increments from the ages of 21 to 25. Finding the Federation would only concede a minimum at 21, usually raised by the same amount whenever craftsmen got an increase, the union fixed its own scale and instructed the members not to take less, after the manner of manual unions in the last century. Enticement was rife and many firms, federated and non-federated, paid the union scale because they could only get draughtsmen by doing so.

In 1951 the Derby association complained that the position was farcical and damaging to the prestige of the Federation. Some firms, they said, were even offering the union's rates in their advertisements. The association urged the Board to be more realistic and negotiate agreed scales for draughtsmen up to 25, and tracers up to 21. The Board were against this. The Federation had always taken the view that the proper way to deal with the salaries of staff employees was by periodic reviews on the basis of merit, having regard to ability displayed, degree of responsibility and value to the employer. It would be wrong, they thought, to give increases merely on the score of age. Automatic increases could have the result that firms would subsidise less useful individuals at the expense of the more able. Young employees might think they no longer needed to demonstrate their merit. So the Board continued to resist claims for wage-for-age scales even after the scientific workers, later in 1951, were awarded one by the Industrial Disputes Tribunal.

In 1954 the Shipbuilding Employers' Federation conceded graded increases ranging from about 8s. 6d. a week to 10s. 6d. at 25 and over, but the Federation would only offer the 8s. 6d. at 21 which had been given to skilled manual workers in that year's settlement. Instead of going to arbitration, the draughtsmen submitted domestic claims to individual firms, sometimes followed by threats of a strike or overtime ban. A special Board meeting in June was informed that 121 firms were affected. Twelve overtime bans were in operation and there had been a number of token strikes. Some firms had yielded and this was straining the loyalty of others. There was considerable irritation with the shipbuilding employers and demands for closer liaison between the two federations such as existed on manual workers' questions. But after much argument, the Board decided to concede the same increases as in shipbuilding. A referendum was taken on whether to offer a wage-for-age scale, but there was a majority against of 63.8 per cent to 27.7 per cent of the Federation's voting capacity.

Support for the negotiation of a scale tended to grow, however. In 1956 the London association, strongly opposed by Birmingham and others, put to the Board the case for a scale for draughtsmen. Training, they said, took place in two stages, first in the workshops and then, from 19 or 20 onwards, in the drawing office. Taking account of national service, a man had probably only two years' drawing office training when he was 23 and was seldom regarded as fully qualified before he was 25. A scale would avoid the dissatisfaction caused by irregular increases, would attract a good type of boy and encourage him to return after national service, and would regularise the existing position in many firms and eliminate the recruiting advantages of industries and non-federated firms which recognised a scale. The union had gained considerable prestige from its ability to enforce a unilateral scale.

The opinion of members was tested again but the majority were found to be still strongly against it. Not until 1965, following a shipbuilding court of inquiry and settlement, did the Federation make a wage-for-age scale agreement. By then the draughtsmen were pressing for a scale rising to 30 and the agreement included an increment at the age of 30 above the 25-year-old minimum.

In the meantime there had been a hardly less long-drawn-out struggle over a claim by the staff unions for three weeks' paid holidays. This was first presented in 1953, when the unions said it would help to restore the difference in status between white collar and manual workers, who had got a second week's paid holiday the previous year. The employers repeatedly rejected the claim, pointing out that the staff had been given 3s. a week more than manual workers because they had no increase in holidays. Social distinctions, they contended, were not so clearly defined as they had been and it was a matter of personal preference whether young people took clerical or manual jobs.

Again the draughtsmen embarked on a series of domestic claims. After some success with shipbuilders in Scotland, they brought such pressure on engineering employers there in 1956 that Scottish members were provoked to complain of Federation inaction. The draughtsmen followed successes in Scotland with successes in the North-east, and there were numerous strikes. The biggest, in which ASSET members joined, affected 3000 workers in a dozen De Havilland undertakings. After a reference to a committee of inquiry, the firm settled for three weeks for those with five years' adult service. The Federation in 1958 advised members that if they felt obliged to increase holidays, they should not concede more than that. The proportion of staff receiving only two weeks' holiday had fallen in two years from 74 to 54 per cent.

The Federation stuck to their policy but in 1961 an inquiry showed that 47.2 per cent of member firms employing 64 per cent of the staff wanted a national agreement. An offer was made in 1965, after the manual workers had been conceded extra days, but the draughtsmen were by then pressing domestic claims for four weeks.

All this time the Board had been trying to stop firms using the vacancy list which the draughtsmen's union issued regularly to its members. By such advertising, the Board said in 1953, employers were committing themselves to the union's wage-for-age scale. Similar advice was given in respect of the journals of other unions, such as that of the foremen.

In 1957 Kenneth Allen confessed that his firm had used the vacancy list 'because the livelihood of our employees is being jeopardised by a shortage of draughtsmen'. This shortage, he argued, had been seriously aggravated for federated firms by a policy which failed to face the facts and channelled the available draughtsmen into non-federated firms. Some other federated firms were using the list and most were paying the union's rates or more.

Independent contract drawing offices had sprung up all over the country and now employed thousands of men. These and non-federated firms, free to use the vacancy list, absorbed most of the recruits. So federated firms were starved of draughtsmen.

Macarty told Allen that his action gave his firm an advantage over federated firms not using the list. Allen replied that federated firms were being forced to use contract drawing offices but he promised his firm would not repeat the advertisements. The Federation arranged to see the vacancy list regularly and tell associations when any of their members were found to be advertising in it.

Contract drawing offices, providing drawings for firms on a contract basis, were another of the Federation's headaches. The Board's attention was first drawn to them in 1955, when the West of England association complained that they were growing in numbers and enticing draughtsmen away from federated employers. But it was said that some districts were worse hit than others and for the time being the Board contented themselves with advising associations to watch the position.

In 1961 the Board discussed the situation again and advised that: 'Employers should not make use of contract drawing offices which have been established by enticing draughtsmen already in employment and which offer the services of these draughtsmen at grossly inflated charges. These contract drawing offices do nothing to remedy the shortage of draughtsmen; they merely take advantage, at the expense of employers, of the existing shortage.' However contract offices continued to flourish. In 1967 the Federation accepted the inevitable and altered their constitution to allow membership to establishments, such as design offices, not employing manual workers. This was part of constitutional amendments designed to recognise the attention now paid by the Federation to white collar workers.

The Indemnity Fund had already been revised to allow for payments for firms affected by eligible staff strikes. Now, the Board proposed that the membership and Indemnity Fund subscriptions should in future be based on the wage and salary bill combined, the voting power of each firm being separated into two parts, one related to their wage bill, the other to their salary bill. This produced an outcry from companies employing large numbers of staff, on the ground that the Federation devoted less time to staff than to manual workers. So the plan was altered to provide that the contribution should be 7d. per £100 on manual wage bills and 4½d. per £100 on staff bills, with payments to the Indemnity Fund and levies in the same proportion.

By 1960, after a decade's experience of guerrilla warfare by the draughtsmen's union, the patience of members was becoming exhausted. The Manchester association told the Federation that the situation was causing them extreme concern. They wanted national agreements and hinted that in their absence they might make their own local agreements. From then on such complaints came at frequent intervals.

It was reported to the Board in July 1961, that in the preceding two years there had been thirty failures to agree with the draughtsmen at Central Conference, of which five had been followed by strikes and another six by strike threats which brought concessions. Some strikes were long but the strikers, because of their high benefits, suffered little or no loss while the employer suffered serious loss and almost always made concessions in the end. Short of a general lock-out, it was hard to see what could be done. The policy committee thought a lock-out was impracticable. They stressed the need to reduce the shortage of draughtsmen by training more of them – something the Board had been urging for years.

Two years later a special sub-committee on draughtsmen's activities was set up. This committee too thought a general lock-out was impracticable and advised against suggestions that draughtsmen should be locked out when they refused work transferred from another establishment, that companies in dispute should receive support from a special levy or that such companies should have recourse to contract drawing offices. In a further report in 1964 the committee finally concluded that the only possible concrete proposal was to train as many draughtsmen as possible.

The North-east Coast association were not satisfied with this. Two of their members at the time were threatened with strikes in support of a wage-for-age scale going up to 30, and the association asked to be allowed to order a district lock-out if their members agreed. The Board understood their frustration and admired their spirit but doubted 'the efficacy or wisdom' of what they proposed. Such a lock-out would involve only 7 or 8 per cent of the union's members. The union would probably levy its other members so that those affected would get full pay and the struggle might well be prolonged. Ultimately the North-east firms might feel impelled to call for support in a national lock-out and it was doubtful if federated employers would be willing to agree to this. Moreover in the existing industrial and political context (a general election was due) the time was not appropriate. The following month the association reported that their own members had shown themselves reluctant to support a lock-out.

Events seemed to be moving towards a crisis. Having got a wage-for-age scale agreement up to the age of 30 in 1965, the draughtsmen were now pressing firms for four weeks' holiday.

> The activities of DATA [the draughtsmen's union] are caus-ing us grave concern and we are continually considering ways and means to combat these activities [said Stephen Brown in 1966 in his final presidential address]. So far it would appear that faced with guerrilla activities, the only solution available to us would be some retaliatory action in the form of a lock-out, either on a regional or a national basis. Whether such a deci-sion would ever be taken, having regard to all its implications, is perhaps somewhat doubtful.

No one would describe that as a call to action, but soon after Gordon Baker took over from Brown there was a meeting of rep-resentatives of some fifty member firms employing some 70 to 80 per cent of all the draughtsmen, and from that meeting emerged a plan.

The Federation drew up a 'staff charter', a comprehensive set of proposals for standard conditions of employment for staff workers, acceptance of which they believed would give a prospect of peace in the industry. Salaries were not included but it covered hours of work, holidays, overtime and shift working, holiday and sick pay, periods of notice and redundancy arrangements. It was the first time the Federation had considered a construction ini-tiative on staff conditions.

The significance of the plan was that the proposed conditions would be standard – that is to say they would be applicable to all the staff workers covered by the negotiations. They would establish uniformity in place of the chaotic variations between different firms resulting from the guerrilla warfare of past years. Some firms had already conceded more favourable terms in one respect or another. They would stand still. Other firms with less favourable conditions would be expected to raise them to the standards set if an agreement was reached.

Member firms would be expected to act together and to give an understanding not to negotiate or volunteer any domestic changes in the future. In return they would have an assurance of support from other federated firms if they were singled out for industrial action on a demand for a more favourable concession.

If there was failure to agree on any item, the Federation would be prepared to go to arbitration and accept the findings. If agreement was reached, any future changes would only be made as a result of national negotiations between the Federation and the unions.

The challenge came in the next stage of the programme. If there was no agreement and the unions refused arbitration, the Federation would advise members to apply the conditions unilaterally. And the unions would be told that if thereafter any member were subjected to direct action by its staff in support of a change in conditions, the firm would be fully supported by federated members generally – 'if necessary to the extent of a national lock-out of members of the union or unions concerned'.

All the proposals were negotiable and it might be an agreement could be reached. It might be that the unions would hold back from a national stoppage. It might be that the Government would intervene before it took effect. But approval of the programme would imply that members were prepared to take part in a national lock-out if necessary.

In June 1966, the programme was put to association meetings. There was a very large majority – 88.64 per cent of those voting – in favour of the proposed charter, which was generally welcomed as a constructive initiative. But in reply to the question whether their companies would implement the subsequent measures contemplated by the Board, 22 per cent said 'No' and in addition there was a small number of abstentions. Not only were more than a fifth of the members unwilling to risk a lock-out, but they included one or two of the biggest groups. The CBI pressed the Federation strongly not to contemplate a stoppage except as a last resort. In view of these circumstances, the Board felt they could not proceed with their programme of action.

Baker and Jukes set themselves to find out why some companies were unwilling to commit themselves to collective action and found there were nearly as many reasons as companies. Some, including at least one big group, took a view similar to that taken by Tangye in 1897 – that it would be morally wrong to lock-out workers who had served them loyally and with whom they had no quarrel. Others were motivated by purely commercial considerations, fearing the loss of staff or orders or both to non-federated firms. Some were unwilling to face the loss of business during a stoppage and some feared that the lock-out would not be universally observed by members. Some thought it would be a better policy to give substantial financial support to individual firms which resisted the draughtsmen.

A lock-out which failed would leave the Federation in a worse position than ever, so they decided instead to try and get an independent inquiry. The position was complicated by the submission of wage claims by each of the staff unions during the summer and in July 1966, by the Government wage freeze. However the charter was offered at a meeting with all the staff workers, including the supervisors, at the end of August.

The unions rejected the idea of standard conditions in principle and offered instead to negotiate a charter of minimum conditions. Since this would have left them free to continue their campaigns at plant level, it would have defeated the Federation's objective of establishing stable agreed working conditions. An offer to go to arbitration was rejected by the unions and negotiations finally broke down in December.

In February 1967, the Federation asked the Government to refer the conditions of employment of staff workers to the Prices and Incomes Board, a move which the unions 'deplored'. In the same month the shipbuilding employers, who had been experiencing the same troubles as those in engineering – and had threatened a lock-out in 1965 – started a national lock-out of their draughtsmen in reply to a strike for higher pay at Swan Hunter's on the Tyne. The Federation urged their members not to give work to strikers or suspended draughtsmen, pointing out the temporary nature of the service such men would be able to give. The shipbuilding employers were unable to bring effective pressure on the union's finances since only 1700 or 1800 draughtsmen were affected and, by a levy on those at work in other industries, the union were able to distribute dispute pay at a level little below the men's normal salaries. In April the Government, after Cabinet level consideration, referred the pay and conditions of both manual and staff workers in engineering to the Prices and Incomes Board.

The Federation had put off negotiations on the staff workers' pay claims until July when the Government's six months of severe restraint, which followed the six months of incomes freeze, came to an end. An agreement was then reached with the clerical

unions, but negotiations with the draughtsmen broke down and in
August 1967, they gave notice to end the 1965 agreement.

Some Board members talked again about collective action if
individual members were attacked but it was decided to wait to
see what the PIB had to say. Its report, when it arrived, was not
helpful to the Federation. It recommended that there should be
national negotiations with staff unions on minimum conditions
of employment, that there should be national negotiations on
principles for fixing the pay of supervisors and that the employers
should reconsider their attitude to the Foremen & Staff Mutual
Benefit Society. The Federation did not allow their policies on
any of these matters to be deflected by the report.

New pay negotiations in 1968 were conditioned by Government insistence, as part of their incomes policy, that there should
be a productivity element in agreements. The draughtsmen's
annual conference rejected a proposal from the Federation seeking the union's constructive involvement at domestic level in work
measurement, the establishment of work standards and control
procedures, and the right of firms to get external help on techniques to promote efficiency. A new form of words had to be
found before an agreement was reached in June. When it came,
the Department of Employment and Productivity regarded it
with some suspicion but let it go through on condition that they
were given a report on its operation in six months' time.

A piece of gamesmanship by the draughtsmen about this time
was a demand that when employers' references were going
through the Procedure, the union should make all the arrangements, name the time and place of conferences, appoint the
chairman and generally control the proceedings. All these things
were normally done by the employers whichever side was responsible for the reference. But the draughtsmen said that unless
there was seen to be complete mutuality in the operation of the
Procedure, the agreement was bound to appear to union members to bear the character of an employers' administrative document rather than of an instrument for settling disputes in which
both parties had equal responsibility and interest.

The Board recognised there was a certain logic in this argument, but did not think federated members would relish being
invited to make submissions before a panel of union members in
the union's offices. However they feared a blunt rejection might

damage the standing of the agreement, and accepted that in future there should be a chairman of the employers' side and a chairman of the union side, of equal standing, and that it should be customary for the side against whom a reference was brought to open the proceedings. In return for this, and on grounds of administrative convenience, the union did not press the point about requiring employers to attend at their offices or other ground of their choosing. Central conferences continued to be held at Broadway House.

In December 1969, a new national agreement was negotiated with the draughtsmen to run for 15 months, but the union continued energetically to press domestic claims. And in April 1970, the union's annual conference decided that their next claim should be for the largest increases in their history, ranging from £8 5s. a week at 21 to £5 15s. for those 30 or over, with existing differentials maintained. The proposed claim was so monstrous as to make it unlikely that agreement could be reached and it had the effect of rousing in the employers a new determination to resist. Under the terms of the 1969 agreement, a new claim could not be lodged until the beginning of 1971 to take effect in April. Both sides had therefore nine months to prepare for the struggle which seemed inevitable.

The draughtsmen pursued the policy which had previously paid off. Their members put forward a large number of domestic claims, energetically pressed, in the hope of getting such big increases in key plants that their national claim would involve little more than a levelling-up operation. More than 200 such claims had been put forward by the end of the year, but few resulted in increases on the scale demanded. Moreover they encountered such determined resistance from one of the biggest employers in the industry, Rolls-Royce, who forced a 13-week stoppage at Coventry, that they were involved prematurely in heavy financial costs and had to abandon hopes of an easy victory.

The draughtsmen's second step was to try to tie up the contract drawing offices, who employed 10,000 to 12,000 workers, so that they would be not merely neutral but unwilling allies of the union when trouble broke out. Their hold over the offices was through an 'approved list'. Any firm giving work to offices not on the list was liable to get into trouble. The union now asked the offices to sign an agreement providing for the closed shop and undertaking not to do work for a client firm in dispute with the union. At the same time the draughtsmen were negotiating a merger with the Amalgamated Union of Engineering Workers which came into effect in 1971 and seemed likely to improve their chances of getting practical support from manual workers.

The Federation, on their side, worked out a long-term salary policy for white collar workers in the same way that they had drawn up their charter of conditions four years earlier. The objective put forward was to arrive at a situation in which national negotiations would establish national minimum rates for about half a dozen defined categories of technical, supervisory and clerical staff with national agreed guidelines for grading and salary ranges. There would be no national general increases and no wage-for-age scales above an agreed age of adulthood. The policy was submitted to association executives for comment but was never formally approved.

In any case, it was not expected that the draughtsmen would accept these principles, and the Federation had lengthy discussions on the form that collective resistance might take if the union took aggressive action. The expected claim was submitted in January 1971. An increase in minimum rates only was offered and negotiations broke down in March.

By that time the Federation had completed their preparations for a struggle. A general lock-out was still regarded as impracticable unless the union attack was on a national scale, which was thought unlikely. So it was agreed that, while national action would be met by national resistance, guerrilla action would be met by guerrilla resistance. At first it was suggested that every firm should be expected to withstand a strike in support of excessive demands for at least four weeks before conceding improved terms, but the idea of a minimum time was later dropped because of the different circumstances of different companies. The Federation hoped firms would resist as long as was practicable. It was left to associations to work out supporting measures. Some associations established 'action committees' to advise firms and some arranged for regular meetings of the larger employers of draughtsmen.

Great importance was attached to informing local associations of any action by the draughtsmen or any intended offer by firms

- a letter from the president was sent to every member firm appealing for their co-operation in this. Special emphasis was also placed on 'retaliatory escalation'. This meant sending home workers taking part in action short of a strike until normal working was resumed. Limited action to be escalated in this way might take many forms and be given various names – strikes by selected groups, token strikes or walk-outs, refusal to carry out normal duties or handle sub-contract work, bans on overtime, or the various euphemisms for going slow such as 'working to rule' and 'working without enthusiasm' and 'withholding co-operation'.

After all these preparations by both sides, the threatened showdown did not take place. By the end of 1971, there had been comparatively few disputes. The Federation received reports of 600 settlements which provided for general increases averaging about £3 a week – most firms conceded less but some of the biggest firms rather more – well below the union claim of from £5 15s. to £8 5s. At least a dozen firms threatened retaliatory escalation, but in each case normal working was resumed without the necessity of carrying out the threat. Union pressure on contract drawing offices also fell away.

The reason for the anti-climax was that the union's funds were under greater pressure than at any time since the war. In 1970 they paid out nearly £450,000 in dispute pay compared with less than £200,000 in 1969, largely because of the Rolls-Royce stoppage which was said to have cost them £250,000. In addition they were for the first time faced with a heavy burden of benefits to unemployed members. By the end of 1970 some 1600 were out of work and more than £55,000 had been paid in unemployment benefit during the year. Unemployment doubled again by the middle of 1971 and the cost in that year was more than £270,000.

The union kept their funds at about the £1m. mark by means of levies but that was £300,000 less than a couple of years earlier and worth less still because of inflation. Their 1971 conference cut strike pay from 80 to 60 per cent of the basic wage and urged members to leave it to the leaders to choose points of confrontation and not embark on 'useless and expensive' adventures.

While all this was going on, the three clerical workers' unions – the Clerical and Administrative Workers and the white collar sections of the two general workers' unions – were also moving away from national bargaining. As part of a pay settlement in

August 1970, the Federation conceded a 'final' general increase as well as higher minimum rates on condition that the unions would discuss a new pattern for future national negotiations which would exclude general increases. In the meantime, domestic claims were not to be based on arguments of general application

In 1971 the unions offered to abandon claims for national general increases if there was an obligation on member firms to negotiate for periodic general increases, if they gave up relying on merit reviews as an alternative, if they were prepared to discuss the salary structure, and if in domestic negotiations the union were entitled to present arguments which would previously have been adduced in national negotiations, such as movements in prices and wages in other industries. At first the Federation would only agree not to put any restrictive conditions on domestic bargaining, and the unions reverted to a claim for a general increase as well as higher minimum rates.

Negotiations on new minimum rates broke down but eventually, in December 1971, an agreement was reached that, 'bearing in mind the difficulties created by bargaining at both national and domestic levels,' the three unions would not present claims for general increases, though national negotiations on minimum rates might be held from time to time. To secure this concession, the Federation had gone a good way to meet the union requirements. They said the agreement should enable domestic salary negotiations to be pursued with more confidence and realism and recommended that federated companies should take into account that general increases would not be negotiated nationally. They fully accepted that in domestic negotiations the unions and their members (and employers) were free to make use of any argument. The Federation also recommended that where job grading schemes were not in existence, serious consideration should be given to any claim for the introduction of such schemes where the numbers warranted it and that information should be available to union members on the principles on which such schemes were operated.

The change was acceptable to the Clerical and Administrative Workers' Union because their membership in the engineering and shipbuilding industries (mostly in engineering) had risen from 26,500 in 1959 to more than 80,000 in 1971 and they attributed this largely to their development of plant bargaining and grading schemes which enabled members to be closely involved in what they were doing. It had also been helped by arrangements for the check-off (deduction of union dues from pay).

The Association of Supervisory Staffs, Executives and Technicians had expanded even more rapidly on the basis of company and plant bargaining, and had abandoned its pressure for national wage negotiations, so that at the end of 1971 none of the white collar unions was seeking national general wage increases. In 1960 ASSET had appointed as general secretary a man of 34 named Clive Jenkins who soon established a reputation in the trade union movement for the ingenuity, unconventionality and success of his leadership. He made a point of getting as much information as possible about any company with which he was negotiating. One of his novel moves was to buy shares in the largest companies such as the General Electric Company, British Leyland, Rolls-Royce and Plessey so that he could, if need be, attend shareholders' meetings and challenge their policy. The union acquired a modern, lively-minded image which probably appealed to many technicians more than the old-fashioned, militant solidarity of the more powerful draughtsmen's union.

ASSET's growth received two big fillips. The first was the 1968 merger with the 22,000-strong Association of Scientific Workers, which had not been expanding as fast as the other white collar organisations, to form the Association of Scientific, Technical and Managerial Staffs. The second came a year later when a law was passed which prevented the Foremen and Staff Mutual Benefit Society from continuing its rule excluding union members from the society. Jenkins had been working for this for years, using every pressure his fertile mind could devise. Both the Prices and Incomes Board and the Donovan commission had expressed disapproval of the rule.

Eventually the last of several private members' Bills, with Jenkins behind them, was passed by Parliament. Some 50,000 working foremen and other staff were now free to join ASTMS without sacrificing the society's benefits. The society at that time had 2740 contributory members (firms), nearly 60,000 ordinary members, and 13,700 pensioners. Its funds exceeded £18,400,000 and it was paying nearly £1,400,000 a year in benefits.

When the merger with the scientific workers took place,

ASTMS inherited two quite different procedure agreements and asked the Federation for a discussion on their relationships. They had in mind a new Procedure and the establishment of national guidelines for assessing the pay of supervisory staff, for the grading of technicians and for the relationship of supervisory and technical staff to productivity deals negotiated for manual workers. But federated associations were sharply divided as to whether staff should be involved in productivity deals or whether their remuneration should be fixed within a framework of grading structures accompanied by merit reviews.

In view of this the union accepted that a joint working party which had been set up should limit itself to an agreed discussion paper which the Board commended to members for consideration in spite of the opposition of four associations with more than 40 per cent of staff voting power. A 'commend' was a novel instrument with less force than a recommendation.

The object of the paper was to provide logical and constructive bases for domestic wage bargaining. It set out considerations which would help in reaching domestic salary structures and assess the contribution of staff to productivity agreements. Criteria for the negotiation of salary and job grading structures for supervisory staffs were agreed. In return it was suggested that the union should not claim general national increases or press nationally or locally for wage-for-age scales and should accept the principles of job evaluation and efficiency techniques.

The claim for procedural revision was suspended because the Federation were preparing new procedural proposals to put to all staff unions on lines similar to those proposed for manual workers, but differences between the unions prevented progress. The draughtsmen were no longer willing to sit at the same table as ASTMS. So the Federation decided to include this problem in the case they were preparing for a hoped-for reference to the Commission on Industrial Relations on white collar recognition problems in the industry.

The growth of ASTMS had produced bitter jurisdictional struggles. Their membership overlapped that of the draughtsmen, who were expanding in the technical field, particularly after the scientific workers had come in. In addition to that, first the boilermakers and then, about 1965, five other manual unions claimed negotiating rights for staff grades, including supervisors. The

Federation refused to consider this unless they were prepared to combine for domestic negotiations with other unions such as ASTMS and to separate their organisations for supervisors from their manual workers so as to preclude the possibility of supervisory staff being disciplined by those whom they were employed to supervise. The manual workers showed no inclination to co-operate with ASTMS so the Federation decided to wait and see what the Donovan commission had to say about it. But the commission had nothing specific to say, though it drew attention to a shipbuilding procedure agreement which encouraged supervisory staff below the level of head foremen to retain their former union membership.

A number of inter-union disputes resulted from these rival claims, some of them causing serious loss which the employers could do nothing to avert. At Girling's factory in Bromborough in 1968 members of the AEU refused to work with ASTMS charge-hands and a large section of the motor industry was laid idle for want of the brakes made by the firm. A long strike by draughtsmen at C. A. Parsons in 1970 forced the firm to grant them a closed shop at the expense of ASTMS and in breach of the Federation procedure agreement.

The settlement also necessitated notices of dismissal to members of the United Kingdom Association of Professional Engineers. This resulted in the first recognition case to be referred to the Commission on Industrial Relations under the Industrial Relations Act. The growth of professional trade unions like UKAPE, claiming recognition, especially after the passing of the Act, added new complications to the confused situation. ASTMS had moved into the field of junior management in a number of companies and the CAWU were also becoming involved.

The solution the Federation had in mind was the establishment of a council on which all five staff unions would be represented and any manual union which could show significant membership. There would be separate panels of the council to cover clerical, technical and supervisory employment. Each panel would agree on joint bargaining units at domestic level or spheres of influence. But at the end of 1971 there appeared to be no hope that the unions would accept this. There was some anxiety in the Federation lest the creation of bargaining units under the Industrial Relations Act would encourage the indiscriminate scramble for members across the traditional clerical, technical and supervisory boundaries.

The draughtsmen's financial position made them less ready than formerly to carry their inter-union disputes to extreme lengths. This may also have been partly due to stronger pressure from the TUC to refer inter-union disputes to them, partly to the passing of the Industrial Relations Act and partly to the knowledge that the Federation were urging that staff recognition problems in the industry should be referred to the Commission on Industrial Relations. Nevertheless conflicting union claims in the white collar field remained a perpetual menace.

Present and Future: April 1972

The Clock Turns Back – But the Federation Still
Grows – Facing the Challenge of Plant Bargaining –
The Power to Lead

A hundred years ago, in April 1962, the Iron Trades Employers'
Association was formed to organise collective resistance to firm-
by-firm demands by the engineering unions. Today, strangely
and unexpectedly, employers find themselves in many respects
back where they started. The manual workers' Procedure for
avoiding disputes, pride of the industry since 1898, disappeared
at the end of last year. The manual workers' unions have broken
off national negotiations and are once again attempting to pick
off employers one by one, or in some areas returning to the
district claims which were once the rule. At the same time a new
Industrial Relations Act has reduced the immunities of those
unions which decline to register to something like the level they
possessed after the legislation of the 1870s. And the maintenance
of full employment, which has so affected the balance of industrial power since the Second World War, has apparently ceased to
be the top priority for governments of either party.

The changes may or may not last. The industry-wide Procedure may be revived, national negotiations resumed.* The Act
may not survive the next general election. Full employment may
be restored. But whichever way these things go, the basic long-
term developments now taking place in the character of the
Federation may be expected to continue.

The representative capacity of the Federation is still growing.
With the changing structure of the industry, the appearance of
ever more and larger groups, there have from time to time been
rumours that one or other of the giants will drop out. But they
are still there. Smaller firms have not left because there is no

* See note, p. 240.

longer a national Procedure. In spite of mergers and closures, the number of member firms, which was at a record of 4826 in 1971, now exceeds 4850.

This may be partly because the termination of the Procedure coincided with the introduction of the Industrial Relations Act and Code of Practice and the Equal Pay Act. In the strange new industrial relations world thus created, many firms need information and guidance – the Federation's guidance has been of high quality – and some body on which they can rely if they get into difficulties. By the time they have adjusted themselves to the new laws, they will have had an opportunity to assess the value of the new functions upon which the Federation has embarked. And with Britain in the Common Market, many will be needing help to understand European ways in industrial relations.

But most members may be expected to stay in for reasons outside the formal machinery of conciliation and negotiation and outside the legislative and other guidance that goes down from Broadway House. There is going on all the time unobtrusive help to members resulting from informal contacts between union and employer officials, frequently resolving difficulties without their resulting in a strike or even in a reference to the Procedure. The telephone lines between the district offices of the unions and the local associations are constantly hot. In fact this kind of firefighting remains the main association activity, and is an important part of Federation work. Some firms which have hitherto relied on the associations to resolve their problems will no doubt have been stimulated by the new legislation to re-examine their industrial relations policy for themselves and take more positive lines, but that will not mean they will want to abandon their right to draw on the knowledge and experience of association and Federation officials when they need it.

Much of this history has unavoidably been concerned with conflict, with the great trials of strength and with the continual guerrilla warfare between powerful organisations whose interests are in some respects opposed to each other. But, coincidental with the struggles, contacts are all the time maintained between two groups of men who know and understand each other and the problems they may face and whose interest is to resolve difficulties rather than create them.

The move away from national to plant bargaining on wages

was already taking place – and was deliberately encouraged by the Federation – before the CSEU broke off national negotiations. This was mainly because the negotiated rates had long ceased to be standard rates and had become minimum rates. In the later 1930s, wage drift made its appearance and increased during and after the war, so that workers have been getting increases both at national and plant level. If the Federation thought they could prevent this by stopping local increases, they might well have preferred to do it that way. Indeed the 1964 package was an attempt to stop local bargaining except in special circumstances, but it was only partially successful.

The basic motive was to stop double increases. Since local increases could not be prevented, the Federation has in succeeding years tried to avoid national general increases. National bargaining still had value because it could settle minimum earnings levels and certain conditions which were accepted as standard by the unions, for instance the length of the working week, holidays and overtime rates. The white collar charter was an attempt to establish the same principle of standard conditions for staff workers. Member firms were to be left free to devise their own wage and salary structure. Increasing importance has been given to the fact that they would also be free to make bargains taking into account measures to improve efficiency or productivity as was provided in the 1968 package.

Plant bargaining is here, but it has its risks as well as its advantages. It puts the unions in a position to pick off firms one at a time. Manual workers have been doing that to some extent since double bargaining developed. The draughtsmen have done it consistently and with considerable success since the war. The end of national increases expands the scope for local leap-frog claims as well as the scope for productivity bargaining. Though the issue seemed to have been settled during the period of the package deals, there are still federated employers who believe that national general increases have a stabilising effect. The long controversy which stultified the Federation's wage policy during the 1950s may not yet be finally resolved. It might even be possible, if unemployment were to continue at a high level, to re-establish standard rates, but that is perhaps not probable.

When claims are directed to individual firms, as the Federation at present accepts that they should be, employers feel the need for mutual support to hold their line, just as they felt it a hundred years ago. Various ways have been adopted in the past to resist demands regarded as unreasonable. One way was to bring in blacklegs to take the place of trade unionists on strike. That is still attempted occasionally, as it was by Roberts Arundel at Stockport, who left the Federation, and by Fine Tubes at Plymouth, but it is hardy practicable for a big firm and difficult for any in the present state of union organisation and public opinion.

A second method was to give collective financial help to firms picked on. This is still done through the Indemnity Fund, but in 1970 the Indemnity Fund was threatened with collapse. In that one strike-ridden year it paid out £1,600,000. This was twice as much as in 1969, itself easily a record and the first time that payments exceeded income. Tax adjustments and the skilful handling of investments cushioned the loss, and there is still a substantial amount in the kitty, but it was apparent that that the fund could not stand many more years of indemnities on that scale.

It was the first time, with the possible exception of a brief period in the early 1930s, that the Federation has had any kind of financial worry. The contribution income of the general and indemnity funds is insulated against inflation by the system of relating contributions to the wage and salary bills of members. Income rises automatically as wages and salaries go up. The general contribution was 1s. for every £100 paid in wages from the first beginnings of the Federation until 1968, though in the early years there was also an entrance fee, and it has remained at roughly the same proportion altogether since it was divided between wages and salary bills. There has always been a surplus and it became the practice to allocate 75 per cent of it to the Indemnity Fund. But the expansion of the Federation's activities in the past few years has reduced the annual surplus, so the Indemnity Fund has benefited less.

The Indemnity Fund was therefore faced with reduced income from the general fund at the same time as greatly increased payments. Because it always showed a healthy balance, and because it was regarded as an obstacle to recruitment, contributions to the Indemnity Fund, which are compulsorily paid by new members in five annual instalments, have been made a reduced proportion of wages bills. At the beginning of 1913 they were

30s. for every £100, in 1948 this became 15s. for every £100, in 1966 10s. for every £100 and in 1968 5s. 10d. for each £100 in wages and 3s. 9d. for each £100 in salaries.

Payments out, with no insulation against inflation, were naturally increased from time to time. In 1913 they were 30s. a week for each man involved, after the first fortnight of a stoppage, with smaller sums for women and juveniles. In 1924 this was raised to £1 16s. a week, in 1948 to £2 14s., in 1961 to £5 and in 1966, with a still rising balance, it was over-optimistically doubled to £10. But the payments in 1969 and 1970 went far beyond anything that had been envisaged. Total indemnities from 1913 to 1945 added up to less than £250,000, while the fund had paid some £330,000 as its contribution to the Federation's administrative expenses. Accumulated funds then amounted to about £1m. – nearly 90 per cent of total contributions.

So the crisis in 1970 was something quite new. There were long discussions about the future of the fund. Though new members were only paying about one-third as much, proportionately, as their predecessors half a century earlier, the contributions were thought still to inhibit companies from joining the Federation, while the financial benefits provided, though on occasion they may have saved small firms from disaster, were no longer sufficient to provide meaningful benefits to larger firms – or to weigh much with them when set against the loss of export orders and customers and other liabilities involved in a long stoppage.

The Federation could have imposed a levy under the fund's rules, but this was not thought likely to be acceptable. The possibility of raising a fighting fund on a bigger scale was considered but ruled out as impracticable. Some members thought the fund had outlived its usefulness. But the Industrial Relations Act may have effects that cannot yet be assessed. Possibly it will reduce the number of strikes. Sometimes firms will be able to obtain compensation if the strike is an unfair industrial practice.

Eventually it was decided to review the whole 'philosophy' of the fund in a few years' time and meanwhile halve the benefits. This reduced them to £5 a week for a man, £2 10s. for juveniles and women, and payments ranging from £2 10s. a week to £1 a week for men, with proportionate amounts for juveniles and women, when output was restricted by action short of a strike.

The result of this, and a falling off in the number of strikes, was that payments in 1971 fell to £500,000 and the immediate threat to the solvency of the fund was removed. The Federation was able to make substantial additional payments to firms resisting the manual workers' claims in South Lancashire in 1972.

Nevertheless, for the moment, at least, the Indemnity Fund is unlikely to be an important factor in encouraging resistance to unreasonable demands on individual firms. This leaves the third method used in the past – collective retaliation. The employers in the last century found that the only conclusive answer was the lock-out, at first usually at district level, then at national level. As late as 1926 they were prepared to stop the industry in support of a single comparatively small employer if they thought a principle was involved.

There have been one or two examples of collective actions since the war. In 1955, it may be remembered, the employers imposed a ban on overtime and week-end work in reply to the spider-men's guerrilla strikes. That may hurt the men more than the employers on outside sites but would not do so in factories where much depends on week-end maintenance. The engineering employers never agreed on a collective lock-out of draughtsmen, much as they have talked about it, though the shipbuilding employers did. The most effective collective action in recent times was in the dispute which resulted in the ending of the Coventry toolroom agreement in the autumn of 1971.

The Coventry employers, after going through the Procedure and failing to agree, gave notice to end the agreement. From June the unions imposed a district ban on overtime and co-operation and from September introduced a weekly strike on Mondays. The following month the employers replied to this with a weekly lock-out on Tuesdays. The men retorted with a continuing strike but soon afterwards a settlement was reached. The employers achieved their objective at a cost in lost production which was estimated at £50m.

At the time of writing (April 1972), South Lancashire employers are concerting individual resistance to claims on wages and conditions covering the district.

Federated firms have been prepared to fight when all have been attacked together, as they were in 1954 and 1957 and again in 1968, but until the Coventry dispute they had not fought over a collective initiative of their own. And they have not been prepared to stop their works in support of another member even though they know they may be next on the union list.

There have been various reasons for this. The lock-outs and threatened lock-out of the past were seldom over wages. They were over matters of 'principle' – which meant such questions as the manning of machines, restrictions on overtime or the closed shop. But it is nowadays taken for granted that firms must struggle over such things individually, as best they can. The closed shop has been stopped, but by law not by collective action. There are indeed no matters of principle in the old sense. The nearest thing to it since the war, perhaps, was the draughtsmen's wage-for-age scale. Most of the issues in dispute have been wage issues and it is very difficult to mobilise support for a single firm on wages when levels of earnings vary so widely. One firm asked to lock out in support of another might well find it was already paying higher wages than were being demanded from the firm attacked. If wages were standard it would be a different matter. It would be much easier to get support for a firm in danger of being forced to concede the 35-hour week than for a firm resisting a wage demand. And it is more reasonable to demand resignation from a Manchester firm granting a reduction in hours than from one conceding an increase which, while much larger than the Federation approves, still leaves it paying less than a similar firm in Coventry.

Another obstacle to collective action is the changed structure of industry. In the old days the man on the spot was responsible only to himself. He might face bankruptcy but not dismissal by the heads of a conglomerate or multi-national company, with its headquarters in London or the United States, preoccupied with short-term financial results. When a strike begins, according to one managing director, the distant owners say, 'Show them they can't have everything their own way.' In the second week of the strike, they say, 'Can't you get a reasonable compromise?' And in the third week, they say, 'For God's sake, get them back somehow.'

Firms find it more difficult to face the financial consequences of a stoppage. 'The balance of bargaining power has shifted in some way which suggests that the cost of resisting, of risking industrial action has increased, and on a short-term calculation of least-cost, firms find it cheaper to concede,' said the research department's paper on 'Wage Inflation and Employment' in 1971. Among the reasons advanced were the ability of unions to prolong industrial action without undue hardship to their members, whose families receive payments from the State, the increase of overhead costs as a proportion of total costs because of the increased quantity of fixed capital per head, the increased integration by firms which enables small groups of employees to threaten total production and the decentralisation of collective bargaining which increases comparability arguments because of the greater number of comparisons that can be made, and of the greater number of disparities, anomalies and inequities that can be pointed out.

The paper said that the diminution of industry's resistance to inflationary wage claims was tied up with the attrition of their finances. In extreme cases, becoming increasingly common, the closeness to bankruptcy of many hard-pushed concerns, unable to get further extensions of credit from the banking sector, and already burdened by high interest-rate charges, had meant that no interruption to cash-flow could be tolerated. The interesting conclusion was reached that 'the re-establishment of a stable collective bargaining atmosphere may well depend on a change of emphasis in favour of stronger central bargaining, at Federation level, and less emphasis on the plant-bargaining philosophy that arose out of incomes policy and Donovan'.

These are reasons why the individual firm is apt to give way, and they are also reasons why the firm is reluctant to face a stoppage in support of others or as part of a collective action. There is another reason for reluctance to take collective action. The success of the general lock-out used to depend on bankrupting the unions and starving out the workers. Union finances are still highly vulnerable, but the workers, relying on social security payments and income tax refunds, can endure a long dispute without strike pay and without going hungry if they feel strongly enough, as the miners did in 1972 and the post office workers in 1971. But they are bound to suffer to some extent, and in today's environment there are employers who, quite apart from commercial considerations, would find it distasteful to lock out their workers because of union action against another firm. Nevertheless the increasingly arrogant and aggressive policies of the

engineer's amalgamation and the draughtsmen have done a great
deal to consolidate the employers. They could eventually force
the employers into positive collective action, as did the ASE
in 1897.

There has appeared during the present struggle in South Lancashire a new pattern or collective resistance, based on the oldest
of all, described by Adam Smith in the last century: 'Masters are
always and everywhere in a sort of tacit but constant and uniform
combination not to raise wages of labour above their actual
rate. To violate this combination is everywhere a most unpopular
action and a sort of reproach to a master among his neighbours
and equals.'

The employers in the Manchester district have formed themselves into 'action groups' of neighbouring firms who are in constant touch with each other about what they are doing in reply to
the union claims. So long as the other members of the group
stand out against unreasonable demands, each is encouraged to
do likewise. The others strengthen his will if he weakens, because
he knows that to concede shorter hours or an excessive increase
makes him an object of reproach.

It is being suggested that this form of organisation might be
extended to cover the whole Federation area. With many variations, it is already being adopted in a number of associations as a
means of handling plant bargaining and overcoming bureaucratic dangers arising from the increased size of associations. The
essential objective would be to enable employers to discuss and
exchange information with their neighbours, and to feel they are
participating in the work of the organisation.

Such 'district clubs' of, say, fifteen to twenty firms, might in
time come to establish their own guidelines on local wages,
salaries and conditions in consultation with their associations
within a national framework.

It may be that a continuation of the 1971–2 level of unemployment, reinforced by the union-restrictive elements in the
Industrial Relations Act, would eventually make possible a return
to something like the imposed quiescence of earlier years. But a
continuation of unemployment is not assured. Neither is a
continuation of the Act. In any case, it would be a slow process
accompanied by much restlessness. The demand for participation
that has spread over the world, in many other sides of life than the
industrial, will not easily be extinguished.

The problem of the inflationary use of plant bargaining is there, and the shift in workers' power from the centre to the shop floor has made it hard to handle. Irresponsible claims in the factories are increasingly receiving union backing. Hence the need to resist. But some employers in engineering and other industries have sought for new forms of management which take into account the shift in power. There have been experiments in 'management by consent', 'employee involvement', 'workers participation', 'joint regulation' and so on. Such forms of management recognise that working groups have forced their way into a share of decision making on many aspects of their working lives, but in a disorderly, unregulated, often destructive way. They aim not to destroy but to harness the emergent forces so that they will at the same time make a constructive contribution to the prosperity of the firm and increase the rewards of the men employed in it.

The Federation was never from 1898 a purely defensive organisation. It has now ceased to be a body, as it was for years after the Second World War, which regarded its functions as going little beyond replying to an annual wage claim and operating the Procedure. The research department and the advisory service have given it a new dimension. The industrial relations department works out programmes for the settlement of wages and conditions which will allow for the free development of new management methods.

The list of the department's constructive initiatives since 1964 is an impresive one – two package deals, a white collar charter and the long-term white collar salary policy, the new Procedure for manual workers and the still-born procedural plan for white collar workers, and the negotiating framework both for clerical workers and supervisors.

It is in a sense irrelevant that most of the initiatives have either been a limited success of failed altogether. The first package deal did something, the second was swamped by the national wage explosion. The manual workers' procedural plan resulted only in the loss of the existing Procedure. Responsibility for the final stage would have been shifted from the Federation in any case. The result of the breakdown was that it was shifted to companies instead of to associations. The white collar charter was rejected by the unions and they would not even sit down together with the

mployers to discuss the suggestion for a new Procedure. The
ong-term staff salary policy has not got acceptance by federated
members. Positive achievements have been the agreement with
he clerical unions on a framework for negotiations and the
discussion document agreed with the supervisors.

It is a pity that the Federation entered upon its constructive
phase in a period when the policies of the most powerful manual
and white collar unions were becoming increasingly destructive.
The point, however, is that the Federation now knows where it
wants to go. It will return to the principles embodied in its various
initiatives, no doubt modifying them as circumstances change. It
is no longer merely reacting to events. It is attempting to shape
them.

At the heart of the new Federation policies is the encouragement of new factory relationships based on shared responsibility.
But it was not illogical for the Federation to reject Hugh Scanlon's interpretation of the *status quo*. So long as the workers continue to accept trouble-makers as leaders in some factories and
so long as unions tolerate or even encourage them, managements
cannot afford to offer them more ammunition. But the object of
the new forms of management is to create a climate in which such
conditions wither away and the argument about the *status quo*
becomes meaningless – as indeed it is now in many establishments.

The advisory service aims to help managements to create that
kind of climate. It reflects a reversal of older Federation concepts,
a reversal which perhaps began with Eddie Robertson's paper in
1968 in which he wrote that productivity bargaining 'involves an
acceptance not merely in intellectual but in emotional terms of
the inescapability of shared responsibility with regard to efficient
manpower utilisation and the effort-wage bargain' and concluded
that it could assist in the management of change.

This was followed by the 1968 package with its provision for
productivity bargaining in the factories. Productivity bargaining
is no longer an 'in' term but the new attitude is nowadays reflected in many Federation documents. One last year, dealing with
the usefulness of job evaluation in preparing the way for equal
pay, for instance, suggested that companies wishing to introduce
job evaluation should set up joint committeees in which all
aspects are freely discussed and developed. Modern thinking, it

added, tends to the view that full consultation is conducive t good industrial relations and acceptance of a job evaluatio scheme, particularly if employees can share in its preparation an have some voice in the construction of the wage scales. One o the first steps in Marsh's programmes of change in the factorie is always the setting up of a joint committee. Pat Lowry's propo sals for joint works committees and a national joint council a part of a reshaped Procedure embodied from another angle th departure from the old conception of management prerogative.

The advisory service's emphasis is on 'improving compan effectiveness' and 'providing potential for higher earnings' bu helping companies to do these things invariably involves, onc the whole of a company's mode of operation has been examined a process of change in which the workers are consulted an involved, with managements leading rather than commanding. I this is to have a broad evolutionary effect on management an worker attitudes in the industry it will have to be spread mor widely than is possible through a nucleus of advisers at Broadwa House. By the end of last year the service had helped some 15 companies to carry out a comprehensive programme of change with results which gratified the companies. Even allowing that th larger groups will not need such help, or will not think they do that is a small proportion of the 5000 federated firms.

For the new ideas to permeate the industry, the co-operatio of the associations is essential. So far only four of them have appointed their own productivity advisers to work in co-operatio with those at Broadway House. There are still many association which are too small to provide such services. Six of them – Aber- deen, Dundee, Barrow, Rochdale, the Border Counties and Bel- fast Marine – each have a membership which employs less than 10,000 workers altogether and pays less than one half per cent o the Federation wage and salary bill. Five more – Northern Ireland, Bolton, Preston, Mid-Anglian and South Wales – have a membership employing less than 50,000 and paying less than two per cent of the total wage and salary bill.

There are many employers and many association officials who insist that their traditional negotiating and fire-fighting roles must remain their predominant function. 'There is a danger that the advisory service will overshadow the real work of negotiation,' one association official said to me. 'It must be kept under control.'

'Our job is to haggle,' said another. 'Anyone can sell a tea-break, but real productivity agreements are a job for consultants.' 'It is nice to have the service available,' said a third, 'but the prime purpose of the Federation is still the handling of industrial relations, which remains a matter of battle and conflict, and the need is for the Federation to be a war horse able to fight its battles.' 'The advisory service is an attempt to preserve the Federation for the wrong reasons,' said one well-known employer.

Some employers are critical because no charge is made for the the service. They do not see why everybody should have to pay for assistance given to a few individual firms. But Broadway House sees no reason why this service should not be offered freely just as are its services in the fields of industrial relations, training, safety or the law.

Supporters of the new development – and there are enthusiasts in the associations as well as critics – would none of them dispute that industrial relations are the prime concern of the Federation. Where they part company is over the assumption that the advisory service is something separate from industrial relations. In fact it goes back to the very roots in helping to improve the direct relationship between managements and workers in the factory. To find its fulfilment, the service may eventually have to merge with the industrial relations department.

The decision the Federation as a whole will have to make in the next few years is whether to be satisfied that the service should remain an isolated group, giving help to a few members here and there, or whether it should be developed into a major part of the Federation's work. That would mean making it the centre of a widespread network involving all sides of the organisation's activities.

Not only would the enlarged associations have their own advisers, and safety and training officers expand their contribution, but industrial relations officers at association level would become as much concerned with helping firms to introduce arrangements likely to prevent disputes as with settling disputes. This might mean that they would need enough training in management to give at least a preliminary diagnosis when firms find their industrial relations are hindering rather than helping efficiency. The aim might be to work towards a system under which one or another association representative would keep in touch with every member firm. The management training centres might come to devote less of their attention to courses and seminars and more to in-plant training. In national and local negotiations, the employers' representatives would be primarily concerned, as indeed they often have in recent years – to create a framework within which the reform of factory relationships could proceed smoothly.

No one doubts that in many factories wage systems are out-of-date, differentials have not been established on a proper basis, shop stewards are hampered rather than helped to do their jobs, overtime is not related to the need for it, and in many ways manpower is not used to the best advantage. To the extent that recent legislation and the Code of Industrial Practice have made the managements re-examine their arrangements, the Federation's new policy will have its opportunity. If it is taken, the next history of the Federation may not be about the employer's power to manage, but his power to lead.

Appendix A

The Declaration

This is the document which workers had to sign in order to get employment with members of the Central Association of Employers of Operative Engineers after the 1852 lock-out. The names are fictitious.

Declaration by the undersigned, on engagement in the employment of

Messrs Master and Boss, Back Street, Manchester

I, **John Worker,** do hereby honestly, and in its simplest sense and plainest meaning, declare that I am neither now, nor will while in your employment, become a member or contributor, or otherwise belong to or support any Trades' Union or Society, which, directly or indirectly, by its Rules, or in its meetings or transaction of its business, or by means of its officers or funds, takes cognizance of, professes to control, or interferes with the arrangements or regulations of this or any other manufacturing or trading establishment, the hours or terms of labour, the contracts or agreements of employers or employed, or the qualifications or period of service. I do also further declare, that I have no purpose or intention to call in question the right of any man to follow any honest calling in which he may desire to engage, or to make what arrangements, and engage what workmen he pleases, upon whatever terms they choose mutually to agree.

(Signed) **John Worker**
Dated the **twentieth** day of **February, 1852**
(Signed) **A. N. Other**
Witness.

Appendix B

Objects of the Employers' Federation of
Engineering Associations, 1896

(1) To promote and further the interests of the Federation, of the Federated Associations, and of the Members of such Associations generally; and, in particular, to protect and defend those interests against combinations of workmen seeking by strikes or other action to impose unduly restrictive conditions upon any branch of the Engineering Trades;

(2) To secure mutual support and co-operation in dealing with demands made, and action taken by, workmen or combinations thereof, on all matters or questions affecting the general and common interests of the said trades, including therein such questions as interference with Foremen, unreasonable demands for wages, minimum rates of wages, employment of apprentices, hours of labour, overtime, limitation of work, piece-work, demarcation of work, machine work, and the employment of men and boys on machines;

(3) To protect the Federated Associations and the Members thereof against strikes or disputes with workmen or against losses incurred by acting in conformity with the decisions or recommendations of the Federation or the Executive Board;

(4) To give to Members of the Federated Associations all such assistance pecuniary, legal, or otherwise as to the Federation or the Executive Board shall appear proper or desirable;

(5) To act jointly by federation or otherwise, and to co-operate with any other Association or Federation in furtherance of the objects of this Federation;

(6) To promote the formation of Conciliation Boards, or other provision for the equitable settlement of all differences between Members of the Federated Associations and their workmen.

(7) To watch over all legislative measures which may affect, or tend to affect, the interests of the Engineering Trades; and

(8) To do all such other things as are in the opinion of the Federation or of the Executive Board, incidental or conducive to the attainment of the above objects or any of them.

Appendix C

How to Win a Lock-out

Extracts from a speech to the Manchester District Engineering Trades Employers' Association by Sebastian Ziani de Ferranti on 31 December 1897. (Ferranti, whose inventions had already won him the description of the British Edison in the newspapers, had moved his works from London to Hollinwood, on the borders of Manchester and Oldham, in 1896.)

It is quite clear that the public and the men, and everybody in this country in fact, must realise that the employers are fighting for law and order, and fighting against socialism. It is not the ASE simply, it is absolutely socialism, and that socialism would ruin the country – masters and men as well. We cannot do anything, I consider, but fight it out to the last, and I am delighted to find, from what gentlemen who have spoken have said, that there is absolute unanimity in this Federation. I am afraid I cannot say anything more to encourage you. If I could I would do, I feel, however, that you are beyond encouragement, that you have your own views, and that you realise just as fully as everybody else that there is that one course only to be pursued.

There is, however, a second course which I venture to name to you, that is, do all that you possibly can to push your business forward in the way of getting fresh men. I have had personally at Hollinwood a very difficult and trying experience. Still I am glad to say that the success is a very great and real one, for we have now one hundred more men than we had before the dispute started. We have been able not only to make good, but we have been able to make progress; furthermore, the output is much greater than it was before the dispute, because now people are willing to work. Before they were determined not to work. After all the difficulties that we have gone through in the process of getting fresh hands, training men, and picking up men all over the country, I do not think the difficulties are as great as is the advantage to be gained and the good from doing it. I think that one of the strongest things that we can do today is to show the ASE that they are not masters, by our getting in a large number of men and getting our works going. I do not think really that we can afford simply to hold together and show them that we are determined in that way. I think we want to do something even more positive, and make a better showing still by getting our works going.

If I may be allowed to do so, I will tell you roughly the course that we pursued. In the first place, we got proper lodging accommodation all ready. In the second place, we got our own police protection in the form of private policemen and ex-soldiers. Then we advertised, and we got in a number of applications, and of course any amount of rubbish. We housed those men, who were quite useless as workmen, in the works; and we went on doing this, losing the first 50 or 100 before we got any to stop, until we were in the majority, that is to say we had so many men that the pickets outside could not very well intimidate them. They were too many.

Then by degrees we got those men off our premises into lodgings. We did not let them find lodgings for themselves. We found suitable lodgings for them in places where we could rely upon their being properly cared for. Of course a great many houses would not look at taking men from us. The next process was to advise the police of every name and house where any of our men were stationed; and those houses were carefully watched, and I may say efficiently watched by the local police to give the men complete protection there. So we went on, all the new hands being taken into the works and lodged there for some time, then being passed out to suitable lodgings where they were protected and cared for, and by those means we got an advantageous position.

Another fortunate thing was that the Oldham newspapers took up as a very great scandal the very wicked inducement by which we got men to come to us. We paid their fares; we had people to meet them and protect them; we housed them free for a certain length of time; we guaranteed them continuous employment after the dispute was over, that is for everybody who worked satisfactorily and well; and we did everything that could reasonably be expected. This was published by the newspapers, and

I am pleased to say that although I felt very uncomfortable when I first read it, it was copied by every paper in the country, and the result was a very large number of applications.

The next process was to get on a number of young lads. This is all a work not of the last three months; it was all done before the last three months. We got on a large number of young fellows, principally from the technical schools, those who attended night classes. My experience is this. Those young lads in from three weeks to a month can do in most cases the work of experienced machine men and engineers. I am simply astounded at it, but still there is the fact. Most of them appreciate what it is to use a gauge within three weeks or a month. They turn out work much better and several times over more quickly than our experienced mechanics did before. I admit that our shop was a hot-bed of society men, and it therefore did far less than others.

Then we come to the last process in what we have been doing. We have got to the point of having been able to dispense with the services of all those who are inefficient; and I think today the shop is full of a far better and more hard-working class of men that it has ever been my pleasure to see in it before. It is a real pleasure to go through the works and see how cheerfully and well business is progressing. I should rather not have said this from my own point of view, but I think it is very important that you should get your works going and push them forward without the ASE, and for that reason I have told you these few facts to show you what can be done, and what I am sure you will be able to accomplish if you put your hands to it; and I am sure that it will materially shorten the period of trouble, and will bring the strike to an end more quickly than it would otherwise come to an end; and it will give you a very real advantage in a nucleus of men entirely outside the Society.

Appendix D

Terms of Settlement, 1898

GENERAL PRINCIPLE OF FREEDOM TO EMPLOYERS IN THE MANAGEMENT OF THEIR WORKS

The Federated Employers, while disavowing any intention of interfering with the proper functions of Trade Unions, will admit no interference with the management of their business, and reserve to themselves the right to introduce into any federated workshop, at the option of the employer concerned, any condition of labour under which any members of the Trade Unions here represented were working at the commencement of the dispute in any of the workshops of the Federated Employers; but, in the event of any Trade Union desiring to raise any question arising therefrom, a meeting can be arranged by application to the Secretary of the Employers' Local Association to discuss the matter.

Nothing in the foregoing shall be construed as applying to the normal hours of work, or to general rises and falls of wages, or to rates of remuneration.

NOTE. – No new condition of labour is introduced or covered by this clause. It simply provides for equality of treatment between the Unions and the Federation by reserving for all the members of all the Trade Unions, as well as for all the Federated Employers, the same liberty which many Trade Unionists and many employers have always had.

Special provision is made in the clause and in the subsequent 'Provisions for avoiding future Disputes,' to secure to workmen, or their representatives, the right of bringing forward for discussion any grievance or supposed grievance.

1. *Freedom of Employment*. – Every workman shall be free to belong to a Trade Union or not as he may think fit.

Every employer shall be free to employ any man, whether he belong or not to a Trade Union.

Every workman who elects to work in a Federated workshop shall work peaceably and harmoniously with all fellow employees, whether he or they belong to a Trade Union or not. He shall also be free to leave such employment, but no collective action shall be taken until the matter has been dealt with under the provisions for avoiding disputes.

The Federation do not advise their members to object to Union workmen or give preference to non-union workmen.

NOTE. – The right of a man to join a Trade Union if he pleases involves the right of a man to abstain from joining a Trade Union if he pleases. This clause merely protects both rights. The Federation sincerely hope that a better understanding will prevent any question of preference arising in the future, and advise the members not to object to Union workmen.

2. *Piecework*. – The right to work piecework at present exercised by many of the Federated Employers shall be extended to all members of the Federation and to all their Union workmen.

The prices to be paid for piecework shall be fixed by mutual arrangement between the employer and the workman or workmen who perform the work.

The Federation will not countenance any piecework conditions which will not allow a workman of average efficiency to earn at least the wage at which he is rated.[1]

The Federation recommend that all wages and balances shall be paid through the office.

NOTE. – These are just the conditions that have been for long in force in various shops. Individual workmen are much benefited by piecework.

A mutual arrangement as to piecework rates between employer and workman in no way interferes with the functions of the Unions in arranging with their own members the rates and conditions under which they shall work.

3. *Overtime*. – When overtime is necessary the Federated Employers recommend the following as a basis and guide: –

[1] In reply to an inquiry as to the interpretation of this paragraph the employers' secretaries on 21st January, 1898, wrote to the general secretary of the ASE stating that the general note (appended to the explanations) which disclaims any intention of reducing the wages of skilled men 'applies both to time wages, and to piece-work earnings – in the latter case there is no intention of interfering with the usual practice of making extra payment for extra effort.'

'That no man shall be required to work more than 40 hours overtime in any four weeks after full shop hours have been worked, allowance being made for time lost through sickness or absence with leave.

In the following cases overtime is not to be restricted, viz.: –

Breakdowns in plant.

General repairs, including ships.

Repairs or replace work, whether for the employer or his customers.

Trial trips.

It is mutually agreed that in cases of urgency and emergency restrictions shall not apply.

This basis is to apply only to members of the Trade Unions who are represented at this Conference.

All other existing restrictions as regards overtime are to be removed.

It is understood that if mutually satisfactory to the Local Association of Employers and the workmen concerned, existing practices regarding overtime may be continued.

NOTE. – These overtime conditions are precisely the conditions now in operation in various places, though in many Federated workshops no limitation whatever exists at the present time. In many cases this will be the first attempt to regulate or prevent excess of overtime.

4. *Rating of Workmen.* – Employers shall be free to employ workmen at rates of wages mutually satisfactory. They do not object to the Unions or any other body of workmen in their collective capacity arranging amongst themselves rates of wages at which they will accept work, but while admitting this position they decline to enforce a rule of any Society or an agreement between any Society and its members.

The Unions will not interfere in any way with the wages of workmen outside their own Unions.

General alterations in the rate of wages in any district or districts will be negotiated between the Employers' Local Association and the local representatives of the Trade Unions or other bodies of workmen concerned.

NOTE. – Collective bargaining between the Unions and the Employers' Associations is here made the subject of distinct agreement.

The other clauses simply mean that as regards the wages to be paid there shall be (1) Freedom to the employer; (2) Freedom to the Union workmen both individually and in their collective capacity – that is to say, collective bargaining in its true sense is fully preserved; and (3) Freedom to non-unionists.

These conditions are precisely those in operation at present on the North-East Coast, the Clyde, and elsewhere, where for years past alterations of wages have been amicably arranged at joint meetings of employers and representatives of the Trade Unions.

5. *Apprentices.* – There shall be no limitation of the number of apprentices.

NOTE. – This merely puts on record the existing practice and is to prevent a repetition of misunderstandings which have arisen in some cases.

6. *Selection, Training, and Employment of Operatives.* – Employers are responsible for the work turned out by their machine tools, and shall have full discretion to appoint the men they consider suitable to work them, and determine the conditions under which such machine tools shall be worked. The employers consider it their duty to encourage ability wherever they find it, and shall have the right to select, train, and employ those whom they consider best adapted to the various operations carried on in their workshops, and will pay them according to their ability as workmen.

NOTE. – There is no desire on the part of the Federation to create a specially favoured class of workmen.

PROVISIONS FOR AVOIDING DISPUTES

With a view to avoid disputes in future, deputations of workmen will be received by their employers, by appointment, for mutual discussion of questions, in the settlement of which both parties are directly concerned. In case of disagreement, the local Associations of Employers will negotiate with the local officials of the Trade Unions.

In the event of any Trade Union desiring to raise any question with an Employers' Association, a meeting can be arranged by application to the Secretary of the Employers' Local Association to discuss the question.

Failing settlement by the Local Association and the Trade

Union of any question brought before them, the matter shall be forthwith referred to the Executive Board of the Federation and the central authority of the Trade Union; and pending the question being dealt with, there shall be no stoppage of work, either of a partial or a general character, but work shall proceed under the current conditions.

NOTE.—A grievance may be brought forward for discussion either by the workman individually concerned, or by him and his fellow workmen, or by the representatives of the Union.

In no instance do the Federated Employers propose conditions which are not at present being worked under by large numbers of the members of the Allied Trade Unions.

The Federated Employers do not want to introduce any new or untried conditions of work, and they have no intention of reducing the rates of wages of skilled men.

These conditions, with relative notes, are to be read and construed together.

It is agreed that there shall be a resumption of work simultaneously in all the workshops of the Federated Employers on Monday morning, 31st January, 1898.

Parties mutually agree that the foregoing shall be the terms of settlement.

Appendix E

The Federation Offices in 1911, by S. A. Hibbitt.

(Sid Hibbitt joined the Federation as a messenger boy in 1911, was head of the statistical department when he retired in 1962 and was still doing some work for the West of England Association in 1971.)

I was 14 years and 3 months old when I joined the Federation as its most humble and junior member on February 1, 1911, the year after the Federation had moved their headquarters from Glasgow to 24 Abingdon Street, Westminster. In the early years of the century it was normal practice for commercial and industrial offices to employ an office boy to carry out such duties as despatching and mailing correspondence, filing, telephone operating and making himself useful in any direction required.

Good standards of conduct, and a stiff white collar and bowler hat, were essential. The boy was expected to continue his education at evening classes, in subjects likely to be helpful to him, on three and sometimes four evenings a week from 7.30 to 9.30 p.m. Complete obedience was expected of him by everyone in the office. But he knew that if he used his intelligence, was obedient and showed an interest in his work and surroundings, coupled with the ambition inherent in most youngsters, he could climb from the bottom rung of the ladder.

My starting salary was 10s. a week, which was of course worth considerably more than it is today. Even in those days, however, a 10s. did not go all that far. The fare from my home to the office was 8d. return, which for a six-day week (no five-day weeks in those days) represented a weekly outlay of 4s. or 40 per cent of my salary. In modern times that would be looked at as out of all proportion, but I have no recollection of feeling any resentment or dissatisfaction. I was very happy from my first day in an office with colleagues who treated a new recruit with great kindness.

The building was a fine Georgian terrace house with imposing hall, wide staircase and lofty rooms. Stables at the back had been demolished to make a nice boardrom and typeroom, connected to the main building by a corridor, so that the house itself was occupied entirely by staff. The files were kept in rooms under the street level. The front rooms looked over the Embankment Gardens and the first floor windows gave a good view of the opening of Parliament.

Mr Smith I remember as a very stern man with a face of granite and steel-blue eyes, clean-shaven with slightly gingery hair. He never gave praise and a member of the staff, when called in to see him, was never asked to sit down. Alexander Siemens, the chairman of the Board at that time, often looked in from his office, which was near by. And occasionally I would see Sir Andrew Noble, a very old and awe-inspiring gentleman. Of union leaders who came in, the one I remember best is Arthur Henderson, general secretary of the ironfounders' union at that time.

Mr Smith brought four senior members of the staff with him from Glasgow and Mr J. McKie Bryce, later to become the secretary, came over from the Board of Trade as his chief assistant. In addition there were four clerical workers in the general office, six female shorthand-typists, a commissionaire and myself, making a total personnel of 18. The typists were the only females on the staff. Nobody, not even Mr Smith himself, had a personal secretary.

By modern standards the Federation was small, consisting of about 700 firms with a total employing power of between 200,000 and 250,000, practically all male workers. The engineering industry was then concentrated in the north of England and Scotland. In 1911 our statistics showed that 83.6 per cent of the workers in federated firms were employed in districts north of Birmingham and the remaining 16.4 in midland, southern and western districts. Fifty years later the proportions were 44 per cent and 56 per cent. In 1911 the number employed by members of the North-east Coast Association was 38,500 and the London Association 6,600. In 1961 the numbers for manual workers in those two areas were 70,500 and 236,200 respectively.

In 1911 the telephone service, run by the National Telephone Company, was not used much. The only facility in the offices, apart from an instrument in Mr Smith's office, was a telephone booth in the mailing department. To take a call, a person had to leave his office and go down to the booth. The number of calls was pretty limited, otherwise the waste of time would have been considerable. No telephone operator was employed, all calls being the duty of the office boy.

When an urgent reply was desired, the means adopted in those days was the telegram. We had special blocks of telegraph forms printed with our telegraphic address. Some of the telegrams were of great length and were, in effect, letters sent in reply to an urgent inquiry. It was my duty to write these telegrams out in printed letters and deliver them to the post office.

In less than a year I was promoted to be junior clerk in the general office. My main duties were now in connection with the annual inquiry which the Federation made regarding the rates of wages paid to all classes of workpeople and the numbers employed at each rate. From the information supplied by this inquiry, which was a pretty formidable one, the Federation Rate Book was prepared and issued to each association annually. I was also associated with the compilation and issuing of what were termed 'Advice Notes' and 'Rate Papers'.

It must be remembered that up to the General Wages Agreement of 1917, all wage claims (for advances or reductions) were negotiated on a local basis. It was most important therefore that all federated associations should be closely informed of all claims and that the Federation should have complete and up-to-date information on the overall situation. The Advice Note gave information regarding the district and classes of workpeople affected and the unions involved and the amount of increase or decrease claimed. The Rate Paper, which was linked to the appropriate advice note by a serial number, gave the result of the claim and the rate which became effective after the change.

The wage structure of the era was a simple one. Majority time rates had become established on a district basis for most classes of workpeople and there were no additions to the rates in the way of national bonus, compensatory or lieu payments or any of the other methods by which wage rates are enhanced today except for piece-work, overtime and some limited merit rates. It was therefore possible to get a complete picture of the wage situation.

Appendix F

Managerial Functions Agreement, 1922

I.—GENERAL PRINCIPLES

(*a*) The Employers have the right to manage their establishments and the Trade Unions have the right to exercise their functions.

(*b*) In the process of evolution, provision for changes in shop conditions is necessary, but it is not the intention to create any specially favoured class of workpeople.

II.—PROCEDURE FOR DEALING WITH QUESTIONS ARISING

(1) GENERAL

(*a*) The procedure of the Provisions for Avoiding Disputes so far as appropriate, applies to:—
  (i) General alterations in wages;
  (ii) Alterations in working conditions which are the subject of agreements officially entered into;
  (iii) Alterations in the general working week;
but such alterations shall not be given effect to until the appropriate procedure between the Federations and the Trade Union or Unions concerned has been exhausted.

(*b*) Where any alteration in the recognised working conditions, other than specified in Clause II (1) (*a*) hereof contemplated by the Management will result in one class of workpeople being replaced by another in the establishment, the Management shall, unless the circumstances arising are beyond their control, give the workpeople directly concerned or their representatives in the shop, not less than ten days' intimation of their intention and afford an opportunity for discussion, if discussion is desired, with a deputation of the workpeople concerned, and/or their representatives in the shop. Should a discussion not be desired, the instructions of the Management shall be observed and work shall proceed in accordance therewith. Should a discussion take place, and no settlement be reached at the various stages of procedure which are possible within the time available, the Management shall, on the date intimated, give a temporary decision upon which work shall proceed pending the recognised procedure being carried through. The decision shall not be prejudicial to either party in any subsequent discussion which may take place.

(*c*) Where any class of workpeople is displaced by reason of any act of the Management, consideration shall be given to the case of workpeople so displaced with a view, if practicable, of affording them in the establishment work suitable to their qualifications.

(*d*) Questions arising which do not result in one class of workpeople being replaced by another in the establishment and on which discussion is desired, shall be dealt with in accordance with the Provisions for Avoiding Disputes and work shall proceed meantime under the conditions following the act of the Management.

(*e*) Where a change is made by the Management involving questions of money payments and as a result of negotiations in accordance with the recognised procedure, it is agreed that the claim of the workpeople is established, the decision so arrived at may be made retrospective on the particular claim to a date to be mutually agreed upon, but not beyond the date upon which the question was raised.

(*f*) Where any local agreement conflicts with the terms of this agreement, the provisions of this agreement shall apply.

(*g*) Nothing in the foregoing shall affect the usual practice in connection with the termination of employment of individual workpeople.

(2) Provisions for Avoiding Disputes

(*a*) When a question arises, an endeavour shall be made by the Management and the workmen directly concerned to settle the same in the works or at the place where the question has arisen. Failing settlement deputations of workmen who may be accompanied by their Organiser (in which event a representative of the

Employers' Association shall also be present) shall be received by the Employers by appointment without unreasonable delay for the mutual discussion of any question in the settlement of which both parties are directly concerned. In the event of no settlement being arrived at, it shall be competent for either party to bring the question before a Local Conference to be held between the Local Association and the local representatives of the Society.

(*b*) In the event of either party desiring to raise any question a Local Conference for this purpose may be arranged by application to the Secretary of the Local Association or to the local representative of the Society.

(*c*) Local Conferences shall be held within seven working days unless otherwise mutually agreed upon from the receipt of the application by the Secretary of the Local Association or the local representative of the Society.

(*d*) Failing settlement at a Local Conference of any question brought before it, it shall be competent for either party to refer the matter to a Central Conference which if thought desirable may make a joint recommendation to the constituent bodies.

(*e*) Central Conference shall be held on the second Friday of each month at which questions referred to Central Conference prior to fourteen days of that date shall be taken.

(*f*) Until the procedure provided above has been carried through, there shall be no stoppage of work either of a partial or a general character.

(3) Shop Stewards and Works Committee Agreement

With a view to amplifying the provisions for avoiding disputes by a recognition of Shop Stewards and the institution of Works Committees IT IS AGREED AS FOLLOWS:—

(a) *Appointment of Shop Stewards*

(1) Workers, members of the above named Trade Unions, employed in a federated establishment may have representatives appointed from the members of the Unions employed in the establishment to act on their behalf in accordance with the terms of this Agreement.

(2) The representatives shall be known as Shop Stewards.

(3) The appointment of such Shop Stewards shall be deter-mined by the Trade Unions concerned and each Trade Union party to this Agreement may have such Shop Stewards.

(4) The names of the Shop Stewards and the shop or portion of a shop in which they are employed and the Trade Union to which they belong shall be intimated officially by the Trade Union concerned to the Management on election.

(b) *Appointment of Works Committee*

(5) A Works Committee may be set up in each establishment consisting of not more than seven representatives of the Manage-ment and not more than seven Shop Stewards, who should be representative of the various classes of workpeople employed in the establishment.

The Shop Stewards for this purpose shall be nominated and elected by ballot of the workpeople, members of the Trade Unions parties to this Agreement, employed in the establishment.

The Shop Stewards elected to the Works Committee shall, subject to re-election, hold office for not more than twelve months.

(6) If a question falling to be dealt with by the Works Com-mittee in accordance with the procedure hereinafter laid down arises in a department which has not a Shop Steward on the Works Committee, the Works Committee may, as regards that question, co-opt a Shop Steward from the department concerned. An agenda of the points to be discussed by the Works Committee shall be issued at least three days before the date of the meeting if possible.

(d) *Functions and Procedure*

(7) The functions of Shop Stewards and Works Committee, so far as they are concerned with the avoidance of disputes, shall be exercised in accordance with the following procedure:–

- (*a*) A worker or workers desiring to raise any question in which they are directly concerned shall, in the first in-stance, discuss the same with their foreman.
- (*b*) Failing settlement, the question shall be taken up with the Shop Manager and/or Head Shop Foreman by the appropriate Shop Steward and one of the workers directly concerned.

(*c*) If no settlement is arrived at the question may, at the request of either party, be further considered at a meeting of the Works Committee. At this meeting the O.D.D. may be present, in which event a representative of the Employers' Association shall also be present.

(*d*) Any question arising which affects more than one branch of trade or more than one department of the Works, may be referred to the Works Committee.

(*e*) The question may thereafter be referred for further consideration in terms of the 'Provisions for Avoiding Disputes.'

(*f*) No stoppage of work shall take place until the question has been fully dealt with in accordance with this Agreement and with the 'Provisions for Avoiding Disputes'.

(e) *General*

(8) Shop Stewards shall be subject to the control of the Trade Unions and shall act in accordance with the Rules and Regulations of the Trade Unions and agreements with employers so far as these affect the relation between employers and workpeople.

(9) In connection with this Agreement, Shop Stewards shall be afforded facilities to deal with questions raised in the shop or portion of a shop in which they are employed. Shop Stewards elected to the Works Committee shall be afforded similar facilities in connection with their duties, and in the course of dealing with these questions they may, with the previous consent of the Management (such consent not to be unreasonably withheld) visit any shop or portion of a shop in the establishment. In all other respects, Shop Stewards shall conform to the same working conditions as their fellow workers.

(10) Negotiations under this Agreement may be instituted either by the Management or by the workers concerned.

(11) Employers and Shop Stewards and Works Committee shall not be entitled to enter into any agreement inconsistent with agreements between the Federation or Local Association and the Trade Unions.

(12) For the purpose of this Agreement the expression 'establishment' shall mean the whole establishment or sections thereof according to whether the Management is unified or sub-divided.

(13) Any question which may arise out of the operation of this Agreement shall be brought before the Executive of the Trade Union concerned or the Federations as the case may be.

Appendix G

Numbers of Engineering Strikes 1949–70

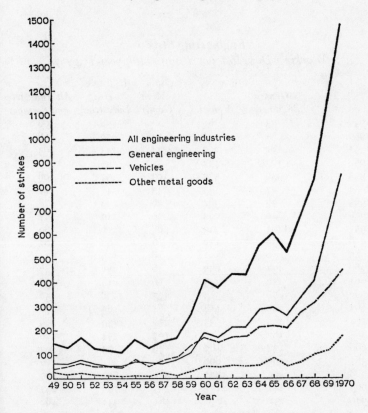

From 1949 to 1970 the numbers of employees in the various sectors changed as follows:

General Engineering:	1,568,200 –	2,283,200
Vehicles:	965,400 –	842,400
Other Metal Goods:	626,000 –	639,000
Total:	3,159,600 –	3,765,500

Source: Department of Employment

Appendix H

Engineering Strikes –
Working Days lost per 1,000 employees 1949–70

	General Engineering	Vehicles	Other Metal Goods	All Engineering Industries	All Industries and Services
1949	33	62	11	38	90
1950	31	133	11	59	68
1951	82	259	14	123	83
1952	107	432	31	195	87
1953	330	533	103	354	106
1954	27	85	43	49	117
1955	36	362	26	139	178
1956	40	293	20	119	97
1957	1404	719	368	1006	389
1958	38	132	6	62	161
1959	50	539	18	173	244
1960	194	653	46	291	137
1961	122	545	66	219	136
1962	1076	1323	435	1038	257
1963	105	448	64	183	78
1964	155	533	56	230	99
1965	182	1058	107	374	126
1966	133	463	49	193	103
1967	204	666	110	291	122
1968	569	1371	336	709	207
1969	442	2221	165	793	297
1970	731	1836	461	932	480

The official figures are for 'stoppages of work due to industrial disputes in the United Kingdom' but practically all were strikes.

The figures are swollen in 1953 by a national one-day strike in the industry, in 1957 by the beginnings of a national strike, in 1962 by two one-day strikes and in 1968 by one one-day strike.

Changes were made in the basis for calculating the engineering figures in 1964 and again in 1966 but the effects are not substantial.

Source: Department of Employment

Appendix I

ENTICEMENT OF WORKPEOPLE 1952

(Extracts from a circular to his members from Sir Ernest Field,
director of the Scottish Engineering Employers' Association.)

18th February, 1952.

All members are earnestly reminded that, in the interest of
federated firms in general and in their own ultimate interest, they
should never offer inducements of any kind which may reasonably
be expected to entice workpeople away from another federated
employer.

This applies to

Advertisement of vacancies.

Applications to, or interviews with officials of Employment
Exchanges or scheduled employment agencies.

Correspondence, or at interview, with prospective employees.

Inducements take many forms, the most common of which are
offers of

Time rates higher than are normal for the job.

Overtime which is not really necessary in the interest of production at the time.

'Easy' bonuses or other increments.

Systems of alleged payment by results which bear little or no
relation to effort and are in effect what are now commonly
referred to as 'Gift Schemes'.

'Merit', 'Experience' or 'Ability' increments paid without
any real regard to the possession of those qualities, or
before there has been sufficient time properly to assess
them.

In short, any payments or conditions of employment which are
not in accordance with the known policy of the Association: a
policy which, though not always to the liking of the individual,
is intended to and generally does operate in the best interests of
our members as a whole.

I must also stress the proved fact that the results of enticement are of only transitory advantage to a firm and of boomerang effect: sooner or later, the labour position being what it is, the losing firms are forced into the position of having to adopt the same methods to fill their vacancies; with obvious effect on the wage structure and costs: the spiral extends, with illusory advantage to the workers but with real harm to the industry.

If we continue to raise our wage levels bit by bit by this haphazard succession of increases not genuinely related to output, what will our position be when we eventually come, as we are bound to, to the condition of keen competition; particularly from foreign countries?

Some members may say 'Why repeat what we already know?' My answer is that by the way in which some firms help to bait the trap which is being set for employers, they do not appear always to remember, and this letter is intended to be a sincere, and I hope helpful, reminder.

There are two other points of great importance:

1. Firms which have their headquarters or associated firm in another district, e.g. in England, are not in order in introducing here any more favourable wages or conditions which may have been established at their headquarters or associated firm. Such firms are required to observe the wages and conditions of the district in which their works are situated. Efforts by their workers to obtain any more favourable conditions applicable elsewhere should be resisted and the claim reported to the association.

2. Members who, by reason of their products, do not have to consider costs or the fear of future competition to the same extent as the majority, have precisely the same obligations to the association as have other members less fortunately circumstanced.

'Enticement' is outstandingly one of our present difficulties which cannot be overcome without genuine goodwill, on the part of *all* concerned, to do so.

There are at least two ways in which to test the validity of a proposed action:

1. Conscience: How would you feel about it if another member did it?

2. Consult the association.

Appendix J

The Growth of the Federation, 1910–71

(At the end of the lock-out of 1897–8 more than 700 firms were taking part. As the Federation reconstituted itself, the number of member firms rose in a couple of years to more than 800 and remained betwen 800 and 900 until 1910, for which year the first figures of the numbers employed are available.)

Year	Number of Firms	Full-time Manual Workers Employed				Full-time Staff Workers Employed	Total Full-time Manual and Staff Workers
		Adult Males	Junior Males	Females	Total		
1910	816	175,400	40,900	*	*	*	*
1911	818	203,300	54,300	*	*	*	*
1912	803	*	*	*	*	*	*
1913	810	235,900	61,800	*	*	*	*
1914	744	263,500	65,000	*	*	*	*
1915/16	*	*	*	*	*	*	*
1917	1,186	*	*	*	*	*	*
1918	1,469	439,600	*	*	*	*	*
1919	2,380	507,100	*	*	*	*	*
1920	2,440	514,800	125,700	58,300	698,800	*	*
1921	2,600	339,100	92,400	17,200	448,700	*	*
1922	2,690	*	*	*	*	*	*
1923	2,573	343,500	94,600	45,700	483,800	*	*
1924	2,493	430,000	109,700	53,900	593,600	*	*
1925	2,389	452,000	115,200	56,100	623,300	*	*
1926	2,233	405,000	99,300	49,300	553,600	*	*
1927	2,175	392,600	95,400	45,800	533,800	*	*
1928	2,119	393,600	97,000	48,600	539,200	*	*
1929	2,069	397,800	100,200	50,400	548,400	*	*
1930	2,024	365,600	93,400	45,200	504,200	*	*
1931	1,968	290,400	73,500	42,000	405,900	*	*
1932	1,870	264,300	68,100	46,100	378,500	*	*
1933	1,847	292,100	72,400	47,800	412,300	*	*
1934	1,821	353,100	85,300	59,700	498,100	*	*
1935	1,806	381,000	95,000	65,900	541,900	*	*
1936	1,825	454,100	116,300	70,700	641,100	*	*
1937	1,880	519,800	134,100	79,300	733,200	*	*

Year	Number of Firms	Full-time Manual Workers Employed				Full-time Staff Workers Employed	Total Full-time Manual and Staff Workers
		Adult Males	Junior Males	Females	Total		
1938	1,981	558,100	143,900	73,100	775,100	*	*
1939	2,023	625,200	156,000	80,000	861,200	*	*
1940	2,157	769,700	185,500	125,800	1,081,000	*	*
1941	2,346	862,900	177,700	236,200	1,276,800	*	*
1942	2,711	970,700	174,400	406,200	1,551,300	*	*
1943	3,161	1,066,800	168,700	592,700	1,828,200	*	*
1944	3,467	1,086,800	142,700	531,600	1,761,100	*	*
1945	3,571	*	*	*	*	*	*
1946	3,636	870,900	88,700	182,900	1,142,500	*	*
1947	3,794	928,900	84,000	176,600	1,189,500	*	*
1948	3,858	930,300	80,900	160,900	1,172,100	*	*
1949	3,934	969,700	89,100	156,400	1,215,200	*	*
1950	3,970	975,800	90,500	153,200	1,219,500	*	*
1951	4,048	1,012,500	91,000	157,000	1,260,500	*	*
1952	4,148	1,047,200	95,000	170,800	1,313,000	*	*
1953	4,227	1,053,500	104,600	163,600	1,321,700	*	*
1954	4,259	1,045,900	110,600	171,400	1,327,900	413,500	1,741,400
1955	4,266	1,080,000	115,800	185,700	1,381,500	439,000	1,820,500
1956	4,303	1,116,000	121,500	182,600	1,420,100	471,200	1,891,300
1957	4,347	1,088,800	121,300	167,600	1,377,700	503,200	1,880,900
1958	4,389	1,104,400	126,600	171,900	1,402,900	528,500	1,931,400
1959	4,375	1,075,800	123,700	165,300	1,364,800	549,200	1,914,000
1960	4,397	1,088,700	124,700	178,900	1,392,300	551,300	1,943,600
1961	4,402	1,143,100	126,400	189,200	1,458,700	579,000	2,037,700
1962	4,480	1,146,400	132,400	187,500	1,466,300	595,300	2,061,600
1963	4,472	1,098,100	127,000	179,000	1,404,100	586,300	1,990,400
1964	4,445	1,112,800	127,500	194,800	1,435,100	601,400	2,036,500
1965	4,497	1,147,300	127,900	205,400	1,480,600	631,900	2,112,500
1966	4,643	1,165,100	131,400	208,000	1,504,500	666,500	2,171,000
1967	4,738	1,121,600	128,900	200,000	1,450,500	667,400	2,117,900
1968	4,751	1,067,000	119,700	196,100	1,382,800	673,800	2,056,600
1969	4,682	1,077,600	120,800	198,000	1,396,400	686,900	2,083,300
1970	4,734	1,080,000	121,000	200,600	1,401,600	700,700	2,102,300
1971 (May)	4,826	1,055,500	†99,400	187,900	1,342,800	705,700	2,048,500

* No record available.

† Junior Males: Prior to 1971 – aged 20 and under; 1971 – aged 19 and under.

In 1900 the annual wage bill of member firms was rather less than £15m. In 1970 the annual wage bill was about £1,600m. and the annual salary bill about £900m.

Appendix K

The Federation in 1971

Association	No. of Firms	Full-time Employees			Voting Power (Percentage of total)
		Manual	*Staff*	*Total*	
London	1,001	224,687	184,680	409,367	20·1
West Midlands	768	243,085	91,395	334,480	19·1
South Lancashire	432	130,640	62,543	193,183	9·4
East Midlands	332	115,815	67,846	183,661	8·2
West of England	351	85,627	55,818	141,445	7·1
Scottish	357	92,482	41,667	134,149	6·7
Coventry	118	66,484	30,683	97,167	5·1
North-east Coast	188	73,523	28,302	101,825	4·7
West Riding	414	73,997	28,304	102,301	4·3
Sheffield	146	60,571	23,250	83,821	3·7
East Anglian	74	26,705	27,436	54,141	2·2
South Wales	129	33,879	9,178	43,057	1·8
Mid-Anglian	71	21,614	16,309	37,923	1·8
Preston	76	25,433	11,763	37,196	1·7
Bolton	138	23,396	9,154	32,550	1·4
Northern Ireland	112	21,113	6,068	27,181	1·1
Belfast Marine	2	5,020	3,671	8,691	0·4
Border Counties	20	3,938	1,668	5,606	0·3
Rochdale	46	4,322	1,593	5,915	0·3
Barrow	5	4,653	1,954	6,607	0·3
Dundee	26	3,102	1,515	4,617	0·2
Aberdeen	20	2,777	881	3,658	0·1
TOTAL	4,826	1,342,863	705,678	2,048,541	100·0

Voting power is related to wage and salary bills, not to numbers employed, which explains, for instance, why Coventry has a bigger vote than the North-east Coast or West Riding, though employing fewer people.

On staff questions the voting may be related to salary bills only and on manual workers' questions to wage bills only. While the West Midlands combined vote is smaller than that of London, its members' vote on manual questions is considerably larger (21.7 per cent to 16.3 per cent).

In addition to full-time workers, federated firms employ 77,500 part-time workers.

The 65 largest federated groups, which have 65 per cent of the voting power, and an employing capacity ranging from some 200,000 down to 4500 are the following:

British Leyland Motor Corporation
General Electric Company
Rolls-Royce (1971)
Hawker Siddeley Group
Joseph Lucas (Industries)
Plessey Company
Guest, Keen & Nettlefolds
Tube Investments
British Aircraft Corporation
    (Holdings)
Philips Electronic & Associated
    Industries
Standard Telephones & Cables
Reyrolle Parsons
Babcock & Wilcox
Vickers
Clarke Chapman-John Thompson
Smiths Industries
Ferranti
British Steel Corporation
Thorn Electrical Industries
Birmid Qualcast
Associated Engineering
International Computers
    (Holdings)
Dunlop Holdings
Dowty Group
Delta Metal Company
Westland Aircraft
Ransome Hoffman Pollard
E.M.I.
Stone-Platt Industries
Weir Group
Renold
Sears Engineering (Sears Holdings)
John Brown & Company

Alfred Herbert
Hoover
Birmingham Small Arms Company
Davy-Ashmore
Averys
Simon Engineering
International Combustion
    (Holdings)
Honeywell
Rank Organisation
Short Bros. & Harland
Wilmot Breeden (Holdings)
The British Oxygen Company
F. H. Lloyd Holdings
Whessoe
Thos. Firth & John Brown
Foster Wheeler-John Brown
    Boilers
Slater Walker Securities
    (Industrial Group)
Caterpillar Tractor Company
The Skefko Ball Bearing Company
Crane
International Harvester Company
    of Great Britain
Thos. W. Ward
Alcan Aluminium (UK)
Otis Elevator Company
Staveley Industries
Laird Group
Mather & Platt
Sheepbridge Engineering
George Kent
Westinghouse Brake & Signal
    Company
Anderson Mavor

At the other end of the scale there are about 2500 federated firms with less than 100 employees each.

Not all the firms in some of the groups are federated.

The following table gives estimates of the number of federated establishments, grouped according to the size of the establishment, based on an inquiry made in January 1971. For purposes of comparison figures are also given for a similar grouping of firms registered with the Engineering Industry Training Board in 1970. While the scope of the Federation and the Board are not identical, the figures may give a general indication of the extent to which firms of different sizes federate.

Range of Numbers Employed	Engineering Employers' Federation		Engineering Industry Training Board
	No. of Establishments	Percentage of Establishments	No. of Establishments
1–24	640	11·3	11,874
25–99	1,720	30·5	7,568
100–249	1,375	24·4	2,659
250–499	845	15·0	1,195
500–999	565	10·0	751
1,000–4,999	460	8·2	585
5,000–or more	32	0·6	48
TOTAL	5,637	100	24,680

There are more federated establishments than federated firms because some firms have more than one establishment.

Appendix L

Presidents of the Federation

Colonel Henry C. S. Dyer	Armstrong, Mitchell, Newcastle, later Armstrong, Whitworth	1896–8
Sir Andrew Noble	Armstrong, Whitworth, Newcastle	1898–1915
Andrew P. Henderson	D. & W. Henderson, Partick	1916–17
Bernard A. Firth	Thos. Firth & Sons, Sheffield	1917–20
Sir John Dewrance	Dewrance & Co., London	1920–6
Sir Archibald Ross	Hawthorn Leslie, Newcastle	1926–30
Dr Alexander Campbell	Hunslet Engineering Company, Leeds	1930–4
Sir John Siddeley	Armstrong-Siddeley, Coventry	1930–7
Sir Charles W. Craven	Vickers-Armstrong, London	1937–40
George E. Bailey	Metropolitan-Vickers, Manchester	1940–3
Greville S. Maginness	Churchill Machine Tools, Manchester	1943–6
Philip B. Johnson	Hawthorn Leslie, Newcastle	1946–9
Sir Robert Micklem	Vickers-Armstrong, London	1949–51
Sir William Wallace	Brown Bros., Edinburgh	1951–3
Sir Percy Mills	W. & T. Avery, Birmingham	1953–6
Frederick C. Braby	Fredk. Braby & Co., London	1956–8
Sir Kenneth Hague	Babcock & Wilcox London	1958–60

F. Vincent Everard	Belliss & Morcom, Birmingham	1960–2
Sir Kenneth Allen	W. H. Allen, Sons & Co., Bedford	1962–4
A. J. Stephen Brown	Stone-Platt Industries, London	1964–6
Gordon M. Baker	C. A. Parsons, Newcastle	1966–8
F. James Fielding	Fielding & Platt, Gloucester	1968–70
Denby C. Bamford	Chadburns, Liverpool	1970–2
Thomas Carlile	Babcock & Wilcox, London	1972–

Appendix M

Chief Executives of the Federation

Thomas Biggart (Sir Thomas)	1896–1910
(Joint secretary with James Robinson. Allan M. Smith was appointed an additional secretary in 1908)	
Allan M. Smith (Sir Allan)	1910–34
(First sole secretary and treasurer, then Chairman of the Management Committee, then Chairman of the Management Board)	
Alexander Ramsay (Sir Alexander)	1934–53
(Director)	
Benjamin Macarty	1953–66
(Director, then Director-general)	
Martin Jukes	1966–
(Director-general)	

Appendix N

Sources

This book is not intended primarily for students. Those terrible twins, Ibid. and Op. Cit., are not to be found in it. But because it covers virgin ground, I think I should say something about sources.

There has been no earlier history of the Federation, but some material is to be found in two Federation publications:

> *Thirty Years of Industrial Conciliation* (1927) and
> *Looking at Industrial Relations* (1959).

The Scottish association have an incomplete manuscript history of the association by Edward J. Lancaster (1965), particularly useful on the early days. Some information is also to be found in *The Engineering Industry and the Crisis of 1922* by Dr A. Shadwell (1922); *The Employers' Challenge*, a study of the national shipbuilding and engineering dispute of 1957, by H. A. Clegg and Rex Adams; *Industrial Relations in Engineering* by A. Marsh (1965); and 'The Role of the Industrial Federation in the 1970s', a paper by Martin Jukes for the Industrial Educational and Research Foundation.

There is no general history of employers' organisations. Clegg has a chapter on them in *The System of Industrial Relations in Great Britain* (1970). Research Paper 7 of the 1965 Royal Commission contains two studies: 'The Functions and organisation of Employers' Associations in Selected Industries' by V. G. Minns and 'A Survey of Employers' Association Officials' by W. E. J. McCarthy. Histories of individual employers' organisations are few. There is one of the Shipping Federation by L. H. Powell (1950) and one on the master printers by Ellis Howe (1950). In general, employers' organisations have been neglected by academics.

Engineering employers, collectively or individually or both, gave published evidence to the Royal Commission on the Organisation and Rules of Trade Unions (1867–9), the Royal Commission into the Working of Labour Laws (1874–5), the Royal Commission on Labour (1891–4), the Royal Commission on Trade Disputes and Trade Combinations (1903–6), the Industrial Council inquiry into industrial agreements (1912), the (Balfour) Committee on Industry and Trade (1924–7) and the Royal Commission on Trade Unions and Employers' Associations (1965–8).

Courts of Inquiry reported on national engineering disputes in 1922, 1948, 1954 and 1957. The National Incomes Commission reported on the 1963 engineering agreement in 1964 and 1965. The National Board for Prices and Incomes dealt with 'Pay and Conditions of Service of Engineering Workers' (Report 49, 1967), 'Pay and Conditions of Service of Staff Workers in the Engineering Industry' (Report 49 Statistical Supplement, 1968), and 'Pay and Conditions of Service of Engineering Workers' (Report 104, 1969). They also reported (No. 68, 1968) on 'Agreement Made Between Certain Engineering Firms and the Draughtsmen's and Allied Technicians' Association'.

Many publications of the Board of Trade and later the Ministry of Labour and its successors contain relevant material.

Numerous histories and studies of trade unions and industrial relations have references to employers' organisations, though often without much knowledge or impartiality. The names of the more important ones will be familiar to students of industrial relations. I shall mention some later but for the moment content myself with acknowledging that *The Story of the Engineers* by James B. Jefferys (1945) has been a desk-side book and that I was helped by an unpublished thesis 'The Amalgamated Society of Engineers 1880–1914' by B. C. M. Weekes, which the author allowed me to read. There are histories of the unions of boilermakers, foundry workers, vehicle builders, electricians and others.

In the main I have relied on Federation and local association archives. The Federation have kept massive quantities of material of all kinds, including minute books going back to 1895, circular letters to associations and members, verbatim reports of meetings with the unions from the earliest days, central conference reports, wage statistics and financial records. A long room in the basement at Broadway House is packed tight with it and there is an overflow into a smaller room. But much material up to 1965 is on microfilm – 1,750,000 items – on the first floor. Miss Lily Cartwright was my ever-pleasant guide through the labyrinth. The use of the microfilm is time-consuming and I am sure that there is much of interest still to be unearthed by students with more years in front of them than I have.

The larger associations have many ancient and modern records in various states of order and disorder. Most go back to first beginnings but those of Coventry and Liverpool were destroyed by German bombs during the war and those of the West of England by a fire. At Birmingham I found all the minute books from 1897 to 1970 waiting for me in a long row on the shining boardroom table, with for good measure an exercise book containing the record of a 54-hour dispute, sadly muddled by both sides in 1871. Glasgow and Belfast have records going back to 1865 and 1866.

Lucky finds included the minutes of Biggart's committee of employers' organisation secretaries, at Glasgow, the verbatim report of the 1897 machine question conference, at Newcastle, and letters written during the great lock-out to Leslie Field, the association secretary, at London.

Generally I resisted tempting by-ways but in Manchester I found myself in the Ferranti archives at Hollinwood, where were family letters to Basil de Z. Ferranti during the 1897 lock-out, and spreading family trees which included several Doges of Venice. I also spent some hours with the Armstrong papers in the Newcastle City Archives, trying vainly to find out why the Tyne employers did not join the Iron Trades Employers' Association when it was formed – a puzzle which was in danger of becoming an obsession although, since it was nearly a quarter of a century before the Federation, it could be argued that it was not of vital importance to my history.

To continue more or less chronologically:

Chapter 1. My main source for the 1852 lock-out is Thomas Hughes' account for the National Association for the Promotion of the Social Sciences included in their 'Report on Trade Societies and Strikes' (1860), supplemented by trade union histories and occasional other references.

Chapter 2. For the 1871 strike there is *A History of the Engineers' Strike in Newcastle and Gateshead* by J. Burnett (1872) and *The North-East Engineers' Strikes of 1871* by E. Allen, J. F. Clarke, N. McCord and D. J. Rowe (1971). On the Iron Trades Employers' Association I have depended more than I liked on their *Record 1872–1900* (1901). The *Record* says that the minutes and papers of the association were handed over to the executive of the Federation but I have not found them. *The Story of the Wallsend Slipway and Engineering Company, 1871–1897* by William Boyd (1911) offers some explanation of why the Tyne employers did not join the association from the beginning, but I am conscious that I have not unearthed the full story. Ben Roberts prints the manifesto of the National Federation of Associated Employers of Labour as an appendix to *The Trades Union Congress 1868–1921* (1958). The Shipbuilders and Repairers National Association have the minutes of the National Federation of Shipbuilders and Engineers (1889–1898).

Chapter 3. The verbatim report of the 'Machine Question' conference (1897) is fascinating. On the eight-hour day I made use of G. D. H. Cole's *History of Socialist Thought*, vol. 3 and *A Year's Experiment and its Results at the Salford Iron Works* by William Mather, MP (1894), and numerous references elsewhere. The letter from Colonel Dyer to Miss Potter quoted in this chapter is in the Webb Collection at the British Library of Political and Economic Science. Material on the 1897 lock-out is abundant. Apart from the Federation's records, the 'Notes on the Engineering Trades Lock-out' issued by the ASE and contemporary reports in newspapers and engineering journals, I found interesting material in an evaluation of the dispute by R. O. Clarke in *Economica*, May 1957. On strike-breaking organisations there is *The Apostle of Free Labour* by William Collison (1913) and an article by John Savile, 'Trade Unions and Free Labour' in *Essays in Labour History* (1960). Some light on the character of employers' leaders is thrown by *Benjamin Chapman Browne: Selected Papers on Social and Economic Questions* (1918), *Viscount Pirrie of Belfast* by H. Jefferson (1947), *Alfred Yarrow, His Life and Work* by Lady Yarrow (1923), *Siemens Brothers 1858–1958* by J. D. Scott (1958). I might also mention George Barnes' autobiography, *From Workshop to War Cabinet* (1923) and D. C. Cummings' *A Historical Survey of the Boiler Makers and Iron and Steel Ship Builders' Society* (1905).

Chapter 4. I found *The Workers' Union* by Richard Hyman (1971) interesting on the formation of the Midlands Employers' Federation. There was useful material in the evidence to and report of the Industrial Council's inquiry into industrial agreements.

Chapter 5. War histories by G. D. H. Cole and others. Lord Askwith: 'Memorandum on Employers' Associations' (to the Ministry of Reconstruction, 1917) and 'Industrial Problems and Disputes' (1920). B. Pribicevic: *The Shop Stewards' Movement and Workers' Control 1910–22* (1959). Alexander Ramsay: *Terms of Industrial Peace* (1917). *The Employer*, the monthly publication of the National Employers' Federation, 1918 to 1919. The Whitley Committee reports, the minutes of the National Industrial Conference provisional committee, an essay on the National Industrial Conference in *The Sociology of Industrial Relations* by V. L. Allen.

Chapter 6. The North-east Coast Association have conveniently preserved two scrap-books of documents, newspaper cuttings, etc. about the 1922 lock-out. There was a debate in the House of Commons on it on 20 March 1922, and there is the report of the Court of Inquiry. The Federation and AEU both published pamphlets putting their case. The Federation produced pamphlets on a number of subjects in this period. A collection of Allan Smith's personal papers was lent to me by his son, the late Alex Campbell-Smith. Howard Gospel let me see the manuscript of an article by him containing new matter on the behaviour of employers' organisations in regard to the Mond–Turner talks. Books with relevant matter are *Men and Work* by Lord Citrine (1964), *British Engineering Wages* by R. S. Spicer (1928) and more by Ramsay – *The Greater Problems of Industry* (1924) and *The Economics of Safeguarding* (1930).

Chapter 7. War Histories again. Wal Hannington: *The Rights of Engineers* (1944). AEU reports on Joint Production Committees. Perhaps I should mention here two useful books on white collar unions: *The Growth of White-Collar Unionism* by George Bain (1970) and *A History of the Association of Engineering and Shipbuilding Draughtsmen* by J. E. Mortimer (1960).

For the period since the Second World War, I have relied a great deal on personal contacts to supplement the records. There are some whose memories go much further back than that. The recollections of Sid Hibbit, author of the earlier appendix about things in 1911, remain as clear as a bell. Danny Maher, a Federation official dealing with Central Conference from 1933 to 1971, gave me colourful sketches of Central Conference characters of the past. Miss D. M. Carey, Allan Smith's secretary, and Miss Winifrede Miles, Ramsay's secretary, contributed sidelights on their characters. I have questioned the president and all the past presidents from Braby onwards, former officials including Ben Macarty, Alan Swinden, Pat Lowry, Ernest Happold, and Sir John Barraclough, a number of union leaders and many others.

The quotation from Lord Butler of Saffron Walden on page 179 is from his memoirs, *The Art of the Possible* (1971).

Since 1950, the Federation has produced a printed annual report and since September 1969, a monthly publication, *EEF News*. There has also been a series of research papers and in the last two years an annual economic review.

Index